I0024998

fl. 1868-1892 Lyndon

# Margaret

A Story of Life in a Prairie Home

fl. 1868-1892 Lyndon

**Margaret**
*A Story of Life in a Prairie Home*

ISBN/EAN: 9783744685245

Printed in Europe, USA, Canada, Australia, Japan

Cover: Foto ©Thomas Meinert / pixelio.de

More available books at **www.hansebooks.com**

# MARGARET:

A STORY OF

# LIFE IN A PRAIRIE HOME.

By LYNDON.

FIFTH THOUSAND.

NEW YORK:

CHARLES SCRIBNER & CO.

1868.

Entered according to Act of Congress, in the year 1868, by

CHARLES SCRIBNER & CO.,

In the Clerk's Office of the District Court of the United States for the
Southern District of New York.

WHATEVER IS GOOD IN MY BOOK

I DEDICATE TO THE MEMORY

OF

# MY MOTHER.

# MARGARET.

## CHAPTER I.

She hath no scorn of common things;
  And, though she seem of other birth,
Round us her heart entwines and clings,
And patiently she folds her wings,
  To tread the humbler paths of earth.    Lowell.

"I say, Aunt Margaret, why don't you tell us the story you promised to, about that lamp that did such queer things?"

"If your aunt ever gets through gazing out of the window, I should be glad to hear the paper read."

"Oh, dear, that's always the way; Jack and I never want to hear a story, but what somebody wants something. It's meaner than any thing"—and George kicked his heels harder than ever against the wall, as he lay on the floor with his legs at right angles with his body.

There was little in the scene upon which Margaret Crosby had been looking out for the last half hour, with her elbow on the window-sill, and her chin in her hand, to attract and interest one. Even when brightened by sunshine and green trees, and grass and waving grain, it was monotonous; but now, in the deepening twilight of a dull day, late in October, when fields, woods, and sky all wore a cold, gray hue, it was fairly desolate; and Margaret's face had a dreary look. It was evident that the scene was in keeping with her mood. But the gloom was banished when she heard her father's voice; and she rose quickly from the window.

"It is a shame, father, that I have kept you waiting all

this time; but I got into a web of tangled thoughts, and there is no telling when I should have come out of it, if you had not spoken."

"Your tangled webs are more interesting to yourself than to others, Margaret," said her sister Fanny, from her easy-chair by the fire.  "You might be a little more considerate, I think, and not sit speechless an hour together, when we are so entirely dependent upon each other."

"It was rather hard, I confess, Fanny, for me to deprive you, for so long, of my wit and wisdom ; but when a body comes suddenly upon her thirtieth birth-day, how can she help a few meditations upon her great antiquity ? "

"How disagreeable you are, Margaret ! That is the second time to-day that you have harped upon your age. Do choose some other topic ! "

"I suppose I may wait till to-morrow, and read the paper myself," said her father, fretfully.

"You shan't wait another minute, father.  Georgie, you just run up-stairs and bring the Gazette from my bureau, while I light the candle and coax the fire a bit."

But George only muttered something about Jack's going, and about stories and promises.

Margaret's "Oh, Georgie ! " brought his feet down from their protracted elevation ; but before he had edged himself away from the wall, rolled over and slowly regained, first his hands and knees, and then his feet, the candle stood on the little table between the lounge, where Mr. Crosby lay, and Fanny's easy-chair, the fire was blazing, and Margaret had brought the paper herself.  Just then the kitchen-door opened, and a man in his shirt-sleeves, with an old felt-hat on his head, appeared.

"I say, Miss Crosby, be you through with that 'ere newspaper ? coz, if you be, I'd like ter borry it a spell."

"No, Jotham, I am just going to read it to my father. When I am through with it, I will let Jack bring it to you in the kitchen."

"Oh, if you're agoin' ter read it out, I don't mind sittin'

down an' listenin'. It's a mighty sight easier ter hear readin'
nor ter read yerself."

Margaret's face flushed a little, but she made no objection
to this addition to her audience, having learned wisdom by
sorry experience.

Fanny gave an impatient hitch to her chair as Jotham,
the man-of-all-work on the farm, seated himself near the
fire, comfortably tilting himself back against the wall; but
the reading proceeded. It was worth while to hear even a
stupid country gazette read in such clear, ringing tones, and
George and Jack came and stood by their aunt, George
with an arm around her neck.

"Wal, now, that there Congress be a great institution,
I should say. Ef I hed my way, I'd hang 'em all up high an'
dry. The States 'ud be better off for it."

"It's wicked for you to talk like that, Jotham," said
George, indignantly; "Aunt Margaret says we should respect the Government, and when I'm a man I'll fight for it,
if I have a chance."

"I say, Mr. Crosby," said Jotham, coming down on the
four legs of his chair, as Mr. Crosby got feebly up from the
lounge, signifying to Margaret that he was going to bed;
"them fields where the wheat an' oats was is all ploughed,
an' what ther's left I kin do easy in four or five days, an' I
want to take the hosses and plough for Tim Simkins to-morra'
to pay fer a good turn he done me last year. I s'pose you
ha'n't got no objections."

"Margaret, can't you manage such little affairs, when you
know how feeble I am?" said her father, reproachfully.
"I do think you might save my nerves a little more than
you do."

"I had no idea, father, that Jotham was going to speak
to you about this. I think, Jotham, that you had better
finish our own ploughing first, and then, if you have a day's
leisure, you can plough for Mr. Simpkins."

"Oh, wal, if you object to obleegin' a feller like that, I'll
clear out. Ther's plenty of folks as a'n't so sot up as all that

comes to," and my lord Jotham stalked out of the room, slamming the door behind him.

Mr. Crosby made a despairing motion with his hands, as if utterly hopeless of any thing but trouble.

"If you could only learn to be a little more politic, Margaret. What are we to do now? We can't get another man, far or near. I suppose I shall have to go to work. I could dig and plough a few days, and then drop into my grave, and there would be one less care for you."

Margaret was evidently used to such mournful states of mind, for she only stroked his hair softly, assuring him that no trouble should come of this, and she should laugh to see her dear father with a spade or a plough.

"I must say, Margaret," said Fanny, "I think things have come to a pretty pass, if you will let that man have the horses for a whole day, to work for some of his low-lived cronies, and I am deprived for days together of a drive, when my health demands fresh air; you know I am not able to walk."

"I do know it, Fanny, and I only wish I could see you enjoying every possible comfort that you require. But one needs an extra allowance of wisdom to manage the queer men and maids about here. I think I shall prove equal to this emergency, having learned something from our experience with Nancy and Harriet and the rest. I wonder what our next specimen will prove? for I suppose we must try again, though I wish we might be spared."

"It's very well for you to prefer to do without a servant, who are well and strong. I can't expect you to appreciate the trial it is to me," said Fanny.

"Why, mother," said George, "it was your fault that Harriet went away; you made such a fuss about her coming to the table with us, and she wouldn't stay unless she could."

"Well, that is something I never will submit to! It is too much to ask. When another servant comes, I wish it distinctly understood that I shall have my meals by myself."

Margaret sighed, as she left the room to see if her father

needed her. When she came back, the boys clamored for their story, and she readily began : " Well, once upon a time—"

" Now, Margaret, you are not going to tell another of those silly stories ? If you are, I shall have to go up-stairs, and read in the cold."

" Mother," said George, " I just think you are too bad. You've been reading that old novel all day, and now you make a fuss about our hearing a little story."

Mrs. Sinclair deigned no reply, and Margaret said, " Well, my dears, we'll go up-stairs, and after you are snugly in bed, I'll tell about the lamp; then you can drop to sleep and dream about the genii and things."

So the boys scampered up-stairs, with Margaret after them ; and having read their verses, said their prayers, and buried themselves under the clothes, all but their eager young faces, they were soon absorbed in the adventures of Aladdin ; and before very long, they were fast asleep, with visions of magic dancing through their heads.

As Margaret left them, the warm light faded from her eyes, and something of the dreary look came back. But, going to her own little room, she took her Bible to read, saying to herself, " No more retrospection to-night; I have indulged too much already. But these way-marks—what reminders they are." She read on for a time, trying to take the words of wisdom and good cheer home to her tired heart; but the spell of the past was strong upon her, and gradually the hand holding the book dropped into her lap, and her thoughts were far away. Margaret's life in the days to which her thoughts flew back was not like the present, homely and matter-of-fact. She almost doubted her own identity in the pictures that thronged before her.

Their home then was one of comfort and elegance, and their mother was its genius—the embodiment of love, purity, gentleness, and wisdom ; seeming ever, by a touch here and a word or a look there, to smooth the wrinkles of every-day life, to draw out the good, and disclose a bright side to every cloud.

1*

The light faded out of their home when Margaret was thirteen and Fanny fifteen. Their mother died, leaving them to the care of an aunt, their father's sister, who thought nothing too good for the beautiful Fanny, and no sacrifices too great for Margaret to make for her; thus fostering the selfishness, Fanny's besetting sin, which their mother had striven earnestly to eradicate, until she seemed to care for nothing but herself.

As they grew older, Fanny devoted herself to society; and as Margaret cared little for it, but found her enjoyment in books and music, the sisters were nearly as much apart as if they had had separate homes. Margaret formed few friendships; and as her father was absorbed in business, and a man of few words, she often felt utterly alone. But there came a time when every craving of her warm heart for love and sympathy was satisfied.

Robert Russell was a man whom any woman might be proud to love—strong and manly, yet gentle, earnest, true, and wise, with high aims and standards for himself, unfailing charity for others, and a power to love that a lifetime only could exhaust. Margaret rested on his strong heart, grew radiant in the sunshine of his affection, and was happy, as such natures only can be, for one short year.

Then came a cloud, no bigger than a woman's hand, but it spread and spread, and grew blacker, until it covered Margaret's sky, and Robert Russell's as well. One day, the memory of which filled Margaret with unspeakable pain, as she sat in her little room, a letter of farewell came to her, and when it came, the writer was two days on his way to China. Margaret's faith in Robert Russell survived the agony of that time, though she would not harbor the suspicion that pressed upon her as a solution of the mystery.

In a few months after, her sister Fanny was married to George Sinclair, and in three years she was left a widow, with two boys, and little besides—for her husband, though kind and worthy, was unsuccessful; and when, soon after his death, Mr. Crosby failed, they all moved to a western

farm, where they had spent five years when our story opens
—five tedious, dull, unprofitable years to Fanny; five complaining, repining years to Mr. Crosby; and five years of
cheerful toil and care, of self-discipline, and growth in every
womanly and Christian grace, to Margaret.

"I don't think I have utterly failed in drawing the
sweet from the bitter," she thought, as she opened the
Bible again; "but if it had not been for the great and
precious truths and promises of this dear book, what should
I have done? They have never failed me; and to-night,
notwithstanding my backward look, I feel stronger for the
rest of the race."

# CHAPTER II.

Our eyes see all around, in gloom or glow,
Hues of their own, fresh borrowed from the heart.    KEBLE.

THE next morning, almost with the dawn, Margaret was busy in her neat little kitchen; and the quickness and ease with which she accomplished her homely tasks would have charmed a looker-on. It might even have seemed that skimming milk, and making bread, and getting breakfast, were her favorite occupations, for her gray eyes were clear and bright, and there was a certain little air of eagerness in the care she bestowed upon one thing after the other; not so much as if she were in a hurry to see it disposed of, as that she was intent upon doing it as nicely and perfectly as possible. As she worked, she sung sweet snatches of her songs of long ago.

Her dress was the plainest calico, and a checked apron reached nearly to her feet; but she wore a fresh linen collar, and her dark hair, for its beauty and the tastefulness of its arrangement, would have adorned a drawing-room. In fact, through all Margaret did, and all she wore, shone the nameless grace and refinement that no untoward circumstances could conceal.

"Good morning, Jotham," she said, as that individual appeared with his milk-pails.

"Mornin'," was his gracious response.

Margaret went to the pantry, and brought the shining pans for Jotham to strain the milk into, and as she arranged them on the table, she said: "There is something I should like to have you do for me to-day, if you can manage it."

"I guess I ha'n't much more managin to do here," he muttered; "folks as asks favors the hull time an' never grants none, a'n't the kind o' folks fer me."

"You know," said Margaret, nothing daunted by his ill-nature, "I have been wishing for a month past to go and see Mrs. Johnson, down on —— Prairie, but I haven't liked to take the horses from the ploughing; it seemed so necessary that it should be done before the heavy rains come."

"Wal, so it is, I s'pose," said Jotham, taking off his hat and scratching his head.

"Mrs. Johnson's son told me last week that his mother was worse than ever with the rheumatism, and this morning, when I found it was so bright, I thought we'd all take a half holiday, and do several things—go to see Mrs. Johnson, and take some of my crab-apple jam to your mother; you know she was here when I was making it."

"She thought it was mighty good, too."

"We'll take the boys, and I know my father and Mrs. Sinclair will like to go; that is, if you think you can spare the time."

There was a queer expression of mingled suspicion and sheepishness in Jotham's lanky face, as he looked slyly into Margaret's, but as that gave no sign of "wanting to take him in," as he expressed it mentally, he replied, "I shouldn't much wonder ef I could git that ar patch down by the sheep-lot ploughed this forenoon ef I worked pretty smart, an' I guess this week ull finish up the hull on't. Wal, yes, ef you say so, I'll tackle up the team arter dinner, an' go to Miss Johnson's." Jotham bolted from the kitchen, and Margaret, with a merry smile on her face, proceeded with her preparations for breakfast.

"Just in time, my dears," she said, as the sitting-room door burst open and the two boys rushed in, each clamoring for the first kiss.

"You got the first yesterday morning, too, George," cried Jack, as he received a hearty one from his aunt, and gave as hearty a one in return.

"Good reason why; I'm the smartest. I hurry up most, and get dressed first," answered George, as he went hopping about the kitchen on one foot, holding the other up with his hand.

"Oh, George, what a fib! Aunt Margaret, after I was all dressed, and had my hair brushed, he put me into bed again, and then started to run; but I got here 'most as soon."

"Yes, so you did. Now, Georgie, put both your feet on the floor, take this dish in both your hands and put it on the breakfast-table; Jack, you carry this."

"Aunty, grandpa says, why don't we have breakfast?" said George, coming back. "Here, I'll carry the coffee in."

"No, no, Georgie," said his aunt. But she was too late; the handle was hot, and he dropped it as suddenly as he had taken hold of it. The boys stood aghast, and Margaret in dismay and vexation, to see the boiling-hot, fragrant liquid spilled over the floor.

"Oh, George! how could you do such a careless thing?"

"Oh, aunty, I'm sorry—I'm just as sorry as ever I can be."

"Well, never mind, dear; only don't undertake such ambitious things another time. The water is boiling, and I can make more in a few minutes."

"Can't I wipe it up, aunty?" asked George, in a subdued manner, not knowing but that might come under the head of "ambitious things."

Margaret would have preferred to send him into the other room, but he looked so penitent and downcast that she gave him a kiss of forgiveness which sunk deep into his boyish heart, telling him to get the cleaning-pail and cloth, and see what he could do.

Jack wanted to help, but George would not let him. He "sopped" up the coffee and wrung out the cloth a great many times, until the floor was very dry, and until he was quite out of breath with his exertions. Then his aunt told him to wash his hands, for the new coffee was made, and breakfast was all ready.

At the table Margaret made known the little compromise she had effected with Jotham for a ride, instead of a day's ploughing for Tim Simpkins, to the intense delight of the boys, and the subdued satisfaction of Mr. Crosby.

"Nothing could induce me to go on such an expedition," Fanny declared.

"Oh, Fanny, you can't mean that you will not go? I thought it would be such a pleasant little change for you. I am sure you would enjoy it, the day is so bright and bracing," pleaded Margaret.

"I am not so anxious for a drive, much as I need it, as to be willing to go in a farm-wagon, with half a dozen people."

"That need hardly be an objection, one would think, if the half dozen people are your father and children and sister," said Margaret, coldly.

"It would be an objection if it were so many editions of myself," answered Fanny; "my nerves wouldn't bear it. Besides, I am not anxious to cultivate the acquaintance of Granny Johnson and her tribe."

Mr. Crosby saw that Margaret looked disappointed and discouraged, and said, "I think you had better go, Fanny."

"It is useless to urge it, father; it would lay me on my back for a week."

"I know it would lay me on my back for a week if I couldn't go," said George; "wouldn't it you, Jack?"

Jack assented with emphasis.

Margaret was tempted to say "we'll give it all up," she felt so disheartened in her efforts to let a little sunshine into their daily round, and so impatient with her sister's selfishness; but she forced herself to say, cheerfully, "Well, I am sorry my plan does not please you, Fanny; but I think the boys will enjoy it, and it may do father good."

"Hurrah for Aunt Margaret, say I!" cried George; "she knows what's good for boys and grandfathers."

Margaret shook her head, but George could not be suppressed, with such a prospect before him.

"I say, Jack, don't you remember that old woman that looked just like old Mother Hubbard in the books, and how mad she got 'cause I said, 'Mother Hubbard, why don't you give your poor dog a bone?'"

"Yes," cried Jack; "and the poor dog looked as if he never saw any bones—"

"Except his own and Mother Hubbard's," interposed George; "if I'd been him, I'd have picked hers for not giving me any better ones;" and the boys shouted beyond control at their own wit, until their mother retreated to save her nerves. Margaret waited till they had spent some of their wild spirits, before she attempted to show them how thoughtless they had been in talking so lightly of an old woman, and how careless of their mother's comfort and the respect they owed her. She disliked noise so much, and it would be so much more manly for them to be gentle and considerate for her. Margaret wondered how she could have lost patience with Fanny herself, as she talked to the boys of her poor health, and her having so little to make life attractive with that drawback.

The forenoon was a busy one; for, besides the several dainties that Margaret conjured out of small materials, to be left at several doors on the road, with a kind word to add to their sweetness, there were the usual household duties, and little cares for her father and sister; and then the boys' lessons could not be omitted. What firmness and patience were needed to bring their attention down to such drudgery! Margaret's head ached with the effort, but she did not tell them so. Her checks and admonitions were all for their good, and so that their lessons were learned and they were tolerably quiet and good-natured, she cared little for her own discomfort.

At last the happy moment arrived, and, having dashed back to kiss their mother, as she sat by the fire with her book, the boys mounted beside Jotham in his "Sunday-go-to-meetin's," Margaret and her father behind, and they started off. Margaret resolutely put from her all troublesome thoughts, and, exhilarated by the sunshine and the keen air, she chatted gayly with the boys; and even succeeded in making her father forget to shiver and look melancholy; and after they had stopped at Mrs. Johnson's, he would even have confessed, if he had been asked his opinion, that she endured probably more bodily pain than he. But then, some people were born to those things, and he did not allow that he was.

When they stopped at "Mother Hubbard's," where Margaret left something from her basket of goodies, George and Jack jumped down, and patted the dog, giving him some bread and meat from a private supply of their own; but they did not laugh when the dog's queer little owner came hobbling out to welcome Margaret.

A little while before sunset, as they were on their way home by a different road from the one they came, Jotham exclaimed suddenly, "Hello! what's that?"

They all listened, and heard plainly the cries of something in distress, whether human or not was yet uncertain.

"What can it be?" said Margaret. "The sound must come from that little shanty further on. Yes, don't you hear it more distinctly, as we come nearer?"

"You had better turn down this road, Jotham," said Mr. Crosby, "and drive on as fast as you can; it's a very suspicious-looking place, and very lonely."

"Oh, father, no. We must not go on, and leave any thing suffering so. It is a child; don't you hear its cries? Stop at the door, Jotham."

So Jotham stopped, and Margaret, without a moment's hesitation, only heeding her father's warnings, so far as to assure him that there was nothing to fear, got out of the wagon and knocked at the door of the little tumble-down house. No one answered, so she opened it and went in. The cries grew less and less until they ceased, and for some fifteen minutes Mr. Crosby and Jotham watched the small, dingy window, through which they could see a bit of Margaret's shawl. As the door was open a crack, they could hear the clear tones of her voice, as she talked to the inmates, whoever they might be, and their gruff answers.

By-and-by the door opened wide, and Margaret came out, leading a forlorn specimen of black humanity by the hand.

The two forlorn specimens of white humanity that she left behind, a man and woman with sullen faces, made no response to her pleasant good-by, but stood stolidly looking on, while their victim was bestowed on the floor in the back of the wagon.

Then, as they drove away, Margaret explained to her astonished companions that the miserable object she had rescued was a girl of some ten or eleven years, and that she was going to take her home and make a " help " of her.

Jotham gave a low whistle, and the boys leaned this way and that, to gain a glimpse of " little nig."

" Why, Margaret, what folly ! " exclaimed her father. " You surely have taken leave of your senses. She looks more like an ape than a human being."

" No she doesn't, father ; she has bright, intelligent eyes, and, if I am not much mistaken, she has quick wits and a warm heart. But if she proves nothing but a trouble, there was no help for it. I could not leave her to the cruelties of those creatures. I wonder how they happened to settle here. They are an undesirable acquisition to the neighborhood."

When they reached home, Margaret's "help," who seemed to have been gathering her courage and spirits during the ride that took her farther and farther from her persecutors, scrambled from the wagon with the agility of a monkey, and, almost before the horses had stopped, stood leaning against the gate-post, with her hands behind her—her white teeth and her eyes gleaming, as she waited for the others to descend. The boys were down first, and looked at her much as if she had been a wild animal, while she twisted herself about, dug her bare toes into the dust, and thrust her tongue from side to side.

" What's your name ? " asked George

" Miss Linkum," she answered promptly.

The boys laughed loudly, and were joined in their mirth by Margaret.

" Who gave you that name, child ? "

"Dunno; reckon my dad did," she replied, following on as they walked towards the house, still with her hands behind her, and with many contortions of body that greatly edified the boys.

"Who made you?" asked George, curious to know how far her religious education had progressed.

"Specks Massa Linkum did; he made mos' all de brack folks."

The boys were too much horrified at such heterodoxy to laugh, and by this time they had reached the house. Margaret did not care to shock her sister's nerves by introducing her contraband too suddenly, so she took her around to the kitchen-door, bidding the children go and tell their mother about the drive.

"Can you make a fire, Miss Linkum?" asked Margaret, as she laid her hat and shawl on the kitchen-table, and went to the wood-box by the stove.

With a queer little chuckle and an "I reck'n," taking the wood and shavings from Margaret's hands, she placed them lightly together in the stove, and then dropping on her hands and knees, blew the embers that had been covered up in the ashes into a flame, and having put on more wood and shut the stove-door, stood with her hands behind her, showing all her teeth as she looked into Margaret's smiling face.

"How long have you lived with those people, child?" asked Margaret.

"Dunno," she answered, dropping all in a heap on the floor. "'Pears like it was 'mos' forty years."

"Well, poor child, you shall never go back to them, if you would like to live here, and let me teach you to be good and useful. Would you?"

"Reck'n should, Missus;" and the black face fairly shone with satisfaction.

Fanny's amazement at such folly on Margaret's part knew no bounds. "I didn't suppose that even you, Margaret, could do any thing so Quixotic. But pray keep her out of my sight. I shall live in constant terror. And one thing,

Margaret—she must not sleep up-stairs; I never should be able to close my eyes."

So Margaret made her a bedroom out of a closet opening from the kitchen. It seemed like a small paradise to Miss Linkum; and if she knew that there were such things as angels, and that they had wings, she would, no doubt, have been greatly surprised to hear that Margaret, her "magnicefunt Mistis," had none; and she would have been still more so if she could have known what a warm interest she felt in her; how she was planning to make her small means meet over a comfortable wardrobe, and how strong her desire was to let the light of life into her benighted little soul.

# CHAPTER III.

——Yet methinks
You might have made this widowed solitude
A holy rest, a spell of soft gray weather
Beneath whose fragrant dews all tender thoughts
Might bud and burgeon.          KINGSLEY.

"CHLOE! Chloe! where are you?" shouted George one morning, about two weeks after the advent of the individual at the farm first known as Miss Linkum, and now as Chloe. "Chloe! Chloe! what are you at? why don't you come when you are called?"

"Why, here I is, Massa George; don't you see me? I'se been sweepin' yere all dis time," answered Chloe, briskly, as George came around the corner of the house, and found her sweeping away with all her might at the clean flagging in front of the kitchen-door.

"You little scamp, why didn't you answer me before, making me split my lungs shouting at you, and you hearing all the time!"

"Oh, I nebber did hear you, Massa George. I nebber know'd you called me, nebber; an' dat's de trufe;" and Chloe shook her head solemnly.

"You tell awful stories, Chloe. Aunt Margaret will shut you up again, if you don't look out. Come along; mother wants you."

Chloe dropped her broom and darted into the house, leaving George to follow at his leisure.

"Where have you been all this time, Chloe?" asked Margaret, who was hearing Jack say his history-lesson.

"I'se done been sweepin' an' clarin' up, an' been huntin' eggs in all the nesses, an'——"

"I told you not to hunt for eggs any more, Chloe."

"Oh, laus, I done forgot, Miss Marg'et. I'll nebber go near dem nesses agin, nebber; an' dat's de trufe."

"Well, be sure that you don't, unless I send you. Now, go up to Mrs. Sinclair."

"Oh! what's that, Aunty?" cried Jack, seizing hold of Chloe's right arm, and pointing to a big round lump under her left. "It's plain enough to see what she's been doing."

"Come to me, Chloe," said Margaret, "and let me see what you have in your dress."

"Oh, Miss Marg'et, it an't nuffin—'tan't only a awful crack I gin my shin when I was workin', an' it all swolled up; but it don't hurt none," she added, eluding Margaret's hand, and jamming herself against the wall.

Margaret rose, and led Chloe out of the room, much to the disgust of the boys, who were anxious to see the fun.

"Oh, you hurt me *so*, Miss Marg'et—it's so sore!" cried Chloe, as Margaret proceeded to examine the lump in her side.

"Take the apple out, Chloe."

"'Tan't a apple, Miss Marg'et; 'tan't nuffin 't'all, an' dat's de trufe," declared Chloe, looking straight into Margaret's eyes.

"Chloe, mind me at once, and take the apple from your dress."

Without further parley, Chloe stuck her hand into the waist of her dress, and produced a fine pippin, one of a half dozen from a graft that bore for the first time that year; and she thereupon burst into a loud, dolorous cry.

"Chloe, stop crying, and tell me if you took any but this. Tell me the truth."

"I declar' I didn't, Miss Marg'et. Dis one jes' falled off of de closet shef right onto my head, an' I picked um up an' was jes' agoin' to gib um to you, an' dat's de trufe."

"I'm very much afraid that it isn't the truth, Chloe; but I shall find out all about it; and remember, I sha'n't pass it by if you have told me a lie. I must do something to make you feel that lies are dreadfully wicked. Mrs. Sinclair has been waiting for you a long time. You can tell her that I kept you."

Only two apples remained on the shelf where Margaret had put them for safe keeping, and she decided to try the effect of close confinement on Chloe for the whole of the next day.

Chloe had shown no lack of ability to learn, and to do well whatever she was set about. She was really a great help to Margaret in many ways. She could churn, sweep, set the table, and wash the dishes quickly and nicely, if nothing more entertaining claimed her attention; but every thing that went on out of doors seemed to demand her personal supervision. If she happened to be alone, and so much as a dog passed the window, or a wagon went by in the road, down would go dish-towel and dish on the floor, or the stove-hearth, or where not, and out of the door she would dash, either to give chase to the dog, or to perch herself on the gate-post, where she would sit drumming with her heels, and singing bits of plantation-songs, until recalled to duty by some one discovering her desertion.

One day she saw Jotham go towards the pig-pen with a pail of sour milk, and having waited till he had poured it into the trough, and disappeared in the barn—as a general thing she preferred to keep at a respectful distance from Jotham—she started for the pen, with a potato in one hand and a knife in the other, and climbed up to see the pigs eat; it was a favorite pastime of hers. All of a sudden, as she balanced herself across the edge of the pen, she felt herself tipping, and, though she threw potato and knife away, and grasped at the boards, she landed head first in the trough. The consequent commotion among the pigs, and the screams of Chloe, brought Jotham, who rescued her in no gentle manner, and took her to the house, where, in spite of her limpings, and writhings, and other attempts to excite sympathy, her appearance caused shouts of laughter from Margaret and the boys.

For a week Margaret heard her say her prayers every night, and then, thinking that she had been sufficiently drilled, left her to say them by herself, when, instead of kneeling by the bed, and saying, "Our Father," she sat on the floor, and rocking herself back and forth, muttered something in a sing-song tone that certainly was not a prayer.

Margaret never lost patience with her. She had counted the cost when she brought the child from her wretched home, and never doubted that time and care would develop the moral sense of which she seemed so sadly devoid.

Fanny had occasion every day to say, look, or act, "I told you so," as she witnessed Margaret's trials with Chloe; but she had so far overcome her own repugnance as to have her act in the capacity of lady's-maid mornings when she felt languid, and rose late. She even allowed her to brush her long, fair hair—a service that, strange to say, Chloe performed very well, only once or twice, in the course of the half hour, bringing the brush down harder than was comfortable on Fanny's head, and only now and then giving her locks a severe pull. She was not likely to commit any such little carelessness with impunity, for Fanny's slipper was always at hand to administer as condign punishment as her small strength would admit.

Fanny's needing help in performing her toilet did not grow out of its elaborateness. She took care of her beautiful hair as one would of a relic of some lost friend, and often sighed over it, as she thought of the days when it shared universal admiration with her languishing blue eyes and graceful figure. But after it had been brushed till it was soft and glossy, she gathered it up in a careless knot, and put it in a net for the day, while day after day she appeared in a faded loose-gown and little gray shawl. It never occurred to her that it might have a cheering effect if she were to wear some of her many pretty dresses and laces and ribbons, carefully preserved since her retirement from society; but even if it had, it was by far too much trouble to dress up, when there was nobody to look at her save her father and sister and children. Away off on a Western farm, there was no object in looking nice; and when she gave Margaret's dress a thought, it was to wonder how she could spend so much time over it; she must be fond of dress for its own sake.

This morning Fanny was feeling "unusually feeble and depressed," and when Chloe had brushed her hair and performed other services, she told her that she should not leave her room that day, and would have some tea and toast, and an egg, and currant jelly, for her dinner. "And here, Chloe, take this blanket down, and heat it to put around my feet. I have no circulation whatever; and, child, see who is opening the front gate."

Chloe rushed to the window.

"O, laus, I dunno, missus. I'll jes' go an' see," and she started for the stairs.

"Is it a man or a woman?" cried Fanny.

"A man, missus."

In another moment Chloe had opened the door for the visitor without his having the trouble of knocking, and stood in her favorite attitude, hands behind her, and the toes of her shoes digging into the floor, waiting for him to enter, which he did as soon as he recovered from the start her sudden appearance gave him.

George and Jack nudged each other, and laughed behind their books, and George whispered, "Bag of bones!" while Margaret shook hands with him and asked him to sit down, which it took him some little time to accomplish. His joints seemed stiff, and cracked as they bent. His legs were long, and his feet so large as to be in their own way. Being fairly settled in his chair, he set his tall, narrow-brimmed beaver-hat on the floor, took off his cotton gloves and placed them in it, wiped his long face with his yellow handkerchief, smoothed his scanty locks, and laying his hands together, remarked, "Sister Crosby, I hope I see you well."

"Thank you," said Margaret, who had sat quietly waiting to hear the pleasant hope expressed, while the boys held their books tight over their mouths, "I am very well."

"I am most happy to hear it. I hope Miss Sinclair is well?"

2

"Thank you, yes, as well as usual."

"My dear young friends," turning slowly towards the boys, "I hope I see *you* well?"

"They are always well," answered Margaret.

"Well, dear friends, health is a inestimable blessing, and I do feel to hope and trust that you appreciate your privileges. Many of my flock are enjoying very poor health at this present time."

Margaret could not at once reply to that remark, and Mr. Skinner laid his hand over his capacious mouth, and gave a short, loud cough, that might have startled any one hearing it for the first time. It was his method, apparently, of giving a fresh start to his ideas, or filling a pause that was likely to prove an awkward one.

Casting a glance around towards the door, and espying Chloe, he hitched his chair a little nearer to Margaret's, and said, "I see you have a colored individooal here. Is she temporal or permanent?"

"Chloe is permanent, I hope," answered Margaret; "she has been here two weeks already."

"Ah, well, I hope you will not neglect to look after her spiritooal concerns. She has a immortal soul, even if she has a black skin. I would impress that upon you, sister Crosby. We orto oversee the distinctions of color and race, and try to do good to all ages and ranks and colors. When opportunities is set afore you, embrace 'em."

Margaret answered that she hoped she should always do so, and then excused herself, taking Chloe with her to get dinner, it being an understood thing that Mr. Skinner would eat at least one meal with them whenever he came.

Another cough enabled him to remark to the boys that he hoped they loved their books. "Books is very valible, my dear young friends, but while you love your jogaphy, 'rithmetic and spellin', *don't* neglect books that distil good principles into you. I have some tracks here that I can recommend to young persons. Here is one on the sin of gambling. Let me forewarn you never to gamble. Ah,

Miss Sinclair, I hope I see you well," and he rose gradually from his chair, and held out his hand and wrist to Fanny, who entered the room, looking as she never did except when some visitor came. It is not to be supposed that Mr. Skinner could have any interest for her, except that he was a person outside her own home-circle. She had no other reason for receiving him so graciously.

"Oh, mother, you do look so beautiful," cried Jack, throwing down his books, and stroking her pretty blue dress, and then her hair. "I do wish you would fix up so every day."

"There, my dears, run and help your aunt, while I talk with Mr. Skinner; it is so seldom that I have the relief of seeing any body," she said, turning to him, as the boys ran out of the room.

Mr. Skinner coughed, and seeming to consider his feet in the way of his conversing with freedom, tucked them back as far as he could under his chair.

"Are you still a wanderer?" asked Fanny.

"Yes, even so—for the present. My flock is a scattered one, and I take aim to see them all in a pastor's capacity now and then, and I preach here'n there, whenever I can git an audience togather. But I think I see a opening to a settlement now."

Fanny inquired with kind interest into his plans, and while they conversed, Margaret and Chloe set the table, and brought in the dinner; and Mr. Crosby was summoned from his room, where he had been busy all the forenoon looking over old business-papers.

"Chloe," Margaret said, "go and find George. I sent him to lead Mr. Skinner's horse out to the barn for Jotham to take care of, and he hasn't come in yet."

Mr. Skinner, in the capacity of pastor, asked a blessing that included every article of food on the table, touched upon every people and condition, and lasted several minutes. He then set himself energetically to the business in hand, helping himself to things within his reach—and it could hardly be said that any thing was without the reach of his long arm.

Generally, at table, the conversation was confined to Margaret and the boys, but to-day Fanny was bright and animated; and while Margaret deprecated the silly, weak vanity displayed by her sister, she was really glad to see her drawn out of her languor, even by Mr. Skinner.

Margaret was not a little amazed when, rising from the table, that gentleman, with considerable shuffling and several particularly loud coughs, signified to her that he wished to see her alone for a brief season, as he had a few words to say to her that it would be well to say in private.

Fanny looked very curious, as Margaret, secretly annoyed at being detained when she wanted to see about George, who had not come in yet, replied that she would have to ask him into the kitchen, and led the way.

Mr. Skinner stared around the comfortable place, seeing, through the open pantry-door, hints of good things for the outer man, that seemed to encourage the inner, for he coughed, and began:

"Sister Crosby, I have been a-feeling for some time past that my usefulness to my fellow-creaturs would be inhanced if I had a helpmeet and a settled habitation." He stopped to cough, and then continued.

"It is a arduous post, but I am sure you could fill it; and having such a opportunity to take a post of usefulness, you couldn't fail to embrace it."

Margaret managed to quell a merry laugh that almost would come, and answered with a tolerably steady voice,

"No, Mr. Skinner, I can't embrace this opportunity. I don't see that it would add to my usefulness to take the post you refer to."

Mr. Skinner had clasped his hands together, and stood with mouth and eyes opened wide in astonishment, when Chloe burst into the kitchen.

"Oh, Miss Marg'et, it's dre'fful! oh, laus, an't it, though!" and she broke into a dismal cry.

"Chloe, what is it?" said Margaret, catching her arm. "Where is George?"

"Oh, laus, he's done been t'rown off de hoss, an' he's 'mos' dead.  Oh!"

"Where is he, Chloe? tell me, quick!" said Margaret, her face perfectly colorless.

"Down in de field, by de corn-crib;" and Margaret waited to hear no more, but sped across the yard and across the fields, Chloe after her.  Before reaching the place, she was agonized by hearing moans of pain.

"Georgie," she called, "where are you, darling?"

"Here, Aunty," answered a feeble voice; and down close by the corn-crib lay poor George, his face drawn with pain, and pale as death.

Margaret bent over him tenderly, and laid her hand on his head.

"My poor child, what is it?   Where are you hurt?"

"I guess it ain't much, Aunty; but I can't move my arm."

"Well, my love, don't try to move it.  Jotham is coming, and he will carry you home."

A little way from them stood Mr. Skinner's lean, hungry-looking horse, now nibbling at the withered grass, and again casting baffled glances at the yellow corn shining through the cracks in the crib.

Margaret understood it all, and smiled in the midst of her great anxiety for George.  Jotham raised him in his strong arms, and Margaret walked by his side, holding the well hand in hers.  Chloe, seeing that she was unnoticed, seized the bridle of the hungry animal, and dragged him after her up to the house.

When Fanny saw George in Jotham's arms, pale and suffering, she fell into violent hysterics, obliging her father and Jack to devote themselves to her—for Margaret would not leave her charge—while Jotham mounted the lean horse and rode at his utmost speed for the doctor, who lived three miles away, leaving Mr. Skinner to nurse his knees as he watched the gradual recovery of Mrs. Sinclair, and listened

to George's moans, who lay in his little bed up-stairs, tended
by his aunt. In an hour Jotham came back with the sorry
tidings that the doctor was away from home, and would not
be home till midnight. Mr. Skinner, with great alacrity,
climbed upon his horse and rode away, and Margaret quietly
gave Jotham minute directions with regard to splinters, and
got bandages ready. George's arm was broken, she had discovered, just above the wrist, and she would not run the risk
of leaving it till the doctor could come. She understood the
anatomy of the arm, and felt that she could set the broken
bone. George trusted her more implicitly than he would
have trusted the doctor, and bore the pain like a man.

Margaret bore her pain like a tender, strong-hearted
woman, only having to go to the window for air when the
arm was all bound up, and the poor boy lying pale, but quiet,
with a dim impression that an angel was taking care of him;
and in the morning, when the doctor came, he declared that
he could not have done better himself.

# CHAPTER IV.

O my beloved! Art thou so near unto me,
And yet I cannot behold thee?    LONGFELLOW.

"I AM glad the sun shines," thought Margaret, one Sunday morning, as she stood at the door, looking out.

There had been a light fall of snow during the night, that still covered the brown fields with a mantle of glittering whiteness, and rested in soft ridges on the branches of trees and the tops of the fences, and a sky of cloudless blue smiled over all. The air was keen and frosty, making Margaret's cheeks glow; and the sunshine crept into her heart, and shone out through her eyes.

"Oh, Aunt Margaret, isn't this a jolly day?" said George, rushing by her, and taking a slide down the snow-covered walk, then coming back with his collar and neck-ribbon, and a handkerchief to make into a sling for his arm.

"I don't think jolly is a very nice word to apply to Sunday; do you?"

"Well, maybe it isn't; but don't you call this a mighty nice day, anyhow?"

"Yes, I do, Georgie; I've been blessing the sunshine and blue sky, and the beautiful snow, with all my heart, and I'm glad you feel so happy about it, too. What do you think of a ride over to the red school-house this morning, to hear your friend Mr. Thomas preach?"

"Aunty, you don't mean it! Are we truly, sure enough, going?"

"Truly, and sure enough, Georgie. I didn't say anything about it last night, it seemed so likely to storm to-day. I didn't want to disappoint you and Jack; but Mr. Thomas saw Jotham yesterday when he went to the mill, and told him that he was going to preach to-day, and hoped we could all go."

"It's perfectly splendid!" cried George. "I never was so glad of a thing in all my life. Ain't it as much as three miles there? . Are we coming home at noon, Aunty?"

"Not unless you are very anxious to! Mr. Thomas said we must go home with Mrs. Davis to dinner, and go to meeting again in the afternoon."

George gave vent to his delight in various ways, last of all bestowing upon Margaret a violent hug and kiss, and then rushed up-stairs to tell Jack the good news. As Margaret turned back into the kitchen, she found Chloe sitting on the floor near by, and saw that her attention had been devoted to the plans for the day, while her work had been at a standstill.

Chloe threw her apron over her head, and drew it down tight by the corners, as she said, "Ain't I gwine, too, Miss Marg'et?"

"Going where, Chloe?"

"'Long o' you, and Massa George, and Massa Jack."

"We are going to meeting, Chloe. What makes you think you would like to go?"

"I seen ole Missus go times 'nough down in Virginny, an' I'se like to go 'long o' you, Miss Marg'et."

"Well, Chloe, I wish you could go; I should like to take you, and have been trying to think of a way; but I am afraid you will have to give it up this time. You know Mrs. Sinclair will want her breakfast when she gets up, and you know she and my father must have some luncheon. If you are a good child, you shall go the very next time I do."

Chloe went about her work, but with a very dejected air.

"Chloe, do you remember the Bible stories I told you last Sunday?" asked Margaret, as she busied herself about the breakfast.

"Dem ones 'bout dat ar kind Massa. dat cured up all de sick folks? I reckon I does."

"Well, to-night, when I get home, we will have some more stories out of the Bible, and sing hymns, and have a nice time."

Chloe brightened up very much.

"Chloe, bring that bowl of sour cream for the Johnny-cake."

"Dere ain't none, Miss Marg'et. I seed Jotham pour dat ar sour cream into de pig's pail."

Margaret knew that Chloe had a weakness for "clabber," and did not for a moment credit her statement; but said nothing, waiting to see if her awakening conscience would move her to tell the truth, as it had done several times of late.

She did not wait in vain; for, after clattering among the pans and dishes on the table a little, and opening and shutting the stove-door violently, as if to drown a voice she did not care to hear, Chloe darted into the pantry, and called out, "Dat ar was a awful lie, Miss Marg'et. I done eat it up. Please to f'gim'me."

"It was very wrong of you to eat the cream, Chloe; and I'm very sorry you didn't think in time to tell the truth at first. But I am sure you don't mean to tell any more wrong stories. You will soon learn to think before you speak. Of course, I will forgive you, Chloe."

Chloe came out of the pantry hanging her head, and feeling as if she would sooner bite her tongue off than do any thing to vex "Miss Marg'et" again.

Margaret tried to persuade her father to go with them, but he dreaded the cold. So she drew the lounge near the fire, and placed a stand by it with such books and papers as she thought he might want, and left careful directions with Chloe about Fanny's breakfast and the lunch.

There was nothing that Margaret regretted more in their isolated life than not being near a church. She felt it for herself, and still more for the boys, who needed, she knew, every good influence to outweigh that of the inert, self-indulgent lives of their mother and grandfather. Mr. Thomas's church was at Jonesville, eight miles from the farm, and it was very seldom that they could go so far. Except in the winter months, the horses needed Sunday to rest from their hard week-days' work, and in winter the roads were almost impassable. Mr. Thomas had been a kind friend ever since they came to the farm, but he lived too far away to see them often.

He was an earnest, cheerful Christian, and had a large, warm heart, with a great deal of practical wisdom. His mind instinctively sought the beautiful in nature and the hopeful in people, and he always strove to let the light in, rather than drive the darkness out. He was a favorite with old and young, and the people for miles around, gathered at the little red school-house on that bright Sabbath morning.

The benches were all filled, and children sat on desks placed against the wall, and a few men stood back by the door; but there was perfect quiet as soon as Mr. Thomas rose in his desk, and gave out the opening hymn,

"How firm a foundation, ye saints of the Lord."

There was a little delay, and then a full, clear tenor voice sung the first few notes of the grand old Portuguese Hymn, and all followed.

Why did that first strain send such a wild thrill through Margaret's heart? To other ears the voice was a pleasant one, but to Margaret's it was like the sounding of a *reveillé*, awakening the music of long ago, and summoning a crowd of memories, of hopes and fears, of happy love, of joys and woes, which came thronging together upon her heart and brain, while she sat spellbound among the singers, seeing nothing but scenes from the past, gleaming and fading, ever changing; hearing, above the voices around her, above the confusion of sounds, in her own heart, those awakening tones.

The hymn ceased, and with the stillness that followed came a hush upon Margaret's wildly-throbbing pulses, and she sat as one in a dream, mechanically bowing her head when the words, "Let us pray," fell vaguely on her ear, unconsciously following the words of the earnest prayer, mechanically raising her head when the "Amen" was uttered. Then she waited, scarcely breathing, while the Scriptures and

another hymn were read, to catch the first sound of that
voice.  Again it sent a deep thrill to her heart, but now
the memories summoned by the first notes of the sweet *re-*
*veillé* no longer crowded upon her in wild confusion.  A
calm, dreamy sense of a presence crept over her, and never
thinking to wonder or question, or feeling in haste to have
the sense verified by sight, she heard as from afar off the
words of the text: "Thou wilt keep him in perfect peace,
whose mind is stayed on Thee."  She even felt an answering
consciousness as Mr. Thomas dwelt upon the perfect peace
that is made the right of every child of God; upon the perfect faith that brings such peace, and upon the glorious foundation for such faith; and, though the words sounded remote
to her ear, her heart felt their influence, and in the closing
prayer and the benediction, mingling with the sense of the
presence, came gratitude for the peace that had never forsaken her in all her troubles.

The spell came over her again when the bustle of moving
feet and the subdued hum of voices began, and, as in a
dream, she shook hands with one and another, returning
kindly greetings, and waited.

Again that wild thrill, as the voice reached her, saying:
"I must bid you good-by, Mrs. Davis; I am sorry to go, but
I fear there is no help for it."

"Are you really going to leave us now?" asked Mr.
Thomas, pressing past Margaret with outstretched hand.
"I hoped you would at least go to my sister's to dinner."

"Thank you, it would give me great pleasure; but I
must take the midnight train from Jonesville, and I shall
have but little time, as it is, to see my kind aunt."

"Won't you stop on your way back?"

"No——" and Margaret lost the rest, except the words,
"Good-by, good-by."

At these knell-like sounds Margaret turned, and saw a
face with dark earnest eyes, lighted up by a smile that
seemed to Margaret like a ray of brightest sunshine.  An
instant, and the face was turned away, and disappeared in

the crowd of curious people at the door. A moment more, and horses' hoofs and carriage-wheels sounded on the stones in front of the school-house, then along the road, and died away in the distance.

"Why, Aunty, why don't you speak to Mrs. Davis? She has asked you twice if you were ready to come home with her," George said, laying his hand on her arm.

"O, I didn't hear you; yes, I am ready to go home. Let us go at once."

George looked alarmed.

"You don't mean our home, do you, Aunt Margaret? You said we were going to Mrs. Davis's, and she wants us to."

Margaret looked at George and at Mrs. Davis, who was perfectly mystified by Margaret's strange manner, and distressed at her exceeding paleness.

"My dear," she said, gently, "you are not well. Come home with me, and have a cup of tea, and take a rest, and you will feel better. The room is close and warm."

When they reached the house, Mrs. Davis took Margaret up-stairs, and said: "Is there any thing I can do for you, my dear? I don't know whether it is in your body or your heart that you are ailing, but I know there is a trouble somewhere, and if there is any thing I can do to relieve it, you will tell me?"

"Thank you, there is nothing—if you will let me rest a little while."

"That you shall do, dear. Dinner isn't ready yet, and even when it is, you needn't come down." And she went out and left Margaret alone with her new, bewildering agony, and with Him whose promise of peace excepts no circumstances, has but one condition.

When dinner was nearly over, the door opened, and Margaret came in and took her place at the table. She was very pale, and her hair was brushed back from her forehead as if she could not bear its weight; but the look of pain had left her face, and her smile was not forced, as she said, "I am not to blame for being so late; you didn't call me, and I heard no bell."

"No, of course I didn't call you, and I see I was wise, for you look better for the little rest."

"You are a very wise little woman, Jenny," said her brother, "and generally have your wise way; but you did not succeed in keeping Mr. Russell, for which I am very sorry."

"So am I."

"And so are the children," added Mr. Davis. "There was a great lamentation among them when they found he had really gone, though he bade them good-by this morning."

"Yes," said Mrs. Davis, turning to Margaret; "he only came last night, and yet he has carried the children's hearts away with him."

"Who is Mr. Russell, any way?" asked George, who had been hearing his praises from the Davis children.

"He is a gentleman," said Mr. Thomas, "who went to China some ten years ago and made a great deal of money, and has come home to live in New York and enjoy it. And a great deal of good he does with it."

"Well, what has he come 'way out here for, if he lives in New York?"

"He has a sister living in St. Louis, whose husband died very suddenly, and he is going on to settle up his affairs, and take his sister home to New York, if she prefers to leave St. Louis. Is that satisfactory, my boy?"

"You see, Georgie," said Mrs. Davis, "our father and his father lived in New York when we were all children, and we went to school together, and Mr. Thomas and Mr. Russell were great friends. So he came a little out of his way to see us."

"Well, Aunt Margaret, I'm going to China when I get grown up, wouldn't you? And then, when I've found a lot of money, I'll buy a big house in New York, and we'll be as grand as any thing. Won't that be jolly?"

"Yes, but by that time I shall be wearing mob-caps and spectacles; so you must not count on my keeping house for you."

"Ho, ho, ho! as if you could ever get as old as that!"

They all went to meeting again in the afternoon, and no one could have told that Margaret's heart had been so fiercely tried that day—that she was still in the "deep waters," and testing to the full the strength of that promise of peace.

# CHAPTER V.

So tired, so tired, my heart and I.    Mrs. Browning.

It was snowing fast when Margaret and the boys returned home from the little red school-house, and it was nearly dark.

"Come into the kitchen, children, and shake the snow off," said Margaret.

The kitchen was cold and dark—no light and no fire—and Margaret felt disappointed; she had expected better things of Miss Linkum.

"Well, Margaret," was Fanny's greeting, as they entered the sitting-room; "I am curious to know what you will say *now* to the wisdom of taking a little black vagrant into the house, and treating her like a civilized human being."

"What do you mean, Fanny? What has Chloe done?"

"Done! Something that I think you ought to feel very thankful for; but I suppose you will consider it a great affliction."

"You speak in riddles, Fanny. Pray tell me what is the trouble."

"Chloe has gone away," said Mr. Crosby, from the sofa.

"Gone away!" cried the boys, in amazement.

"Yes, run away," said Fanny; "and it's my opinion we are well rid of her, though I should like to know that she didn't carry any thing away with her. To think how I let her brush my hair and be in my room so much—the little ingrate!"

"How do you know she has run away? When did you miss her first?" asked Margaret.

"She went soon after noon," said Mr. Crosby.

"Yes," said Fanny; "she got my breakfast when I woke, and I must say it was quite nice, considering; and when I got up, she laced my boots and did my hair; but when I was through with her, she hung round my chair, asking me questions that I didn't half understand, about how 'Miss Marg'et found out dem t'ings' about something or other, I don't know what; and when I told her I couldn't be troubled with her, she asked if you would be gone much longer. I suppose she wanted to find out if she had time enough to get away."

"Oh, it was not that, I know," said Margaret, with tears in her eyes.

"Well, then she left my room, and by-and-by I heard father calling, and came down to see if any thing was the matter, when he told me that Chloe had just gone off with some persons he had seen prowling around."

"Who were they, father? What did they look like?" asked Margaret, anxiously.

"I think they were the people you took Chloe from. I got up to take a turn or two across the room, and as I passed the window, I saw two very shabby, ill-looking creatures—a man and a woman—walking slowly by on the other side of the road, and looking slyly at the house. I didn't pay much attention to them, but pretty soon Chloe came down-stairs and went into the kitchen, and then I heard her singing out in the yard. By-and-by I heard the sound of persons running in the road. I went to the door, and there were that same man and woman, with Chloe between them, making from the house as fast as they could go. I called, and Chloe looked back, but they only ran the faster—and that's the last of them."

"How could you think the poor child had run away?" asked Margaret, the hot tears falling over her pale cheeks. "She has been stolen by those same cruel wretches. Georgie, run out to the barn, and tell Jotham that I want the horses and wagon again right away. Tell him to make haste."

"You are insane," said Fanny; "it is at least four hours since they started."

"It is madness, Margaret, in such a storm, and so nearly

dark as it is," said her father. " If the child is stolen, I am
really sorry for her; but you cannot find them."

Just then there was a great deal of stamping in the kitchen,
and a moment after, Jotham's head appeared at the sitting-
room door.

"What's this about takin' them hosses out agin to-night?
That's somethin' beyend my carkalations. It's snowin' an'
blowin' like fits."

" It's something very important, Jotham," said Margaret;
"get the wagon as quick as you can, and I'll tell you where
I want to go."

"Wal, I s'pose ther's no help for't. I'm ready when you
be;" and he shut the door not so very gently, and Margaret
put on her things.

"I am only going to see if they have taken her back to
the old place," she said, in answer to her father's remonstrances. "I am afraid it is a forlorn hope, but I could not rest
without doing that much."

It was a forlorn hope, for they found the old shanty deserted, the door partly open and the snow drifting in; and
there was nothing left to show that any thing in the shape of
humanity had ever been there, except the miserable straw
pallet that lay in one corner; and Margaret's heart ached for
poor Chloe—perhaps even then being dragged through the
driving storm by her tormentors.

The evening passed drearily enough. Mr. Crosby was
silent, as usual ; Fanny dozed awhile in her easy-chair, and
then went to bed; the boys were tired and cross, and Margaret felt more utterly sad, hopeless, and desolate than ever
before. The loss of Chloe, strange to say, seemed uppermost.
It was a trouble that she could grasp; it was the certain
misery and degradation of one who had aroused her warm,
pitiful interest, and whose constant proofs of a loving heart,
and quick, bright intelligence, had strengthened that interest
every day.

The other trouble was bewildering, and was to be realized
as her doubly " desolated days " went on.

So, as she lay awake nearly the whole of the long night, hearing the wind whistle around the house, and the snow beat against the window, it was of Chloe that she thought most; and mingling with her pity and anxiety for the poor fugitive, came the question, Why, in going to meet the strange ordeal of that day, need she have left Chloe to such a dreary fate?

When she did sleep, it was to dream wild dreams that were more painful than her waking thoughts. Only once she had a little respite from the terrible dangers, the weary journeys, the hopeless partings from loved ones, that haunted her sleep. For one blessed moment she felt her mother's arms around her, her head resting on her bosom, and she thought that after the long years of separation they were to part no more. But when she looked into those sweet eyes, and began to recount her sorrows, gradually the lovely, tender face faded from her gaze, the warm encircling arms fell from her, and a shadowy, mist-like form floated away, slowly and sadly, leaving her alone and desolate again, to listen with wildly-beating heart to wind and storm, and to feel as if she had been permitted to taste the joys of paradise only to be banished.

Morning came at last, and Margaret lay with her eyes fixed languidly on the snowy panes, through which she could see the few flakes that "still wavered down," when there came a loud continuous knocking at her door, and Jack called,

"Aunty, why don't you come down? We're all of us dressed and ready for breakfast, and there ain't any. Oh, are you sick?" he said, opening the door wider, and coming to her bed. "Why, you are most as pale as the pillow-case, Aunt Margaret. Are you very sick?"

"No, not very," she answered, in a voice so low and weak that Jack hardly knew it, "but I don't feel strong enough to get up this morning. Has Bridget come?"

"Yes, Aunty; she's been here a good while, I guess."

"Has Jotham made the fires?"

"Yes, Aunty."

" Well, Jacky, tell Bridget that I am not very well, and ask her to get the breakfast; and you show her where the things are. You and Georgie can set the table."

" Well, we will, but I should like to do something for you," Jack replied wistfully.

" That will be for me, dear," and Margaret turned away, as if too weary to say more.

Jack went softly down-stairs to tell his grandfather and George and Bridget how sick his Aunt Margaret was, how white and weak. George started for the stairs, and Mr. Crosby followed slowly, thinking how much trouble he had. Jack ran to ask George not to make such a noise, for if Aunt Margaret's head ached, he would make it worse; so George went into the room on tiptoe. She opened her eyes and smiled as her father and George came to her bedside, and looked anxiously at her; but she did not speak. Mr. Crosby felt her pulse, and laid his hand on her forehead.

" You have no fever, child. Does your head ache? Is your throat sore? "

" No, father, I am only tired; I shall be rested by-and-by."

" Why, couldn't you get rested in a whole night? " asked George, in surprise. " I was most tired to death last night, but now I ain't the least bit."

" I shall have Bridget make you a cup of tea, child; that will refresh you," said her father.

" I'll make it myself; I know how," said George; and down he went, confiding to Jotham, who was in the kitchen, that his aunt was very sick.

Jotham declared himself " not at all surprised, arter that harum-scarum ride in the snow," and without consulting any body but himself, when he had shovelled paths for Bridget's convenience in hanging out the clothes, he saddled a horse and went for Dr. Somers.

" Father," said Margaret, as Mr. Crosby turned to leave the room, " will you have Jotham make inquiries about poor Chloe, and have every thing done that can be, to get some trace of her? "

" Yes, I will, though I am afraid it will do no good."

The table was set very neatly, the boys taking pains to have every thing as their aunt liked it; but the breakfast gave proof that every body did not cook as nicely as she did. The beefsteak was fried in lard, the bread was cut in " chunks," as George said, the coffee was muddy, and Mr. Crosby and the boys wondered how many such meals they should have to eat. George's tea was much more successful than Bridget's coffee.

Fanny never knew Margaret to be sick before, since they had measles and scarlet fever together, when they were children, and was greatly surprised and dismayed, when she came down-stairs in the middle of the forenoon, to find the doctor taking off his great-coat, and warming his hands preparatory to a professional visit to her sister. The shock was so great to her nerves, that, if it had not been for the pleasant little excitement of the doctor's unexpected presence, she would certainly have had hysterics. Perhaps the fact that he had very little appreciation of such demonstrations, and had once or twice checked hers, rather too summarily for graceful effect, helped her to restrain her feelings.

" I hope Margaret's case isn't a serious one," she said, as the doctor took up his medicine-chest.

" I hope there is nothing contagious the matter with her," he answered, with a curious twinkle in his keen blue eyes; " but if I find it is nothing serious enough to keep her safe in bed, for a week at least, I shall surely bleed or blister her. I have been wishing for a long time to see the young woman laid by for awhile, and I won't be baulked;" saying which, he went up-stairs.

He shook his head as he met Margaret's languid eyes, that always had a bright welcome for him, and felt her feeble pulse.

" Child, what do you mean by having such a dead-and-alive wrist as that, and such faded-out looking eyes? I expected to find you with a galloping pulse, and a red face, that I could put down at a dose, and then give you some thing to keep you in bed a week or so. What have you been doing ? "

Margaret smiled faintly, and shook her head.

" Don't you shake your head at me, Miss. There is something to pay when any body, especially such a body as you, gets so exhausted and lifeless. Why, you hardly take the trouble to breathe. I am sure I don't know what to make of you ; " and he knit his shaggy brows over his medicine-case.

" Doctor, you know my Chloe, that you thought was so handy and bright when George broke his arm ? "

" Yes. What of her ? "

" Yesterday, while we were gone to church, the man and woman I took her from came and stole her away."

" The dickens they did ! " cried the doctor, looking at Margaret. " Is that the trouble—pooh ! no, of course it is not. Well, can I do any thing about it, I wonder ? I can make inquiries, and look into all the shanties and holes I come to in my rides."

" I shall be so thankful if you will, though I am afraid she is far enough away before now."

" I wish she was here," said the doctor ; " she'd take care of you ! "

" I just want to lie still awhile, and do nothing. That's all, unless you could put my brains to sleep for a little."

" That's just what I would do, if I knew how. I'd like to take them out and see what they've been doing with you, if I could get them back again. Here, take this powder, and have whoever takes care of you put this—who is going to take care of you ? " he said, almost fiercely.

" Oh, I shall have good care."

" Yes, I'll see that you do ; " and he gently arranged her pillows to the perfection of comfort, and left her.

" How do you find Margaret ? " " What is the matter with Margaret ? " were questions asked in a breath by Mr. Crosby and Fanny.

" Where are those boys ? What are they making such a racket for ? " demanded the doctor, going to the kitchen-door, which, when opened, disclosed a scene of direst confusion. It came to pass in this wise: George and Jack had insisted upon washing the dishes after breakfast, and Bridget had yielded willingly enough, being anxious to get the washing done, and go home to her children.

George washed the dishes and Jack wiped them, and with the excitement of their novel occupation, their spirits rose. So, after having a grand frolic over the dish-pan, splashing the water over the floor and themselves, and making a "fa'arful muss," as Bridget said, they seized the opportunity, while she was hanging up her clothes, to rush to the wash-tub, so as to have a larger field for their operations. They were up to their elbows in soap-suds when Bridget came back.

"Och, yez good-for-nothing little spalpeens!" she cried; "away wid yez!"

But the boys only laughed the louder, and splashed the water the more furiously.

"Come, now, be aff wid yez; I'll go sthraight an' tell yer grandfayther av yez;" and with that she laid a hand on each of the boys to push them away from the tub. Quick as a flash, George seized the dipper from the tub, and dashed its contents full into Bridget's face, who screamed and spluttered at the unexpected soapy deluge; and as soon as she recovered her senses, she caught the nearest culprit by one leg and one arm, and was carrying him—he kicking, and she scolding—towards the outside door, probably intending to throw him into the snow, while Jack was tugging at her dress with one hand, and belaboring her back with the other, when the doctor appeared at the door. Fanny and Mr. Crosby followed to see the cause of the uproar.

"Jack, come here, sir!" said the doctor, in tones that obtained instant obedience. "Mrs. Bridget, put that boy down!" George was deposited on the floor, and with great shamefacedness picked himself up; while Bridget, with a rueful expression on her face, dropped a curtsey, saying, "Shure, sir, I ax yer honor's parding; I didn't intind to harm the b'y," and returned humbly to her wash-tub.

"Boys," said the doctor, when he had them in the sitting-room, looking with great amusement at their bedraggled appearance, "I believe you love your Aunt Margaret, and you know she is very sick. Now I want to see how well you can treat her. I don't expect you to cut-up any more such shines, or do any thing to disturb or worry her. What do you think? Is she worth being careful of?"

"I guess she is!" cried George, looking very much as if he would like to fight any body who said she was not.

"Well, we'll see how it goes. Good morning all; I may see you again this afternoon."

And in the afternoon he did come back, bringing with him Miss Patty Hopkins to nurse Margaret. Miss Patty was the doctor's faithful ally, and was always ready, at a half-hour's notice, to go to any of his patients who were not likely to have good care without her.

Her qualifications as a nurse were many, but the chief, in Dr. Somers' eyes, was her implicit faith in him, and her carrying out his instructions to the letter. She was a little woman, and so light on her feet, so noiseless in all her movements, that Dr. Somers declared she must be stuffed with thistle-down. Nothing could possibly be neater and daintier than Miss Patty, as she entered Margaret's room, after having received her directions from the doctor; and she was always just so, from the lovely gray hair that lay in soft waves on her fair though wrinkled forehead, down to the noiseless shoes and white lamb's-wool stockings.

She lived alone with a sister older than herself, and not one half so good and neat as Patty. Indeed, she was the one thorn in Patty's flesh; for, what with her naturally querulous temper and her "rheumatics," she was a very uncomfortable companion.

Margaret did not hear Patty when she entered, and she stood with her little withered hand laid over her mouth, apparently to prevent any word escaping that should waken her patient, looking tenderly at the pale face, when Margaret opened her eyes.

"Oh, Margaret, is that you?" Patty said, smoothing the clothes.

"How do you do, Miss Patty? Have you come to take care of me? How did you know I was sick?"

"Oh, a little bird told me, my dear; and right glad I am to be here, though right sorry I am to be needed," and she proceeded to mix Margaret's powder, consulting her great silver watch to see if it was time, to the very second. Having administered it, she tidied up the room, and did many things for Margaret's comfort, and then sat down to her knitting, chirping occasionally like a cheerful little snow-bird, as Margaret lay watching the flying needles, and feeling a dreamy satisfaction in being taken care of.

# CHAPTER VI.

Knowing this: that never yet
Shure of truth was vainly set
    In the world's wide fallow;
After-hands shall sow the seed,
After-hands, from hill and mead,
    Reap the harvest yellow.      WHITTIER.

FROM the time that Simon and Nancy Stubbs sullenly yielded Chloe to Margaret, they daily quarrelled over it, each charging the other with the folly of letting her go. She had brought water, gathered sticks from the woods near by—in fact, had done all the work that was ever done in the shanty, besides being an object on which to vent their ill-tempers; and they soon decided to get possession of her, and make her fine friends pay them well, if they attempted to recover her. So they bent their energies to the carrying out of this project, never failing some time each day to watch the farmhouse from behind trees or fences; but there was always some one astir about the house, and Chloe never was to be found farther away than the gate-post.

The fated Sunday came at last; and having seen the wagon go by, and concluding that the family would be away for several hours, they started for the farm. But a change had come over the spirit of their plans. They had given up the idea of taking Chloe back to the shanty and making her useful there, or of making money through the interest of her friends; and decided to forsake, quietly and forever, a neighborhood which they were beginning to find was neither comfortable nor safe, and to take Chloe with them to beg and steal what they needed on their journey to some other place. Mrs. Stubbs had grumbled a little at first, when Simon proposed the change, but her objections to a journey in cold weather were overruled by the necessities of the case. Wanderings were by no means contrary to the tastes

3

and habits of this worthy pair. Several small demesnes, in
different parts of Kentucky, had been honored by their
presence; and between their little tobacco-patch in Virginia,
where Chloe had been hired by them from her mistress, and
their coming to farmer Brown's shanty, they had made two
or three brief sojourns. If Chloe had known, when they
suddenly decamped with her from the cabin on the tobacco-
patch, that she was no longer any body's property—that
even her "Ole Missus" had no right to sell or hire her to
any body—she might have made some use of her liberty;
but she did not know that any such wonderful change had
come to herself and her kindred, though she had a vague
notion of Massa Linkum as their father and friend; and so
she followed, obediently and unquestioningly, the fortunes
of Simon and Nancy.

How they expected to make an honest living with only
the half-acre of land on which the shanty stood, and with
no other resources, or that they ever had such expectations,
never appeared; for they attempted nothing beyond raising
a few potatoes. And when their idle, shiftless ways, and by
no means starved appearance, came to be coupled in the
minds of the neighbors with the disappearance of chickens,
vegetables, fruits, and the contents of corn-cribs, it was not
to be wondered at that Mr. and Mrs. Stubbs met dark looks
and cross words which excited their alarm. As Chloe was
used as a cat's-paw in the doing of little mischiefs in which
she could be trusted, she shared the odium that rested on
her master and mistress as long as she lived with them; but
when it became known that Miss Crosby had rescued her
from their cruelty, the greatest sympathy was felt for the
child. So, all things considered, they felt that another
move was inevitable, and their arrangements having been
completed for some days, they were only waiting to get
hold of Chloe. They had used their few pieces of shabby
furniture for firewood, and concluded to resort to extreme
measures if chance did not speedily aid them.

If they had seen Mr. Crosby when he saw them, Chloe

might have been saved; but so sure were they of there being no one in the house save their victim, that they were on
the point of going to the door, when it opened, and Chloe
came out with a leap. They crouched down, one on each
side of the gate, and Chloe proceeded to make footprints in the
soft carpet of snow, singing and talking to herself the while.

She was not allowed to sit on the gate-post and drum
with her heels on Sunday, so after walking in the snow until
it ceased to afford her any amusement, she jumped upon the
gate and swung it open. Instantly a horny hand was placed
over her mouth, another seized her arm, and two dull, ugly
eyes leered at her in front, and she found herself torn from
the gate, and dragged along the road between those two
who were to her the impersonation of all that was hideous
and cruel.

A thrill of hope shot through her heart as she heard Mr.
Crosby's call, and, glancing back, saw him standing in the
door. She made one fierce effort to tear away from her foes,
but it was worse than useless; their grasp tightened, and
they ran the faster, and so they kept on until they were out
of sight of the house, and had gone some distance down a
lonely cross-road. Then they stopped and let go of Chloe,
who sank on the ground, gasping for breath, and striking
her side to stop the sharp pain in her heart, while her captors stood by with grim satisfaction at the success of their
scheme, and recovered their own spent breath.

"Come, nigger, ye've kep' that up long enough," said
Simon gruffly, when Chloe's gasping had changed to a moan,
and she sat rocking to and fro.

"I nebber 'spected to see you no more, nebber," she said,
shaking her head as if she could not be reconciled to the fact
that she had.

"Oh, ye didn't, didn't ye?" Simon answered sneeringly.
"Wal, git up an' come along. We've got to git out o' these
yer diggins mighty quick. Haul her up, Nance," and he
swung a bundle over his shoulder, while Nance gave Chloe
a push, saying, "Git up, can't ye?"

Chloe staggered to her feet and looked around; but, seeing nothing familiar far or near, except her two mortal ene-
mies, she clasped her hands over her head, and, opening her
mouth wide, gave vent to a wild, despairing cry. She would
have thrown herself on the ground again if Simon had not
caught her by the arm and shaken her roughly.

"Look a here, nigger, jest shet up yer head now, or
I'll give ye somethin' to yell at. I give ye fair warnin' ef
ye so much as whimper or open yer head, I'll make ye
smart. Yev' got to be mighty peert on yer feet, too. D'ye
hear?"

So on they started, Chloe with a load of misery at her
heart that was like leaden weights to her feet; but if she
lagged behind ever so little, she was sure to feel a grip on
her arm, or a blow on her back, that reminded her of the
promise of worse things to come.

On they tramped, for what seemed to Chloe a great many
hours, without seeing a human being. She grew dizzy and
bewildered, and Simon and Nancy were watching her uncertain steps with cross looks, when they came in sight of a
little brown house. A faint hope came into Chloe's heart,
and Simon and Nancy held a short consultation, which resulted in Simon's taking the bundle from his shoulder and
giving it to his wife, and their assuming a free-and-easy manner, as if they had nothing special on their minds.

As they drew near, they saw a lumber-wagon standing in
the barnyard, filled with potatoes, and a slovenly-looking old
man just harnessing a couple of rough-coated mules to the
wagon. The fact that the man was about such business on
Sunday may have reassured Simon, for, muttering to Nancy,
"Nothin' to be afeared on, I reckon," he crossed the road
and leaned his arms on the fence.

"Hello, Mister! wher' be you a-goin' with them ar 'taters?"

"I don't know as that's any business of yourn."

"I've got a very pertikelar reason, stranger," Simon answered, with an attempt at a conciliatory manner; "an' I
hopes ye won't take nary 'fence at my axin' ye."

"Wal, if it'll be any 'commodation, I'm goin' to Jones ville with 'em."

"Wal, stranger, wot do ye say to givin' me an' my ole woman an' a nigger gal I've got yer' a lift?"

"I don't say nothin' to't. Me an' my potaters is a big enough load fer my animals."

"Oh, now, be obleegin', can't ye? That poor little nig- ger gal's clean done used up, an' can't go a step furder; an' what's to be done is more'n I know, withouten you takes pity onto us."

"Wal, pile in, then, an' I'll take you on a piece; though you're a pretty rough-lookin' customer," he added, as Simon went to bring Chloe and Nancy.

Chloe was so glad not to have to drag her tired self along, that for a little while she forgot that the mules were carry- ing her away from Margaret faster than her feet would have done; and, if she could only have had some water to mois- ten her parched mouth, would have been almost comfortable, as she sat jammed in between Simon and Nancy.

The slow jog of the mules made the ride of four miles a pretty long one, and when they came within sight of the church-steeple and white houses of Jonesville, it was grow- ing dark; the sky was overcast, and little flurries of fine, sleety snow gave promise of a severe storm. Simon had no notion of entering the village, so he hustled his companions down, and, with a graceless "thankee" to the old man, he hurried them along a road that lay outside the town, where the houses were few and scattered.

Nancy had tied Chloe's apron over her head, and given her one of her own ragged shawls; but the child's teeth chattered with the cold, and her hands and feet ached, as they pressed on against the wind and thickening snow; and as they passed one house after another, where the cows were being milked and driven under shelter from the storm, and the men were hurrying to get to the warmth of the kitchen, Chloe wondered if Simon and Nancy must get as cold and hungry as she was, before they would stop for the night where

they could get warm, and have supper. In all their previous
wanderings, they had never neglected creature-comforts so
utterly, and Chloe little dreamed what their dread of falling
in with some one who had seen or heard of them before,
would lead them to undergo in the way of hardships.

At last, when it was so dark that they could hardly keep
the road, they came to a house where all was still, and one
light shone dimly out through the storm and darkness. Seizing Chloe's hand, and muttering a threat to her, and something to Nancy, Simon led the way, not to the house-door, as
Chloe expected, but across the yard, through the barnyard-
gate; and whispering that they were to stand still till he
came back, he went to reconnoitre. · He soon returned, and
took them to a side-door that opened into the part of the
barn where the horses were, and, groping along behind them,
feeling their way slowly and carefully, they at last reached a
place where they could feel a little hay under their feet, and
there Simon made his companions sit down, informing them,
to Chloe's utter dismay, that this was to be their bed and
shelter for the night. Then, in the darkness, he divided the
cold potatoes and dry bread they had brought in their bundle
between them, and he and Nancy ate greedily. But Chloe
could not eat; her fingers were too cold and stiff to hold the
food; and her teeth could do nothing but chatter; and besides, there was what seemed a frozen lump in her throat,
that made her feel as if she should choke if she attempted to
swallow. So she sat still while Nancy and Simon munched
and muttered to each other, and then lay down on their hard
bed, until her misery waxed so sharp and unendurable that it
suddenly burst out in a low, broken wail, which could hardly
be suppressed, when heavy hands covered her mouth and
beat her head and shoulders, and whispered but fierce
threats met her almost unconscious ears. They laid her
roughly down between them, and Nancy held her there until
she fell fast asleep. Simon soon followed her example, and
by-and-by kind Nature closed poor Chloe's eyes; and let her
forget all her woes—even the biting of the cold—until the

first faint warning of coming dawn awakened her captors, and they hurried her up and away, almost before her eyes were open.

The snow was quite deep, so that their progress was slow and tedious; but before it was fairly daylight, they had left the village some distance behind them, and were very hungry; for, relying upon Chloe's beggings and stealings, they had only provided for one meal. But after she had been to the door of every house they passed for two miles, all she had collected was barely enough to appease their hunger for a time, and their privations did not tend to make them any more amiable. Cross words and grumblings, and blows and pushes for Chloe, were the order of the day, as they tramped on through the untrodden snow, only once or twice getting a lift of a mile or so, on an ox-sled.

Late in the afternoon they came to a shabby little public house, where farmers stopped to water their horses and get refreshment for themselves, on their way to and from markets; and, made desperate by their hardships, and nearly overcome by their long tramp and want of food, Simon and Nancy decided on a bold measure. They walked into the public room, where there was a red-hot stove, and all three were speedily before it, eagerly warming their half-frozen hands and feet, never heeding the scowling looks of the burly landlord and two or three men who were lounging about the room. As soon as Simon began to feel a little thawed out, he went up to the landlord and demanded a supper of ham and eggs, and lodging for the night.

"In course you can hev a supper an' lodgin'," answered the landlord, eyeing Simon's vagabond aspect. "Pay fer it, an' you're welcome to all ther' be in the house."

"I'll pay fer it when I've hed it," answered Simon, doggedly.

"No, you don't," said the landlord, seating himself, as if the matter were ended. "I've hed sich customers afore now. Show me yer money, an' I'll git yer supper, an' not afore!"

The end of the matter was, that Simon, having no money,

and giving mine host more " impidence than he could stand,"
was turned out into the cold with Nancy and Chloe, to find
a supper and bed as best they might.

At a house near by, where Chloe was sent with bitter
warnings from the desperate pair not to come back without
something, she got a few scraps of cold meat and bread, of
which a very small share was vouchsafed her, and again their
cold, comfortless bed was a barn-floor, and again their journey began with the first gleam of gray dawn.

No doubt many kindly eyes had looked on poor Chloe
that day, and many benevolent hearts would have been
moved to keenest sympathy, and to do their utmost for the
forlorn child, if they had but known her sad story. But
with two such birds of prey ready to pounce upon her if she
loitered in her quest for the food they craved so fiercely, or
did any thing to excite their suspicions, how could she venture to make known her griefs? And so, on the third day
of their wanderings, no relief came, except that at one house
they were allowed to warm themselves at the kitchen-fire,
and received a larger supply of food than usual; and then a
kind-hearted farmer took them in his sleigh, until he turned
into a road leading away from the town to which Simon was
bending his steps.

But Simon had conceived a happy plan for spending that
night in comparative comfort. After leaving the farmer's
sleigh, and watching him till he was out of sight, he led the
way back for a little distance along the road they had just
come, until they reached a small school-house, from which he
had seen the scholars and the teacher depart, and caught the
last curl of blue smoke from the chimney, as the door was
locked and the wooden shutters closed.

Looking cautiously around, and making sure that no
person and no house was in sight, he opened one of the
shutters, pushed up the window, got in, and pulled Nancy
and Chloe in after him, closed the shutter and the window,
rekindled the dying fire, and, seating himself before it,
rubbed his hands and laughed, as nearly as Simon Stubbs

could laugh, over the sharpness of his wits. Nancy chuckled too, as she crouched by the stove, but poor Chloe was past being made happy by warmth and plenty to eat. She looked around the little, dimly-lighted room, and at the uncouth figures by the stove, made to look more hideous than ever by the flickering firelight, feeling much as if she were caged with wild beasts that might at any moment tear her to pieces. They paid no attention to her, but basked in the heat of the roaring fire, and talked with unwonted animation and amiability over their plans and prospects; and by-and-by, having finished their cold supper, they grew drowsy, and at length fell asleep.

Chloe, notwithstanding her exhaustion, sat with eyes wide open, going over and over, as if in a perplexed dream, the events of the past three days, which were to her like three long months, until, in the absence of the positive pain of cold and hunger, her benumbed senses gradually brightened, and clear, unclouded thoughts of Margaret and her happy life at the farmhouse came into her mind. Contrasting with the wretched nights she had passed since she was torn away from that pleasant place, came the remembrance of the warm little bed where she had slept so sweetly, and a picture of herself, kneeling by Margaret's side to say her prayers, made her start and almost exclaim aloud. And then, without stopping to think whether she should waken the sleepers by moving, she dropped on her knees, and, pulling her dress over her head, began to pray—not the prayer Margaret had taught her—she could not remember that in her eagerness—but this: "Dear Massa Jesus, I done forgot to say my pra'rs all dis time; please to forgimme, an' do git me away from ole Simon and Nance quick's you can, an' do fotch me back ag'in to Miss Marg'et, an' I won't nebber steal nor lie no more, an' dat's de trufe. Amen."

As she got up from her knees she hit a stick of wood, and glanced at Simon and Nancy, to see if it waked them; but they did not stir; and then a streak of silvery light caught her eye, coming through a chink in the shutter, and,

3*

with a feeling of security that she did not stop to account for, she went to the window and opened the shutter, to see if it were daylight. The moon shone full in her face, at first almost blinding her with its radiance, and somehow it seemed dimly connected, in her simple mind, with Jesus, and her prayer, and Margaret. She opened the window and leaned out. The shining snow looked almost on a level with the sill, and before the idea of escape was formed in her mind, she was running from the school-house as if wings had been lent her.

# CHAPTER VII.

Now am I fairly safe to-night—
And with proud cause my heart is light;
I trespassed lately worse than ever—
But Heaven has blessed a good endeavor.    WORDSWORTH

ABOUT a mile from the school-house where Simon and
Nancy Stubbs had taken lodgings for the night, lived farmer
Truffles, and on the morning after Chloe's escape, his household was in an unusual state of excitement and bustle, owing
to the fact that Mrs. Truffle's aunt Keziah was coming to
spend the day.   It was not so much that Mrs. Keziah Kinney's periodical visits were a pleasure and a present profit,
but Mrs. Truffles had a numerous family of boys and girls,
and her aunt had a large and valuable farm, with no children
to leave it to; and though she seemed likely to outlive many
of her nieces and nephews, the Truffles, and the heads of two
or three other branches of the family, vied with each other
in their devoted attentions, and for days before her visits, as
much cleaning and cooking was done as if for a family-gath-
ering at Thanksgiving or Christmas.

On this particular morning the eldest son, a good-natured
boy of fifteen, who gave no promise of ever knowing what
to do with a farm if he had it, was appointed to go in the
double sleigh to bring the visitor, and many were his mother's tribulations in getting him arrayed in his best clothes
and fairly started.   But at length, having run several times
from the kitchen to the stairs to know if he was not ready
yet to tackle up, having had a hunt for his new cap, which
was found behind the flour-barrel in the pantry, and having
given explicit and repeated directions as to his behavior to
his great-aunt, she had the satisfaction of seeing him drive
out of the barnyard.

"Benjamin! Benjamin!" she screamed, "stop, for pity's
sake.   You hain't got the buffalo-skins."

"Yes, I have, too," answered Benjamin; "they're in behind there."

"Well, spread 'em out over the seat. How it looks to
see 'em all in a heap on the bottom."

"Oh bother, ma, I'll spread 'em out when I git there,"
answered Benjamin.

"Oh dear suz me! I never did! I don't believe he'll
think of it again," said Mrs. Truffles, as she betook her anxious, scorched face back to the oven; while Benjamin drove
leisurely on to his aunt's house, a little distance from the village of Moresville.

No sooner did he stop at the gate than Mrs. Kinney appeared at the front door, so muffled in shawls, cloaks, hoods,
and moccasins, that it was a wonder she could move as energetically as she did. Her sharp eyes, sharp nose, and sharp
chin, were the only possible points for Jack Frost to assail,
and he would not have a chance at those as soon as she
could hold before them her huge yellow muff, which hung
by a string around her neck. At present her hands were
occupied in locking the door and putting the key in her
pocket—she always did that, though she left a trusty woman
in the kitchen—and in piloting her way down the steps and
out to the gate.

"You needn't tie that hoss, Benjamin," she cried in sharp
tones; "I don't wish to wait no longer with all my things
on. Twenty-five minutes by the clock is plenty long enough
to sit a-waitin' for a lazybones of a boy like you. Ef ever I
go to see your mother ag'in (which ain't at all likely, an' I'll
tell her so soon's ever I get there), I'll go in my own shay,
an' not run the resk of bein' baked, as I have been this day,
and then catchin' my death of cold an' rheumatiz, as I'm sartain sure I shall. See ef I don't."

Benjamin had no idea what he was to be witness to, for
all this time he had stood by the hitching-post, with his
hands in his pockets, looking ruefully towards the kitchen,
where he had fully expected to warm himself, and get a sly
cake from the kind-hearted Betty. He came mournfully to-

wards the sleigh as Mrs. Kinney shut the gate with a loud clang.

"A pretty way to send for a visitor, I should say," and she looked wrathfully at the bare wooden seat, and seized hold of the buffalo-robe.

If there had been any neighbors within a quarter of a mile, they would surely have been brought to the spot by the shriek that burst from Mrs. Kinney's lips. As it was, there was no one but the amazed Benjamin to hear it, or to see the old lady stagger back against the fence, and gaze with horror at the object that her seizure of the robes had disclosed—a black face, a pair of sleepy eyes, and tufts of wool surmounting these, that stuck out in every direction. For a minute the head did not move; then it was thrust a little further out of the robes, and examined the situation with its bewildered eyes, that were getting a more wide-awake expression. Then the head settled back, and the eyes were fixed upon the horrified face of Mrs. Kinney.

"Benjamin Truffles," gasped Mrs. Kinney at last, "what's that?" and gathering courage from the sound of her own voice, she continued her inquiries more at length.

"Benjamin, what *is* that thing? Sakes alive, what does it look like?"

"Seems to me it looks like a—like a nigger; don't it?" answered Benjamin, more surprised than he had ever been before in all his life; and he ventured a little nearer, where he could have a better view of the object in question.

"A nigger! how should sich a thing get into that sleigh?" asked his aunt.

"I'm sure I don't know," answered Benjamin, with a blank look which convinced his aunt that he was as much in the dark as herself.

"Well, I should think you'd better know," she said sharply, now fully recovered from her fright. She was too matter-of-fact a woman to be long overpowered by any thing, however suspiciously unhuman it might appear, and this woolly-head, she soon decided, was altogether human.

So she reached out her mittened hand, and gave the robe
a jerk which disclosed an apron, that had evidently been tied
over the woolly head, and a ragged, faded shawl, covering
some small shoulders.  The figure wearing these tokens
of humanity was nearly upset by the sudden demonstration
of hostilities.

"My goodness sakes! what are you a-doin' here, I
should like to know?"

"I dunno."

"Well, who should know, if you don't?  What did you
go an' get into this sleigh for?  Don't you know you
shouldn't get into other folkses sleighs?  Why don't you
speak?  What did you do it for?"

"Dunno."

"Sakes alive! if this ain't too much!  Where be you a-
goin'?"

"Dunno."

"Well, I never did!  What ails the cretur?  Where do
you live? or don't you live nowhers?  Mebbe you don't
know that?"

"I live long o' Miss Marg'et."

"Miss Margot, eh! well, why didn't you say so afore?
Where does Miss Margot live?"

"Dunno; I wish I did," was the sorrowful answer.

"Oh, you've lost your way? or mebbe you've run
off?"

"No, I ain't, I was fotched."

"Well, well, this beats me! but I can't bother with you
no more.  I 'spose Miss Margot lives up to the village—
though, thank fortin', I never heerd tell of such a pusson—an'
if you keep on this road you'll come to it, I guess.  But
don't you go pokin' yourself into no more sleighs and things,
or you'll get took up an' put in jail.  Come, get out, an' let
me get in."

"Does you know whar Miss Marg'et lives?" was asked
eagerly, as the whole of Chloe emerged from the buffalo-
skins.

"No, I don't; how should I?" Didn't I say I'd never heerd on her? Hurry, why don't you? There! I ain't a goin' home with you, Benjamin. Tell your mother that I'm down sick with this day's worriments, an' I'm goin' straight to bed. All this comes of bein' in affable circumstances, an' havin' poor relations pesterin' of you with their false intentions."

At this point she discovered Chloe still lingering, digging her toes into the snow, and looking as if she wanted something.

"What on airth do you stand there starin' at me for? I dare say Miss Margot wants you, an' there's the road. Go home, Benjamin;" and Mrs. Kinney went into the house. Benjamin gave Chloe a farewell stare and went away, and Chloe's wanderings began again.

As she trudged sorrowfully on through the snow, the events of the past night became clear to her. She remembered the flight from the school-house, her getting so tired with running, and creeping into the sleigh in the first barn she came to, and wrapping herself up in the warm skins; and the next thing she was conscious of, was hearing such a dreadful noise, and seeing the old lady and the boy standing by her in that strange place. She knew she must have slept while the sleigh was getting there. The momentary hope that Miss Marg'et was not far away, and that she might see her soon, awakened by Mrs. Kinney's seeming to know her name, gave place to bitter disappointment as she recalled the long journey she had taken with Simon and Nancy, and she felt more lonely and helpless than ever before; but she kept on towards the village, looking wistfully at the houses she passed, for she was very hungry; though she could not bring herself, unmoved by commands and threats, to go to the doors and ask for something to eat.

By-and-by she came to a large open field, just at the edge of the town, where five or six boys were hard at work building a snow-house, and she stood to watch them, wondering how any body could stay out in the cold, if they had a warm

place to go to, and she thought those boys looked as if they
had.

"Hello! here's fun," cried the largest of the group, as
he espied Chloe.  "Come on, boys," and he started across
the field, followed by all the others.

"Hold on," cried another, Henry Newton, the blacksmith's son; "what are you going to do, Jim?"

"Put her in the fortress and storm it," cried Jim.

"Hurrah! that's fun, sure enough," cried a third, as they
all ran on towards Chloe, who saw them coming, but never
dreamed they were coming for her.

"For shame, boys," exclaimed Henry, as the others
caught poor Chloe and started back with her.  "How can
you be so cruel?"

"We ain't going to hurt her," answered Jim.  "She's
going to go inside and be Dixie, and we'll be the North and
besiege her, but we shan't hurt her."

"See how frightened she is," said Henry.  "It's a mean
shame, boys, and I won't play unless you let her go."

"Well, don't then; before I'd be so chicken-hearted,"
said Jim, making Chloe enter the fortress.

"Look here, boys, I'll tell you what; I'll go inside with
Dixie and fight for her; only let me make some ammunition," and he began making balls and handing them in to
Chloe, whom a few words made to understand that she had
a champion in the bright-faced boy.

"Ho! turned traitor, has he?  We'll give it to any
body that dares to fight the North!"

"I ain't a traitor, but I won't see a poor little black girl
abused, even if you do call her Dixie."

So when he had ammunition enough, he went into the fortress, and telling Chloe she need not be afraid, only to hand
him the snowballs, the fight began and was kept up for some
time, the assailants shouting, "Down with the traitor! down
with the Northerner gone over to Dixie!"  And the fortress
was beginning to be considerably battered, and Henry's
ammunition was running low, when all of a sudden the

shouts outside ceased, and the besieged heard the tramping of receding feet. Looking out through one of the loop-holes, Henry saw the besieging army scampering across the field as fast as they could go; and the mystery of such a cowardly proceeding was explained, when he saw the schoolmaster going by, and looking inquiringly at the snow-fortress, and then at the departing boys.

Henry started back, and pulled Chloe away from the opening.

"No wonder they ran," said he, in a whisper; "if Mr. Colton had caught them at such a mean trick, I guess they'd have got something they wouldn't like."

Pretty soon Henry looked out again, and saw that the coast was clear; so he and Chloe left their tower.

"Where do you live?" he asked.

"I don't lib nowhar jes now," she answered.

"That's funny. Where do you live when you do live anywhere?"

"With Miss Marg'et," she replied.

"Who's Miss Marg'et? Does she live near here?"

"Laus, no! she libs a great ways off from dis yer place. I wish I know'd how to git thar."

"Where are you going to stay till you go back to her?"

"I dunno, Massa; s'pects Massa Jesus knows; but I don't."

Henry looked at her in amazement, and then said, "I guess you're cold and hungry, ain't you? and the boys will be coming back; so you just come over to father's shop and warm yourself, while I run home and get you something to eat. If mother wasn't so sick, I'd take you home too; but you see I can't, as it is."

So the kind-hearted boy took her to the shop, where a fire blazed on the forge, and Chloe warmed herself and watched the sparks that flew from the red-hot iron, as it was pounded by the blacksmith's strong arm, while Henry ran home to get the food he had promised. He soon came back, bringing some nice slices of bread and butter and cold corned

beef, and a piece of gingerbread, and watched Chloe awhile
with great satisfaction, as she ate as one might who had
fasted so long in the cold.

"Father," he said, "I'm going to school now; but you'll
let this poor thing stay here till she gets ready to go, won't
you?"

"Of course I will," he answered, glancing from his work
at Chloe. "Where does she belong?"

"I don't know," replied Henry, "and she don't seem to,
either; but I guess she'll find out when she gets warm, and
has eaten her bread and butter. She must stay here, any-
way, till school begins," he added—thinking, but not saying,
that he would not trust the boys, if they got hold of her again.

Chloe ran to the door to take another look at her brave,
kind friend, and as he glanced back before he disappeared
around the corner, she smiled, and nodded her head, and then
went back into the shop. The blacksmith fixed a comfortable
place for her near the fire, where she remained till a broad
hand was laid on her arm, and a kind voice said, "Come,
wake up; it's getting towards night now, and, if you're
going home, it's time you started."

So Chloe got up and left the homely but kindly shelter,
and wandered on through the village-street, and before very
long darkness came down, and lights appeared in the windows. She had not had time to think much of Simon and
Nancy that day, but now that night had come, she could think
of nothing else, and strained her eyes to look into every dark
corner and down every street, expecting to see them spring
up before her; and at every step that sounded behind her,
she started and shivered with fear, lest she should feel that
horny grip upon her shoulder. Where she was to sleep that
night she did not know. She would not have dared to go
into any barn, for fear of lying down beside Simon and
Nancy; and Mrs. Kinney's severity made her afraid to ask
for any thing at any of the houses she passed. So she crept
on in loneliness and terror till she had left the village, and
the houses were few, and the road was quite deserted.

By-and-by she came to a large house that looked very cheerful, with the light streaming from several windows. Chloe stood still to look at it, thinking that if she could only be near such a pleasant-looking place she should feel better. So she opened the gate softly, and walked along the path that led to a little wing on the left. As she stood on the ground, she could see that the room was empty; and oh, how inviting it did look, with that blazing fire in the wide fire-place, the shining andirons, and the bright rug before it! She thought she should like a nearer view, and crept up the steps, and close up to the window. By the fire stood a little table, with the cosiest supper for one person upon it, and an old-fashioned rocking-chair stood by, with a footstool before it. How warm and bright it all looked, and how cold Chloe was. She put her hand on the knob, and it turned, and the door was open and shut again before Chloe knew what she was about. It seemed to her that it all did itself. The next thing, she was sitting on the rug, close by the fire, perfectly oblivious of every thing, except the delight of feeling such warmth, and being out of the possible reach of Simon and Nancy for a while. And there she was, when, in three or four minutes, the door opened. Chloe started to her feet and stood in speechless dismay before a woman in a gayly-flowered gown, a cap with full frills and a bunch of green bows on the top, a large white linen apron, and a little basket of keys in her hand. She, too, was speechless for a moment, and what dreadful punishment awaited her for her unheard-of audacity, Chloe did not know.

"Well, I do declare! what in the name of h'all that's pitiful!"

The tone loosened Chloe's tongue.

"Oh, Missus, I ain't been an' took nuffin'. I ain't tetched nuffin' 'tall, but I'se so cold an' so 'feared of Simon an' Nance. Ef you'd jes' lemme lie out dar in de shine o' de fire an' candles! Oh, please, Missus, don't make me walk in de snow an' dark no more to-night!" and the dread of such a fate so overcame her that she burst into the most bitter crying.

"Why, bless the child! what 'as 'appened to 'er? There, don't cry so. Who are the folks you are so afraid of? Where is your 'ome, and 'ow came you 'ere? But never mind all that now. I won't bother you with any more questionings. It's plenty to know that you are un'appy; and un'appy people are never sent away from this 'ouse without comfort. So now, poor thing, stop crying, and sit down there on the rug again, while I drink my tea. Then I'll bring Mrs. More—that's the lady of the 'ouse—in to see you, and you'll 'ave a nice supper and a warm bed, and in the morning we'll 'ear your story, which I dare to say is pitiful enough."

. Chloe's astonishment dried her tears, and she sat toasting by the fire, watching her new friend as she sipped her tea, and now and then stopped her cup on its way to her lips, to look at Chloe, and ejaculate, "Well, well!" "I never!" "Did you ever!" or some such expression of her inability to solve the mystery before her.

When the little black teapot was empty, and the bread and cakes were disposed of, Mrs. Jenkins, who was Mrs. More's housekeeper, picked two or three crumbs from her lap and put them on the plate, smoothed down her apron, adjusted her cap, and rising, said to Chloe, "Now I am going for Mrs. More, and you stay just as you are till I come back."

In a few minutes the door reopened, and Mrs. Jenkins ushered in Mrs. More, shutting the door softly behind her, as if there was somebody asleep in the room that she would not waken for any thing. Chloe stood up with her hands behind her, and she thought she had never seen any thing so beautiful in all her life, except Miss Marg'et; and her taste was not at fault. Mrs. More was an old lady in a widow's dress, with soft, silvery-white curls, a face full of sweetness and benevolence, and a certain gentle dignity of manner.

"Don't be alarmed, ma'am," Mrs. Jenkins said, in a reassuring tone; though Mrs. More did not seem in the least discomposed as she looked at Chloe.

"Pray be seated, ma'am;" and Mrs. Jenkins shook up the cushions of the rocking-chair, in which Mrs. More seated her-

self, and folding her hands quietly in her lap, listened while
Honora described in her brisk, emphatic way, her finding
Chloe in the room when she came in to her tea, and her distress and fear of being sent away. "I kept 'er, knowing that
you would be very much offended if I didn't. Now, ma'am,
what shall I do with the poor creature?"

"Take her to the kitchen, Honora; give her plenty to eat,
and then put her to bed. Has she told you how she came to
be wandering about so late at night?"

"No, ma'am, I didn't like to question 'er much, when she
was so cold and hungry."

"That was kind. I dare say she will tell her story readily enough in the morning. You need not be afraid, little
girl; if you have no other home, we will give you one here.
Mrs. Jenkins will find something for you to do to keep you
happy, and you shall stay as long as you need our care."

Mrs. Jenkins looked at Chloe triumphantly, nodding her
head, as if to say, "I told you so," and Chloe gazed at Mrs.
More with a spell-bound feeling, hardly able to take in the
good fortune that had befallen her, until that lady left the
room; but her last thought, as she dropped to sleep in her
snug little bed, was a wish that Miss Marg'et could know
how comfortable she was; and she wondered how long it
would be before she got back to her first friend.

# CHAPTER VIII.

The healing of His seamless dress
Is by our beds of pain;
We touch Him in life's throng and press,
And we are whole again.　　　WHITTIER.

"OH dear," sighed Jack, one day as he sat in Margaret's room on a stool, with his elbows on his knees, and his chin in the palm of his hands. He had been standing by the window, examining the frost-pictures, and very likely had found something that looked like Santa Claus in his Christmas accoutrements, for when Miss Patty, who sat by Margaret's bed knitting, said softly, "What's the matter, my dear?" he answered,

"Why, to-morrow's Christmas, and we can't do any thing 'cause Aunty's so sick; can't hang up our stockings, or wish Merry Christmas before daylight, or have a plum-pudding, or any thing at all. Oh, dear me!"

"That's very bad, to be sure," answered Miss Patty; but hearing a slight movement at her side, she shook her head and put her finger on her lips; so Jack said no more. He kept his dejected look and attitude for a little while, and then went down-stairs.

"Miss Patty!"

Margaret's voice was so low and weak that it seemed hardly more than a faint whisper, but Miss Patty heard it, and her knitting was on the chair instantly.

"What is it, my dear?"

"Will to-morrow be Christmas?"

"Yes, my dear, it will, but it's of no earthly consequence; it doesn't matter in the least that I can see, whether it's Christmas or Fourth of July."

Margaret's wan face was flushed, and her lips quivered, showing Miss Patty plainly that she had heard poor Jack's complaint.

"Only," she added cheerily, giving a little touch to the pillows, "if it was Fourth of July, we'd have you out in the warm sunshine, and get some color into those pale cheeks; we would indeed. But it's best as it is, after all, isn't it?"

Margaret shook her head sadly. "The poor darlings; how selfish I have been!"

"Selfish!" cried Patty, looking at Margaret as if she feared she had suddenly become delirious. "I can't think what you mean, my dear; but never mind, don't try to tell me. There, there," she added, soothingly, laying her soft, cool hand on Margaret's forehead, "we ain't going to bother our heads about days and things. We'll just take this little powder; and then shall I say a verse, or a hymn?"

"Not just this minute, please, Miss Patty. How many days have I been lying here?"

"Oh, my dear, I wish I could put days out of your head. Why, let me see," she said, counting on her fingers; "they've been such sweet ones to me, that I am afraid I sha'n't count 'em all. There was Monday, that was the day I came, and Tuesday—oh, my, it's useless! don't make me think of such foolish things."

"I remember," said Margaret, "thinking before—before I was sick—that I must begin about Christmas; and that must have been—"

"Only two weeks ago," said Patty, seeing that Margaret was making a painful effort to straighten things in her mind.

Margaret sighed, and turned her head wearily upon the pillow, and Miss Patty stood looking at her sorrowfully, thinking that it was all her own fault—she ought to have kept Jack out of the room. What would the doctor say, if he should see her now?

"Miss Patty, a week from to-morrow will be New-Year's day, won't it?"

" Yes, to be sure, my dear."

" Well, you must get me well by that time, Miss Patty; and the first thing, you must sing to me."

" To think that you should care to listen to such a poor
voice as mine ! But the words are all the same, ain't they ?
Yes, of course I'll sing ; " and folding her hands in her lap,
and keeping time by a gentle swaying motion back and forth,
she sung in a sweet little quavering voice :

> " The pity of the Lord
> To those that fear His name," &c.

The few slight variations from the original tune of
" Boylston" only added to the quaintness, taking nothing
from the sweetness of the performance. When Miss Patty
ceased, she found that Margaret lay with closed eyes, and
that the flush was all gone ; so she took up her knitting with
a little sigh of relief. But it was not long before she heard
a noise that made her fly to the door. She closed it, all but
a little crack, and stood with one eye on the lookout to see
who came up the stairs, fully determined within herself that
nobody should enter the room.

" Miss Patty ! " said Margaret.

" Oh, my dear, I thought I had sung you to sleep."

" Who is that at the door ? "

" Oh, it's only a little boy, and he's going right away
again ; he doesn't want any thing ; " and Miss Patty opened
the door she had been holding, and gave George the very
gentlest push imaginable, saying, " Go away, Georgie ; you
can't come in here now."

" Let him come, Miss Patty ; I want to speak to him."

Patty looked distressed, but permitted George to come
to Margaret. She held out her hand for his, and warmly
returned his kiss, for the first time since she had been ill.

" Georgie, love, it's very hard for you and Jack not to
have any Christmas. I can't tell you how badly I feel, to
have disappointed you so."

" Oh, my dear, I can't have you talk like that," cried Miss
Patty.

" Do you think you can forgive me for spoiling your
pleasure, Georgie ? "

"You didn't do it a-purpose," said George, to ... depressed by the dismal prospect for to-morrow to ... he had nothing to forgive, while really the tears that filled his eyes were as much of unconscious pity for his aunt's pale face, as for his own and Jack's sorrows.

Margaret smiled faintly, while Miss Patty almost wrung her hands, at what seemed to her George's cruelty.

"Well, Georgie, do you think it would be better than nothing if we kept New-Year's day—hung up our stockings, and had a plum-pudding then, instead of to-morrow?"

"Oh, yes, Aunty," answered George, brightening. "Will you be all well by that time?"

"I can't promise, dear; but I will do the very best I can, and if I'm not able to make the pudding and cook the turkey myself, I will get Miss Patty to do it, and we will keep the day as merrily as we can. Now kiss me, and go and comfort poor Jack."

"When will it be New-Year's day?" asked George.

"Next week, Tuesday, my dear," said Miss Patty, leading him to the door, and shutting it after him.

Margaret looked very tired, and her nurse sat by, feeling more cast down about her patient than she had done before. Somehow, she seemed to be getting beyond her control.

"Miss Patty, do things seem at all comfortable downstairs?" asked Margaret, after a few minutes.

"Oh, very, indeed!" answered Patty, her hand giving a sudden twitch that dropped a whole needleful of stitches. "That is, my dear, as comfortable as could be expected under the circumstances," she added, nervously; "I mean, while you are sick. I couldn't rightly say that every thing is in apple-pie order. But that's neither here nor there to you, you know," she added, recovering her self-possession and some of her stitches. "Providence takes its own ways to make people appreciate their blessings, and we can't prevent it, if we would. For my part, I feel more submissive to your lying here, when I'm down-stairs, than any other time."

Margaret smiled doubtfully, while Patty, having restored

4

her stitches to order, proceeded to knit with unwonted
energy.

"How strange it is that nothing is heard of poor Chloe
yet!" said Margaret, after another few minutes. "I do
wonder where she can be. They must have gone away on
the cars; don't you think so, Miss Patty?"

"I shouldn't at all wonder if they had," she replied, lifting her two forefingers, as if she meditated putting them in
her ears; but seeming to conclude that it would not serve
her purpose in soothing Margaret's anxieties, she began to
sing another hymn, and soon had the comfort of seeing her
sleeping quietly.

Surely, if the extreme of disorder and discomfort, in
Margaret's absence, could have made Mr. Crosby and Fanny
appreciate the blessing of her presence, they must have
learned to do so before this; but the touch of severity with
which the gentle Miss Patty had intimated that she considered the state of things down-stairs, whatever it might
be, a just dispensation of Providence, implied that she, at
least, was not satisfied with the result of the lesson.

Jotham's mother and Bridget Flanagan had been summoned to the rescue two or three times, in the kitchen
department, and were glad to do all they could for Margaret's
sake; but they both had family cares of their own, and could
not come often, or stay long; so that Jotham's clumsy hands
and the boys' unreliable ones were the sole dependence, as
the general thing.

Fanny had been very poorly ever since Margaret was
taken sick. All she could do, and more, was to look into
Margaret's room in the morning, and then crawl down-stairs
to oversee things, that every thing might not go to rack and
ruin; which she did by sitting in the easy-chair by the fire,
and administering reproofs to the boys, and orders to Jotham, or Bridget, if she happened to be there; which orders
might as well have been addressed to the wall, as she truly
asserted.

For all this she felt that she deserved great credit, when

she was utterly unable to leave her bed. But some people were compelled to bear the brunt of life's cares, while others shirked their burdens, never thinking whether the shoulders they fell upon were able to bear them or not.

Such complaints of the disregard of some for the feelings and comfort of others, were sometimes uttered in the presence of Miss Patty, and it required all the little woman's Christian forbearance to keep her from giving Mrs. Sinclair a piece of her mind. She had not fully decided whether Mr. Crosby shared those sentiments, for he was always either shut up in his own room, or lying silent upon the sofa, when she prepared Margaret's meals—the only times that she left her patient.

The meals were regularly and most carefully prepared, though even such dainty bits as Miss Patty could concoct had as yet failed to tempt Margaret. It may have been owing to Margaret's want of appetite, that Fanny found herself able to sustain her arduous cares; she certainly would not have been, with no other nourishment than the bread and tea, or coffee, varied by Bridget's unsavory dishes, upon which her father and the boys dieted.

On this day before Christmas, things seemed to have reached a climax. The boys were first cross and discontented because they were not going to have any fun, and then noisy and hilarious over their prospects for a good time at New-Year's; and their mother scolded them for being so cross about such a trifle, expressing herself to her father and Miss Patty as quite incapable of seeing how any body could bear to be the cause of such disappointments; and then was equally incapable of seeing how any body could be so inconsiderate as to tell excitable boys of a pleasure so long beforehand, and scolded them for being so noisy.

Bridget was there, but she was washing, and had a sick child at home, so that she could hardly be induced to leave her tubs. Jotham was out of sorts at having to do so much " women's work," and when he brought wood into the sitting-room, though that was his business, threw it down by the stove, instead of putting it in the wood-box, making a great noise and no little muss, which, added to the accumulated dust and dirt of several days, made a most untidy room

Then, the table had been set by the boys, who got into a frolic over it, nearly pulling the cloth and all the dishes off upon the floor. They tried to straighten it, and to become quiet, when Mr. Crosby came from his room and sternly reproved them, shutting the door to keep out their disturbance, and their mother almost went into hysterics over their behavior; but the table remained askew, and, with a plate of bread in one corner, butter in another, a dish of unpeeled potatoes, and fried ham swimming in fat, looked any thing but inviting. So, what was Fanny's dismay at hearing a knock at the door, and voices outside.

"Oh, mercy! what shall we do? George, wait!" but she was too late. Before she was fairly out of her chair, or had time to draw her shawl around her, the door was open, and Mr. and Mrs. Thomas and Mrs. Davis entered.

Of course, they took it all in at a glance, but they shook hands, and made their greetings particularly animated and impressive, to cover their own and Mrs. Sinclair's discomposure. If Fanny had acted upon her first impulse, she would have fled from the room; but summoning all her seldom-used graces of manner, and the fortitude that availed her on an occasion like this, however it was lacking at other times, she laughingly apologized for their disorderly plight, and, seating herself, begged her callers to be seated too. So they fell into easy chat, and Fanny, exhilarated by her unwonted effort in the cause of good breeding, and feeling that she had conquered a terrible situation, talked so fluently and pleasantly about the weather, that it was some time before any one had a chance to inquire about Margaret.

"Why, really, Mrs. Davis, I hardly know what to tell you," said Fanny, lowering her voice and looking perplexed.

"I hope she isn't worse," said Mrs. Davis, anxiously. "I saw Dr. Somers the day before yesterday, and he told me she was in no danger."

"Danger! Oh, no. She has no fever, no chills, no pain —no any thing that I can discover. But you know, when one once gives way to weakness of mind or body, it is very apt to get the better of one, especially if one doesn't exert one's self to throw it off. I don't know where I should be, if I gave way to every sense of weakness and languor;" and Fanny threw a great deal of feeling into her blue eyes.

"I should hardly think of its being weakness of mind, in Margaret's case," said Mrs. Davis, in a constrained tone; "and weakness of body is a difficult thing to throw off."

"I can't understand Margaret's being ill in this way," said Mr. Thomas. "The doctor tells me it is nervous exhaustion; I should think that would only be likely to follow a severe mental strain, and hardly then, in a person of Margaret's brave, buoyant disposition."

"It is very peculiar," said Fanny. "The only mental strain Margaret has had was the loss of that black Chloe she had been so interested in; but one would hardly think that could have affected her so."

"Perhaps she had over-exerted herself," suggested Mrs. Thomas. "Had she done any thing that especially taxed her strength?"

"No, nothing more than her usual little household duties," answered Fanny. "She went to meeting that Sunday, but that couldn't have been too much for her."

"To meeting?" said Mrs. Thomas, inquiringly.

"Yes, my dear," answered her husband; "it was while you were in Chicago. I preached in the red school-house, near Jenny's, and Margaret and the boys were there. You know I told you about Robert Russell's being there, and leading the singing."

"Oh, yes, I remember," replied Mrs. Thomas. "And it was the very next day that Margaret was taken sick—was it not, Mrs. Sinclair?"

"She was ill that very day," said Mrs. Davis, looking wonderingly at Fanny, who had started and turned deathly pale, for no possible reason that Mrs. Davis could divine.

" Don't you remember, brother, how wretchedly she looked after the morning service, and her lying down before dinner, and looking so white and worn all the rest of the day ? My heart ached for her ; but there was something in her look and manner that made me feel almost awe-stricken, and I couldn't offer any thing, for her pain seemed to me beyond the reach of human skill. I can't tell why," added Mrs. Davis, wiping the tears from her eyes, " but I have had the strangest, intensest sympathy and solicitude for Margaret ever since that day ; and nothing could have kept me from coming to nurse her, only I knew Patty Hopkins was here, and that she would do far better than I should. Then I have heard from her through Dr. Somers every day or two."

The boys had been very quiet during this conversation about their aunt ; but when Mrs. Davis ceased, George asked, " Has that Mr. Russell been back again ? "

" No, Georgie ; he isn't coming back this way."

" What do you know about Mr. Russell, George ? " asked Mrs. Thomas.

" Why, didn't I hear Annie and Charlie Davis talking about him all noon-time that Sunday, and don't I know that he made lots of money in China ? "

" It was strange," said Mrs. Davis, turning to Fanny, " what an impression Mr. Russell made on our children. He was only there one night, and before church Sunday morning ; yet not a day passes that the children don't wish he would come back. We were sorry he couldn't have stayed to see Margaret. Brother and I had an idea that they would be kindred spirits."

" Indeed ! " Fanny managed to say.

" Mother, I mean to go to China when I'm big ; wouldn't you ? " said George.

To Fanny's intense relief, Miss Patty came down just then.

" Oh, Mrs. Davis, that is you, isn't it ? Well, Margaret got an idea, I'm sure I can't tell how, that it was, and she wants to see you a little minute—about some business," she added, by way of an excuse to Mr. and Mrs. Thomas.

Mrs. Davis followed Patty up-stairs to receive Margaret's commissions for New-Year's presents for the boys; and, thanks to the interruption, Fanny had gained control over herself, so that she could talk coherently for the few minutes that Mrs. Davis was gone, and say "good-by," and see them depart.

When the children saw their mother go hastily up-stairs, they called to her that dinner was on the table; but she answered, "I want no dinner," in a hollow voice, and went on.  Locked in her own room, she sat pale and rigid all the afternoon, for the first time in her life enduring keen and bitter pangs for the sufferings of another, being convinced, beyond the power of a doubt, that she had caused her sister's illness, and long years of loneliness and desolation, of which this was but a faint outward sign.  For the first time in her life she was undergoing a fierce struggle between her better feelings and her selfishness; for she had in her possession, long ago hidden away and forgotten, a sealed letter which she knew, however much she might resist the conviction, would at least bring some comfort and healing to her sister's heart.

She had known at the time that the letter came into her hands—and she blushed to recall how it came to hers, and never to Margaret's—that it would have dispelled the barrier her own words and deeds had conjured up between two loving hearts; and she endured over again the agony of wounded vanity with which she had found that even that last desperate expedient had failed to secure Robert Russell for herself.  Perhaps that stinging remembrance helped to turn the scale against Margaret, and her own better nature.

The afternoon waned, and twilight gathered before she moved from her place.  Then she discovered that it was growing dark, and that she was almost benumbed with the cold.  With resolute fingers she opened the secret place, whose existence even she had almost forgotten, and left the room with the letter in her hand.  Passing her sister's door with her head averted, she went down-stairs, and, putting the letter into the fire, watched it as its folds opened and curled, grew red and blackened, and then fell into pale ashes.

"There," she said to herself, "that is the best thing to do. Now there is no danger of my being tempted to give it to her and awaken hopes that could never be realized; for in all probability he is married, or has forgotten her. And, after all, it may have been only a farewell letter;" but then she recalled the farewell letter that came afterwards, when no reply was sent to this long one. "Well, it's over, and it was the kindest thing for her and me. There was no need of making her hate me for nothing."

For a little while, after their cheerless supper, Fanny sat silent and gloomy by the fire; Mr. Crosby lay with closed eyes on the sofa, and the boys, feeling a hush in the dimly-lighted room, sat in a corner by the stove, talking in undertones. By-and-by Fanny got up, saying, "I am going to bed, father; I am very tired. Good night; good night, children," and went up-stairs. On her way to her own room she stopped to see Margaret, whose eyes brightened at the unusual interest in her sister's manner of asking how she felt, and if there was nothing she could do for her. She was disappointed that Fanny did not kiss her good-night; but it was a great deal for her to show so much interest.

Pretty soon the boys came softly up the stairs, Jack with his shoes in his hand, and George on tiptoe. Miss Patty would have put them gently away, but Margaret said, "Let them come."

"Do you feel better, Aunty?" asked Jack. "I do wish you'd get well. It's as cold and dark as any thing downstairs. Nothing's a bit nice;" and he laid his head disconsolately on the pillow, and Margaret laid her hand tenderly upon his cheek.

"So do I wish you'd get well, Aunty," said George; "and not because of Christmas, either. I'd rather you'd be well than to have forty-nine Christmases all in a bunch."

"There, my dears," said Miss Patty, seeing that Margaret's face was flushed again.

"Oh, let them stay; they do me more good than you can think." So they talked together for a few minutes, and then the boys went to bed.

While Miss Patty was rejoicing that there could be nothing more to excite her patient that night, slow, feeble steps were heard on the stairs, and a gentle tap came at the door.

"My dear father, have you come all the way up-stairs to see me?"

"It's lonely down-stairs," said her father, so sadly, that tears sprang to Margaret's eyes. "How do you feel to-night, my child?"

"Dear father, I am a great deal better to-night; that is, I feel that I am going to be a great deal better. I shall be down-stairs before you think of it."

"Well, I shall be glad. We need you sadly, child."

Margaret took her father's hand, that lay on the bed, and clasped it in both of hers. Then she looked at it, and in his face. She thought he had grown thinner, and older, since she was sick.

"Are you as well as usual, father?" she asked.

"Yes, I believe so," he replied; "but I shall feel better when you get about again. I'll sit here awhile, if you don't mind, and hear Miss Hopkins sing the hymn she sung to-day; I just heard a little of it when the stairway-door was open. Your mother used to sing it."

"Yes," said Margaret, "I remember."

So Patty sung, in a smaller and more trembling voice than ever, while Margaret held her father's hand clasped in hers. When the hymn was ended, neither spoke, but Mr. Crosby kissed his daughter, and went down-stairs.

When they were once more alone, Miss Patty took the Bible, and, putting on her spectacles, read to Margaret, as she always did the last thing at night, if no more than two or three verses. Now she read a good many verses from the twelfth chapter of Hebrews; and when she had finished, Margaret said, "How did you know just what I needed to-night?"

4*

"Oh, I knew, my dear," answered Miss Patty, as she flitted around the room, making things to the last degree tidy, before she should lie down on her little couch; "I knew very well that you didn't want to hear about the 'many mansions,' and the 'rest that remaineth,' and the golden city, to-night."

"No," thought Margaret, "the mansions are ready, but I am not meet for them yet. How could I think of resting, when my race was but just begun? 'So great a cloud of witnesses.' I wonder if mother knows how I have faltered, how I have longed for the rest, while I dreaded to run the race? I *will* lay aside every weight, and run with patience and courage, and when I reach the goal, it will be sweet— 'beyond remembering and forgetting'—'beyond the ever and the never'—'love, rest, and home, sweet home.' But I must not dwell too much upon the prize; that will not help me to run with patience. I must look only to Jesus, my ever-present Friend and Helper. How gently and tenderly He has reminded me to-day that I have something to do, and that life is not valueless and aimless. Aimless! with so much evil in myself to overcome; with father, sister, and the dear children to care for, and so many to whom I can at least give a cup of cold water!"—and, thus thinking, her thoughts gradually grew indistinct, until she fell asleep, and slept more sweetly and refreshingly than she had done for many nights.

# CHAPTER IX.

Ring out, wild bells, to the wild sky,
The flying cloud, the frosty light;
The year is dying in the night;
Ring out, wild bells, and let him die.    TENNYSON.

"On, is that you, doctor?" called Miss Patty from the kitchen-door the day before New-Year's, as Dr. Somers stopped at the gate.

"Yes, I believe it is," he replied, tying his horse. "What are you doing here?" he asked, looking into the kitchen before he went up-stairs, and laughing heartily as he saw Miss Patty. She had on a clean ruffled nightcap, and one of Margaret's checked aprons tied around her neck and again around her waist, and never stopped her business of rolling out piecrust as she answered, "Oh, you may laugh! I'm making a lot of nice things against to-morrow."

"What's going on to-morrow?"

"Oh, Margaret has set her heart on having a grand dinner; and it shall be, if these old hands can make it so!" and Patty nodded her head till her cap-frills danced.

"Humph! this is a fine how-to-do! I'll see about your having a grand dinner without consulting me;" and the doctor went up-stairs.

"What's all this?" he cried, as he opened Margaret's door.

"All for New-Year's day," answered Margaret, meeting his look of pretended horror with a bright smile, that was more like herself, and more welcome to him, than any thing he had seen in a long time, and he stood a minute to enjoy the pretty picture.

A bright, crackling wood-fire burned in the little fire-place, and on one side sat Margaret in a large rocking-chair, made luxurious with quilts and blankets; on the floor was spread a sheet covered with evergreens, in the midst of

which sat the boys, all absorbed in making wreaths and long
strips for festoons, which they had learned to do very skilfully under Margaret's direction.  The winter's sun shone in
upon them, making Jack's curly hair look like threads of
gold, and George's cheeks like crimson pippins.

And how fair and sweet Margaret looked!  She had not
gained a tinge of color, but the old light had come back to
her eyes—at least, it was there now—and her mouth had not
forgotten how to smile—a real sunny smile, as the doctor said
to himself.  She looked enough like a spirit yet, but he
thought they need not be afraid of the wings growing, just
at present.

Miss Patty had spent a full half-hour on Margaret's toilet,
notwithstanding the pressing duties of the day; and though
the doctor only saw the effect of her loving cares, he was
quite satisfied that, however much attention other things
might receive, there had been no lack of it there.

" How dared you get up without asking my leave ? " he
said, coming around to Margaret's chair.

" I wanted to surprise you, doctor," answered Margaret.
" You didn't expect me to get well so fast; did you ? "

" I knew you wouldn't be long about it when you once
got started; but I didn't know just when you would be ready
to begin."

" It took me longer than was necessary," said Margaret,
a shadow crossing her face.

" No such thing," replied the doctor, with a very positive
shake of the head; " not a bit of it.  The only wonder is,
that you weren't longer yet.  But mind you, Miss, I'm going
to look after you as a cat looks after a mouse, from this time
forth—that is, till Mr. Skinner, or some other good man,
comes along to take you off my hands."

The doctor did not see the puzzled expression of Margaret's face, for he was intently watching the boys, and she
could only guess, from the twinkle in the corners of his eyes
and mouth, that he knew something of her almost forgotten
episode with Mr. Skinner; but how, she could not imagine.

"Why, in the name of all that's humane, don't you ask me to come here to dinner to-morrow ? " asked the doctor, turning suddenly from the boys to Margaret. "What do you mean by having a New-Year's feast, and leaving me out, when you know that my wife and daughters are away, and I can't have any at home ? "

"Why," said Margaret, "I never thought of your caring to come ; but I am sure I wish you would, and I will invite you upon one condition : that you let me go down-stairs in the morning, and stay all day."

The doctor shook his head disconsolately. "I see I shall have to eat my dinner all by myself at home."

"But, doctor, you see I can't trust to Jotham's taste in putting up these pretty wreaths and festoons, and I must be there to give directions."

"Boys ! are those things 'most done ? " cried the doctor, starting up.

"Yes, 'most," answered George, too busy to waste words.

"Well, hurry up, and we'll fix 'em ourselves, without any of Jotham's help or your aunt's directions. You daren't say that you can't trust my taste ? "—to Margaret.

"No," replied Margaret, "because it isn't true. I am glad enough to have you do it, and I beg you will come and dine with us to-morrow, Dr. Somers."

"Thank you. I will, with pleasure ; and when I come, I'll escort you down, Miss Crosby. Come, boys ; you've got enough of these festooneries to trim Freedom's Hall, in Jonesville ! " He caught two corners of the sheet, the boys jumped up and caught the other two, and they all ran down-stairs in high spirits, and for an hour Margaret heard their merry voices, as they trimmed the little sitting-room, which Bridget had already made as clean and fresh as possible.

The busy day came to an end, but not before Miss Patty's work was all done. Before dark she took off her cap and apron, and gave a final survey to the rows of mince and pumpkin pies, the turkeys, chickens, and plum-pudding, all

ready for cooking the next day, and bestowed a critical
glance upon the kitchen, which was quite as neat as if Margaret herself had presided there. .

"Here, Bridget," she said, as Bridget appeared, ready to
go home to her children, "here's a basket of things for you
from Miss Margaret, and she wishes you and the children a
Happy New-Year."

"Och! an' did she, indade, the swate angel! an' shure,
if there iver was one on the airth, it's hersel'—bliss the kind
heart iv her!" As Bridget trudged home, she lifted the
cover of the basket, and spied so many good things to eat,
besides several pairs of little bright-colored woollen mittens,
that she went on whispering blessings on Margaret, as if
that had been the first basket of the sort she had ever received from her.

When Patty came up with Margaret's supper, she found
the room all quiet and serene, with the flickering firelight
playing on Margaret's face, giving it the glow of health ; and
as she placed the little stand by her chair, she thought that
of all sweet places on the earth, that little room, with Margaret in it, was the very sweetest.

"Miss Patty," said Margaret, "are you perfectly tired
out with all your cooking ? "

"Oh, my dear, not a bit of it ! I have swept a room, and
been more tired than I am this night. Tired ! no, indeed."

"Is father alone down-stairs, Miss Patty ? "

"Yes, dear, I believe he is. The boys are busy about
something, and Mrs. Sinclair is in her room."

"Well, won't you ask him to come up and take tea with
me ? There is enough for us both, and I know he would like
it. The boys will be good with you."

Mr. Crosby came, and was in no hurry to leave the pleasant place when tea was over.

Margaret felt that she was more to her father than she
had ever been before, and that she could wait hopefully and
labor patiently for their home to become all that she longed
to have it.

Hour after hour of the night, as she lay awake, memories of the past would come, in the presence of the Old Year just dying and the New Year coming in. Once, long ago, she had kept watch for the Old and the New, with one whose high soul responded to every aspiration of hers; whose hand, clasping hers, gave promise of help and guidance through all the coming years.

She had never doubted the truth and nobleness of the heart that spoke through those earnest eyes and that hand. She only felt that she had failed to call forth the deepest love of which it was capable, or it would not so readily have lost faith in her steadfastness. While that was agony enough, it was better than if she had been obliged to mourn over a fallen ideal; and she had grown to think of her lost love as one thinks of friends in heaven. But when she heard his voice and felt his presence, and realized what it was to be near him, even with the shadow of the past enveloping them, she tasted again the bitterness of her loss.

But the bitterness, the shrinking from life's burdens, the longing for rest, and the aching sense of irremediable loss, were gone now; and though she still felt " heart-bare, heart-hungry, very poor " in earthly treasures—in the love that gives, in full measure for all it receives, the hopes that included herself as well as others—she had come to accept this poverty as a mysterious benefaction from her heavenly Father, and to trust that in His own way He would make up to her for the lack of that for which her whole nature cried out; and if it should only be through ministering to others, and keeping her own garments white against her entrance into her heavenly mansion, she would not repine.

It was thus that she could think calmly, and even cheerfully, of all the things that came unbidden into her mind this death-night of the Old Year.

A full hour before the New Year saw the sunlight for the first time, George and Jack opened their eyes wide in the darkness, and began to speculate in whispers upon the contents of their stockings. After waiting as long as they could

—which was not long—George got up and stole softly into
Margaret's room, where the stockings were hung on each
side of the fireplace, and scampered back to bed with them;
and when the first bit of daylight looked in at the windows,
they ran to all the doors, wishing every body a Happy New-
Year.

Fanny was sitting in Margaret's room, soon after breakfast, when the doctor unexpectedly appeared. He lifted his
shaggy eyebrows in surprise, for this was the first time he
had seen Fanny there, and then sat down by Margaret with
the most dejected air.

"I can't come and help eat your turkey to-day," he
said.

"Oh, why not?" exclaimed Margaret and Fanny.

"Why, you see, there's a man—a college-friend of mine,
though he isn't quite as venerable as I am—who has been
threatening to come and see me for a long time. He is a
doctor in St. Louis, and has been tired out for months, and
needing rest; and what should he do but come to my door
last night, when I was fast asleep, like the Man in the good
Book, and ask me to let him in. I didn't send him off, but I
don't know what he will say when he comes to eat such a
New-Year's dinner as my unassisted Abigail can get up. It
serves him right, though, for coming when my wife was
away. But, poor me! what have I done that I should have
to go without so many good things?"

"Why, doctor," said Margaret, "I shouldn't think you
need have waited for an invitation to bring him with you."

"Of course," said Fanny, "we should be delighted to see
him."

The doctor pretended to be very much surprised and relieved.

"He's an old bachelor, by the way," he said, turning
back as he was leaving the room, "and pretty well off, too;
but don't you go to captivating him as you did Mr. Skinner!
I won't have him trifled with." And with a threatening
shake of his head at Margaret, he shut the door.

"What nonsense was that about your captivating Mr Skinner?" asked Fanny.

"Only some of the doctor's nonsense," answered Margaret; "he likes to tease people."

"Well, now, what shall I wear? If I had only known this in time, I might have had a dress made over. Miss Patty sews, doesn't she? My dresses are all so antiquated!"

"Our visitors being gentlemen, will not know whether you are just in the fashion or not," replied Margaret. "Your dresses are all rich and tasteful."

"I do think it is a most dreadful thing to live so out of the world as we do. I can't endure it much longer;" and Fanny went to her own room, where she was busy all the morning selecting her dress and laces and arranging her beautiful hair for the momentous occasion.

Patty helped Margaret to dress, and then went to attend to things in the kitchen, much against her will, leaving Margaret to put a few last stitches in a dressing-gown she had been making for her father before her illness, which, as he had not seen it, she was going to give him for a New-Year's present. The boys were full of business, as boys always are on such days; and even Mr. Crosby seemed interested in the unusual bustle.

"Oh, Fanny, how lovely you look!" was Margaret's involuntary expression as her sister entered her room, a little before dinner-time.

"Do I?" said Fanny, with a gratified smile; "it's strange if I have kept any of my good looks in this wilderness! But even here, there does come a time, once in an age, when one is glad to look well. You look nicely, too," she added, gazing rather doubtfully at her sister's lovely face and becoming dress. "But you have no color, and your eyes are languid. Excitement doesn't brighten you up as it does some people;" and she glanced at her own face in the glass.

"Isn't it strange," she continued, as Margaret did not speak, "that with all my ill health I look so young? I don't believe any one would take me to be older than you."

There was a little sparkle in Margaret's eyes, and the very slightest curl of her lip, as she answered, "I suppose different troubles affect faces differently. Your's does not happen to be one that turns the hair gray and makes the skin sallow;" and then, ashamed of her unnoticed sarcasm, she added, "but you really look much younger than you are, dear, and when you are dressed becomingly, as you are now, look wonderfully well. Here's my New-Year's giftie to you, Fanny. It is not much, but I hope you will think it better than none," and Margaret took from her drawer a dainty little breakfast-cap, made of old-fashioned but exquisite lace, and finished with blue bows.

"Oh, thank you," said Fanny, holding it up; "that's really lovely, and will be very becoming, I know. But when ever shall I have a chance to wear it?"

"To-morrow morning, if you will," answered Margaret, gently.

Just then Dr. Somers' sleigh drove up, and Fanny, having taken a sly look at the stranger from the window, went down to receive him, which she did with a graceful cordiality that amazed Dr. Somers, and put his friend, Dr. Doane, entirely at ease about being an unwelcome intruder at their family feast.

"Well, well!" the doctor said to Margaret, when he had asked how she felt, and scolded her for sewing; "a leopard can't change his spots, nor an Ethiopian his skin; but I have seen more astonishing changes than those would be—transformations, metamorphoses;—can you assure me, though, on your word of honor, that that beautiful, animated, well-dressed woman down-stairs *is* your sister, Mrs. Sinclair?"

Margaret smiled. "You never happened to see Fanny when she felt well and cheerful."

"I suppose she only feels so when there's something to make it worth while," he answered, gruffly. "You needn't frown at me," he added, in answer to Margaret's look of re-

proach. "But come down-stairs, now; you are a match for
the handsomest as well as the best."

They found Fanny and Dr. Doane chatting in the most
animated manner; and Dr. Somers looked on with jealous
eyes to see the impression Margaret made upon his friend.
Her greeting was quite as graceful and cordial as Fanny's,
with the added element of simplicity and sincerity, which he
saw and appreciated, whatever a stranger might do. Dr.
Doane was a tall, slight man, with dark hair and beard, a
broad intellectual forehead, gentle, flexible mouth, and large,
soft eyes; and there was about him an air of refinement and
cultivation.

"Well, Margaret," said Dr. Somers, when he had placed
her on the lounge to rest till dinner was brought in, "how
do you like our decorations?"

"They are perfect," she replied, looking admiringly
around the room. "But what is that?" she asked, as her
eyes fell on an engraving that hung between the windows,
with a wreath over it.

"That? let's see," and the doctor took the picture down
and brought it to Margaret. It was one that she had often
admired in Dr. Somers' parlor, and she knew at once that it
was a gift from him. She thanked him heartily, and while
still examining it, the boys came in, all rosy and excited
over their new sleds, presents from the good doctor. When
they saw Margaret, they dashed their caps on the floor, nearly
stifling her with kisses, in their joy at having her down-
stairs again.

Then Mr. Crosby came in, and after speaking to the
visitors, he bent over Margaret, telling her how glad he
was to have her with them once more, and how thankful for
the new dressing-gown, which he had on. By that time
dinner was on the table, and Miss Patty appeared, with her
face a little flushed, but looking very nice in her clean white
apron, and the new cap, Margaret's present that morning.

The dinner was all very nice, and Miss Patty was more
than rewarded, if she had needed any other reward than

Margaret's satisfaction, for every thing was pronounced perfect, from the turkey down. Every body was cheerful and talkative, and Dr. Somers outdid himself in telling funny stories. When they left the table, they fell into more quiet after-dinner talk. Dr. Doane, fresh from the stir of the city, had much to tell his eager listeners of what was going on in the world of books, music, and art, and his touches upon social life were, to Fanny, like a taste of her old enjoyments.

"I say, Miss Crosby !" Jotham had opened the door from the kitchen, and, with his hands in his pockets, called Margaret's attention in the foregoing manner. "I jest come to wish you a Happy New-Year's, an' to say that I'm much obleeged fer them mittins an' that ar comforter you give me. They'll come mighty handy when I'm drivin' round in the cold."

"I'm sure I hope they will, Jotham," answered Margaret. "I wish you a Happy New-Year, too."

Jotham looked rather sheepish at finding all eyes directed to himself, but still maintained his ground with a reasonable degree of confidence, adding, after a little pause, "an' ther ain't nobody much pleaseder ter see you round ag'in nor I be ;" when he turned on his heel and shut the door.

"Oh, Aunty !" cried Jack soon after, from the window where he sat looking at one of the books that Mrs. Davis had sent to him and George, "here's Mr. Skinner !"

"Oh, it isn't possible," cried Fanny, wondering what the elegant Dr. Doane would think of their having such an outlandish visitor.

"Good !" cried Dr. Somers, "that's capital ; " and he fairly rubbed his hands with glee.

Margaret looked at him deprecatingly, but he only rubbed his hands the more, going to the window to see for himself.

"Margaret, your friend is handsomer than ever—though both he and his horse have the appearance of not having been to dinner."

"Oh, I remember that poor old horse," said Margaret ; "and Georgie, here's a chance for us to return good for evil.

Run and tell Jotham to give him a good dinner, but do not ride him yourself this time."

"That's right," cried the doctor, "to be sure! and here comes his master; you must be as good to him. Love me, love my horse," and he opened the door for Mr. Skinner.

"Come in, sir, come in. How do you do? Happy New-Year to you." Mr. Skinner came in with his accustomed deliberation, and in the course of half a minute had bestowed a scrutinizing glance upon every one in the room, while the doctor stood by, ready to offer him a chair.

Then having set his hat down, and taken off his gloves, he shook hands with each one, and hoped he saw them well. When that solemn duty was performed, he seated himself in the chair the doctor had placed for him, near Margaret.

"We are enjoying quite a spell of weather, sister Crosby," he remarked, spreading his hands out to the warmth of the fire.

"Yes," said Margaret, "it has been very cold for some time."

Up to this time, Mr. Skinner had worn a woollen muffler, that very nearly concealed his head, and his voice came from its folds with a most peculiar effect. But finding that the fire made it superfluous, he gradually unwound it, and hung it on the back of his chair.

"It's rather cold ridin'," he remarked, casting a sidelong glance at the table, set back against the wall, and examining the floor carefully, gave a loud cough.

"I've ben ridin' sence early breakfast-time, barrin a stop I was obligated to make nigh onto a mile from this juncture. One of the runners come off of my cutter, and I was obleeged to have it put on afore I could proceed hither."

"What an unfortunate circumstance," said the doctor. "If it hadn't been for that detention, you would have been here in time for dinner! It would be cruel to tell you of all the good things we had, such as turkey, chicken pie, and plum-pudding."

With every word the doctor uttered, Mr. Skinner's face

grew blanker, and when he mentioned plum-pudding, he dropped his head forward, drew his feet from under his chair to a horizontal position in front of him, and rested his hands on his knees.

"It's a most mysterious dispensation," he said, shaking his head mournfully. "I borryed that cutter because it was small, and I thought it would run slicker an' spryer than a bigger one."

"Well, my dear sir," said the doctor cheerfully, "we live and learn in this world; and most things are learned by experience. This morning's experience will teach you that there's many a slip 'twixt the cup and the lip, if nothing more."

Mr. Skinner did not seem to think that a particularly pleasant or desirable lesson to learn, and seemed so utterly cast down, that Margaret took pity on him, in spite of the mischievous glances from the doctor's eye.

"It isn't too late for you to have some dinner now, Mr. Skinner, if you won't mind its being cold."

"Mr. Skinner, what a favored mortal you are," said Dr. Somers.

But Mr. Skinner was too ecstatic for words; he could only stretch his mouth into a smile, and look at Margaret, as she bade Jack ask Miss Patty to get something ready for Mr. Skinner as soon as she could. And there he sat, his hands and feet shuffling nervously, as he watched the preparations for his repast, seating himself at the table when it was ready; and, nothing daunted by being the only one so occupied, he fell to eating most industriously.

When his hunger was fully appeased, he lifted his eyes from his plate and gazed around the room. The doctor was showing Dr. Doane and Fanny and the boys some puzzles, and tricks with strings; and Margaret, sitting by the fire watching them, having forgotten Mr. Skinner's presence for the time, was somewhat startled when he seated himself at a little distance, and leaning towards her, gave a premonitory cough. His good dinner had cheered him so, that he felt ready for any daring deed, and he had one in mind.

"Miss Crosby"—here he placed his hand over his mouth and coughed again—"Miss Crosby, I have come here to-day with a specified object in view, and, with your permission, I will state it at wonst." He did not wait for her permission, but proceeded.

"You doubtless remember a former occasion, upon which I proffered to you my hand and heart. I have given the subject careful consideration, and have arrived at the inference that you acted unadwisedly; wherefore I have come here this first day of the new year, having previously informed our mutooal friend, Dr. Somers, to give you a opportunity to retrack your decision; and here and now I lay my hand, my heart, my possessions, at your feet."

Margaret had glanced several times at the group in the other end of the room, but they were all busy with the puzzles, and Dr. Somers looked innocently absorbed and unconscious. She was about to speak, but Mr. Skinner interrupted her, saying solemnly:

"Let me forewarn you to act with due deliberation. It is not a or'nary post which I proffer to you; I may say it is a influential one, and this is the last time! This very arternoon I start on my way to a neighborhood where there is a widow! with property! and I shall put up with her while I hold meetin's, and though she may not have the personal adwantages of some, and I don't say that she has, there *is* a inducement. So consider well."

"Mr. Skinner," said Margaret in a low voice, but with a dignity that even he felt, "I wish to hear no more on this subject. Once and for all, I refuse your 'proffer,' and request that you will never renew it." Then she said, in ordinary tones, "Perhaps you would be interested to see Dr. Somers' puzzles," and rose to join her friends. The bewildered Mr. Skinner followed, and Dr. Somers at once addressed his conversation to him; but he soon showed signs of uneasiness, and presently went for his hat, saying that he must travel as far as Jonesville that day to return his cutter, and borrow another for the rest of his journey. His horse was accord-

ingly brought, and having shaken hands with all, he went
out.

"Oh, look!" cried George, "if that isn't funny!"

It was a very funny picture—Mr. Skinner in a little box
of a sleigh, with so low a seat, and so small a space in front
of it, that his knees were as high as his chin, while his angu-
lar horse towered above him, so close to the dashboard that
he nearly kicked it at every step he took.

The afternoon passed quickly and merrily, and the two
doctors went away—Dr. Somers having sent Margaret up-
stairs in Miss Patty's charge, and Dr. Doane having promised to come to tea the next day.

Margaret was tired, but it was a comfortable tiredness,
as she told her father and Miss Patty. She had really
enjoyed the day. The coming of a new character into the
narrow circle of their lives was very pleasant to Margaret,
and she found herself, according to her old fashion, making
an estimate of Dr. Doane, subject to changes when she should
know him better.

How many times poor Chloe had been in her thoughts
through the day, and what a weight it would have taken
from her heart if she could have known that she had escaped
from her captors and was in a safe haven!

# CHAPTER X.

For while he wrought with strenuous will
    The work his hands had found to do,
He heard the fitful music still,
    Of winds that out of dream-land blew.    Whittier.

A PICTURE of the silent, sky-bound prairies, in their un-trodden winter whiteness, was in Robert Russell's mind, in contrast with the turmoil of New York, with its snow black-ened by the tread of many feet, as he entered his counting-house the Monday morning after his return from St. Louis.

"Good morning, Russell, I'm glad to see you back. When did you come in?"

"Saturday night," answered Mr. Russell, as he and his partner, Mr. Kent, walked back to the office.

"Did your sister return with you?"

"No; she could not make up her mind to leave St. Louis at present. All her husband's friends are there, you know," replied Mr. Russell, taking up a pile of letters that lay on his desk.

"See if there is a letter among those from old Mr. Tap-scott," said Mr. Kent. "I shouldn't wonder if he has ap-pealed to you, as he found me unmanageable."

"Is he still in trouble?" asked Mr. Russell, looking for Mr. Tapscott's handwriting.

"He is on the verge of bankruptcy," answered Mr. Kent, "and he has been begging us to renew the note we hold against him, which, of course, is out of the question."

"The note is nearly due, is it not?"

"The thirty-first—to-day," answered Mr. Kent.

"He says that we are his first and largest creditors," said Mr. Russell, reading Mr. Tapscott's letter. "He thinks he could meet his other liabilities, and weather the storm, if we would favor him a little."

5

"I have heard that story several times since you went away."

"And did not think it best to heed it?"

"No; of course not," replied Mr. Kent, with some asperity. "I can't see why we should grant him such a favor, any more than any other of the five hundred men who get involved in the course of a year."

"Mr. Tapscott is an old man—he must be nearly seventy —and I do not know of a sadder sight than an old man left penniless, and obliged to begin life again after forty or fifty years of hard work. He was an old business friend of my father's, and I have known something about him in that way. He failed some twenty years ago, through indorsing for his son-in-law, Mr. Ventnor; and since Mr. Ventnor's death he has had his widow and three of her children to support; I believe the eldest son takes care of himself. Besides that, his wife is an invalid; so, you see, there are special reasons for favoring him."

"Then you approve the extension of that note?" said Mr. Kent, looking extremely annoyed.

"I do, most assuredly," replied Mr. Russell, "but I will not involve the firm in this thing. I will indorse the note, and if it does not save Mr. Tapscott, I will be the only loser. But I know that he is an honorable man, and will do the best he can by all his creditors."

Both gentlemen turned to their desks. Soon after, the door opened, and Mr. Tapscott himself entered the office. He came with painful hesitation, an apology for intruding in his very look and manner; his face was pale and haggard, and he seemed almost too weak to stand. Mr. Russell hastened to greet him and offer him a chair, and Mr. Tapscott essayed to speak, but his lips refused to utter a word.

"I am sorry to hear that you are having trouble in your business," said Mr. Russell; "but if a friendly hand can hold you up till you find your footing again, mine shall not be withheld from my father's old friend. Mr. Kent, may I trouble you for that note?"

Mr. Russell was the senior partner, and besides, nobody ever questioned his measures when his mind was made up. So Mr. Kent moodily handed him the paper. Going to his desk, he made out a new note, giving Mr. Tapscott all the time he desired, and then handed it to him to sign, after which Mr. Russell placed his own name on the back of it, and put it in the hands of Mr. Kent. The old man had been like one in a dream, his eyes never moving from Mr. Russell; but when he saw Mr. Russell's signature, and received the cancelled note, he buried his face in his trembling hands and sobbed aloud. Mr. Russell turned away to give him time to recover himself, which he soon did; but as he wrung his benefactor's hand, before leaving the office, he could only utter, " God bless you! "

After a short silence, Mr. Kent said: " If I should see any other man but Robert Russell do such a Quixotic thing, I should set him down as lacking common sense; and I wouldn't trust him with a business transaction involving a hundred dollars."

" I am glad you grant me the possession of a little of that valuable commodity, in spite of my Quixotic deeds," said Mr. Russell pleasantly.

" By the way," said Mr. Kent, " a man came here, two or three days ago, to see you about your tenement-houses."

" You mention my tenement-houses in rather a disrespectful connection," said Mr. Russell, smiling. " I suppose I am to infer that you consider them another of my foolish schemes."

" I must confess that I do think it rather an eccentric investment for a man of your sagacity."

" Well, I can't say that I look for large profits at present; but I am confident I shall not be a loser in the end; " and Mr. Russell returned to his desk, and for the next few hours his clear-sighted, absorbed attention was given to business.

Only one little interruption occurred. In the course of the morning, one of the clerks came to his desk.

" Mr. Russell, that little Italian girl is here, and seems

very anxious to see you. Shall I tell her that you are en-gaged ? "

"No; I will come to her directly," he answered, laying down his pen.

"Well, Angelica," he said, as he took the hand of a little girl who stood near the outer door, "I'm glad to see you. How are your mother, and Paul, and the little ones ? "

"Mother and the little ones are very well," she replied in a sweet voice, "but Paul is feeling very bad, and wants to see you, sir; and mother said I might come and ask you if you couldn't call to-day; " and she lifted her soft, dark eyes to Mr. Russell's face pleadingly.

"Is Paul really worse, do you think ? " he asked.

"I don't know," answered the child, "only he felt very ill Saturday, and I came to tell you about it; he said he should feel better if he could see you, but you were not here; and when I told him you were to be at home to-day, he kept begging mother to let me come again, till she did, though she said she knew you would be very busy, after being gone so long."

"I am very busy this morning, Angelica, but I am glad you came, and I will see Paul this afternoon. Tell him that I am coming."

The little girl thanked him with her eyes, and hurried home, while he went back to his work.

When Mr. Russell returned from China, having established a prosperous branch of the New-York house, which he left in charge of his brother, every body thought he would retire from business, and enjoy his fortune in elegant leisure; and every body was surprised to find that he remained in the firm, and went every day to the counting-house. He did not love idleness, and knew that he should find more opportuni-ties for doing good, in his own peculiar way, as an active member of the great world, than in the comparative seclu-sion of a man of leisure. Besides, he desired to add to his fortune, that he might have the more to use as opportunities for using it opened before him.

One of his favorite projects was, to provide respectable

homes for such poor people as came especially under his notice, and a block of comfortable, convenient houses, was already completed in a respectable part of the city. To these he bent his steps when he left the office, late in the afternoon; for Angelica's mother had been the first to enjoy the comfort of a change from close rooms in crowded tenements, where eyes and ears shrunk appalled from the sights and sounds that greeted them, to the airy, cheerful apartments of Mr. Russell's planning.

One day, not very long after Mr. Russell's return to America, a little girl came into his office, admitted by one of the clerks, and timidly showed him a small oil-painting, which she wished to sell. Mr. Russell saw that the picture had real merit, and was struck with the child's delicate beauty. Encouraged by his evident interest, she confided to him that her father was dead—that her mother took in sewing, and she crocheted, and made nets, and that was all they had to live on. There were five of them, since her father died, and her brother Paul was sick with a cough and a pain in his chest. It was he who had painted the picture, at little times when he could sit up. Mr. Russell bought the picture, and asked the little girl to come again the next day to tell him if her mother was willing to have him call and see them, as he would like to talk with Paul about his painting. He never knew what glowing descriptions Angelica gave her mother and Paul of the kind gentleman who paid so much money for the painting. But when she came the next day, he walked home with her, and from that time had been Mrs. Sarelli's kind, helpful friend, and the joy of Paul's hitherto tedious life.

Mr. Sarelli was an Italian artist, of real genius, but unknown and without friends in America, whither he came with his young English wife, lured by glowing anticipations of the fame he should win through his beloved art, and the happy home he should make for her who had forsaken all for him. His bright dreams quickly faded before the bitter reality; and after years of painful struggling against the

approach of want and distress to his loved ones, he laid
down his brushes and pallette—poor little powerless weapons,
when they are wielded by the obscure and friendless—and
died, leaving to his oldest child the sad inheritance of his
genius and his delicate constitution.

Mrs. Sarelli had no resource but her needle, and her utmost industry, together with little Angelica's small earnings,
made but a slender purse for the supply of life's necessities
to the five.  The first winter after her husband's death had
been a severe one, and she was glad that Paul could cherish
the fond hope of adding something to their scanty store, by
staying at home and painting; for with an aching heart she
heard the dreaded cough, and saw that his cheeks often wore
a feverish flush.  One or two little pictures were finished,
and pronounced perfect by the loving eyes of his mother and
Angelica, and sold by one or the other, after painful efforts,
for a mere pittance.  Then there were only materials left,
of what had remained of his father's small store, for one
more picture, and no money to spare, as Paul knew, when they
were used.  Long and patiently he worked on that last bit
of canvas, and when he had touched it and retouched it,
lingering over it as one lingers by a friend whom he is to
bid good-by forever, he gave it into Angelica's hands.

His sacrifice was repaid a thousandfold in the friendship
of Mr. Russell, though he had seldom been able to use the
complete supply of materials given him by that kind friend
on his fifteenth birthday.

When Mr. Russell knocked at their door, Angelica
opened it.  Mrs. Sarelli hastened to welcome him, and two
little figures came flying across the room, seizing his hands,
and dancing up and down at his side as he walked towards
the couch where Paul lay, his dark eyes glowing, and his
cheeks burning with the excitement of seeing his friend once
more.  The little ones clung to his hands till he stooped and
kissed them—Edith, with her mother's golden hair and blue
eyes, and little Mary, like the rest, with her father's Italian
beauty.  Then they danced back to their play, leaving Mr.

Russell to sit down by Paul, and hear all he had been doing and thinking since he had been away.

"I shall be well again, now you have come back," said the boy, after they had talked awhile. "I think I shall be able to paint in a few days, and I have such a lovely idea for a picture; I do hope I can sketch it before it fades from my mind. But I don't know what I am to do about the sky. I want a wide stretch of blue sky, with those piles of snowy clouds, just changing to crimson, that I remember to have seen long ago; but I'm afraid I sha'n't succeed in that. I wonder if I ever shall see much sky at a time again!"

"Do you think you can keep the idea in your mind till summer comes?" asked Mr. Russell; "because then I mean to have you see a great deal of sky, and green grass, and trees and flowers, and all the beautiful things to be found in the country."

Paul looked at him with his heart in his eyes, and Angelica and her mother dropped their work in their laps, to wonder what Mr. Russell could mean.

"I did not intend to mention my plan so soon," he said, smiling at Paul, "but I think, after all, you might as well have two pleasures as one; and I do not think the reality will be any the less a pleasure for your having that of anticipation. About fifteen miles from here, on a little hill, stands a little cottage, with a little yard in front, and a little garden behind; with a view of the river and fields and woods beyond, where the sun sets, sometimes in crimson and gold, sometimes in purple and gray, sometimes in yellow and pale green; and there are no red brick walls on any side, to shut out the view of the sky. The little house is occupied now by somebody that I do not know; but I do know the people who will be living there before the roses blossom in June."

Not a word was spoken, but something very like a sob came from Mrs. Sarelli, and Angelica's face was hid in her mother's lap.

"What do you think, Paul?" asked Mr. Russell. "Will you be patient till that time comes, and keep your sky-

pictures till you can sit in the sunshine, and paint the livelong
day ? "

Paul pressed Mr. Russell's hand first to his lips and then
to his heart, and gazed into his face with his eyes full of
happy tears.

Mr. Russell glanced at a pile of shirts that lay on a chair
near him, and said, "I will send Patrick for those on
Wednesday, Mrs. Sarelli, as to-morrow is New-Year's day."

It was not the least of the many acts of kindness that
filled Mrs. Sarelli's heart with gratitude to her friend, that he
spared her the contact with ungracious employers; but this
day her heart was too full for words.

As Mr. Russell rose to go, Paul drew him down, and
whispered, "I have learned that chapter, and it has been the
sweetest comfort to me since I have been sick this time. I
don't think I could have been patient without it."

Mr. Russell whispered a few words of encouragement,
and then said good-by; but that same evening came a knock
at the door, and a package was brought in, containing a
New-Year's dinner, and some useful present for each.

The street-lamps were lighted when Mr. Russell reached
home. His house was not very far up-town. It was the
same old-fashioned, red brick house that his father had built,
when that part of the city was considered quite in the
country; where he and his brother and sister had been born,
and had grown up; where his mother had died suddenly,
soon after his departure for China, and where his sister had
been married.

His sister had lived at home after her marriage, until her
husband's business called him to St. Louis. Her father was
too much attached to his old home to leave it and go with
her, as she earnestly wished, and he lived on with his old servants, who had been so long in the house as to seem a·part
of it. His health failed soon, and he felt that he must
have one of his sons at home, to lean upon in his old age.
Robert came at once, and his father lived only a month after
his return. Now he was alone, and the great house had a

dreary, deserted air, in spite of Janet's efforts to make it
cheerful. Memories of loved ones gone to their rest, and
old times and old friends, met him at every turn, forcing
him, while at home, to live more in the past than in the
present.

"Well, Mr. Robert," was his old housekeeper's greeting,
"I don't suppose you'll be surprised to find your dinner
spoiled and stone-cold."

"I should be surprised to find it stone-cold, Janet. You
would not have the heart to treat me so badly as that."

"I don't know, Mr. Robert; it's an unheard-of circumstance for a member of the Russell family to be late to
dinner;" and old Janet shook her head.

"You will have to forgive me this once, Janet, and let me
have my dinner this minute, for I am very hungry."

"Mr. Robert," said Janet, reluctantly, "I suppose I ought
to tell you that there's a person in the parlor waiting to see
you; I don't presume that she'd much like to wait till you've
been to dinner."

"Is it a lady?" asked Mr. Russell, in surprise.

"I suppose she's a lady, or Reuben wouldn't have put her
in the drawing-room," answered Janet to herself, for Mr.
Russell had hastened to see his guest.

As he entered the drawing-room, a tall woman came
briskly forward to meet him, with little mincing steps, quite
out of keeping with her unusual height. Her dress was an
odd mixture of colors and styles, the prevailing effect being
dowdiness. She had a large worsted bag upon her arm, and
a pair of soiled, crumpled kid gloves on her hands.

"Have I the honor of speaking to Mr. Robert Russell?"
she asked, laying one hand on the bag.

Mr. Russell bowed.

"I am Mrs. Sophronia Brower," she said, with a curtsey,
seating herself, and reaching out for a little mosaic stand,
which she placed before her, as if she were about to deliver
a lecture from behind it.

"It is rather an unseasonable hour for females to be out,

5*

but the man at the door informed me that you would soon return, and I have been waiting in momentary expectation. My business is important, as you will admit, when I state it, which I will do at once, as my time is precious." And she proceeded to open her bag.

Mr. Russell thought of his dinner, and approved of her intention.

" The name of Robert Russell is one which, wherever seen, must command the attention and win the confidence of every person, male and female, far and wide; and *there-fore* I come to him to lead the van—to head a list of illustrious names that are about to commence a glorious work; in short, a crusade against ignorance, vice, and barbarity—to sow a seed that shall speedily grow into a tree, that will overshadow the earth with its benign branches—to kindle a spark that will soon illumine the moral, as the sun now illumines the material world ! "

She paused to gain breath, and having taken from her bag and unrolled a paper at least two yards long—blank except at the top—she held it off at arms-length :

" What a scroll upon which to engrave one's name ! Ah, that I were in the place of him for whom is reserved the honor of heading that glorious tablet ! " She gazed at it in rapt admiration a moment, and then said :

" I know I have only to name the august Society whose unworthy servant I am, in order to elicit your warm sympathy and ardent coöperation. It is ' The Society for the Diffusion of the Knowledge of the Arts and Sciences and Polite Literature among the Heathen.' "

Mr. Russell smiled, but shook his head as his visitor, auguring well for her scroll, held it towards him.

" I am sorry to disappoint you," he said, "but I cannot give you my name."

" Am I to understand that you refuse to countenance so glorious an object? " exclaimed Mrs. Brower.

" The object seems to me rather chimerical than glorious."

" And will you *contribute* nothing ? "

" You could hardly expect me to contribute to any thing of which I disapprove."

" I have heard that you discountenance all benevolent societies," said Mrs. Brower, severely.

" I very sincerely approve of really benevolent societies, and if yours was one for sending missionaries to the heathen, or giving them the Bible, I would willingly contribute, though I have no ambition to put my name to long papers."

" You *may* live," said Mrs. Brower, solemnly, rising and rolling up her scroll, " to see that the surest way to enlighten the heathen mind, and prepare it to appreciate the emblems and figures of the sacred writers, is to teach them to appreciate the grand and beautiful in art and nature and profane literature ; " and securing her roll, she prepared to depart.

" I think the truths of the Bible the means for enlightening and saving men, whether they are heathens or nominally Christians ; " and Mr. Russell bowed Mrs. Brower and her bag out of the door.

After dinner, which Janet had kept hot, notwithstanding her intimation to the contrary, Mr. Russell retired to his sanctum. This room had been his especial retreat almost since he could remember, and had fewer haunting presences than any other in the house. Its coloring was warm, and there, with the curtains drawn, the drop-light shaded, and a blazing fire in the grate, to cast ruddy gleams over the carpet and walls, he spent many happy hours, when he was conscious of no present and no past—only of the charm of some congenial research, or of communion with favorite authors.

To-night he sat musing by the fire over the events of the day ; and it did not take long for the lingering hours of the Old Year to weave around him their magical spell, and close his senses to all, save the pictures which Memory and Fancy might conjure up before him. · Ah, Memory !

> " Needs must thou dearly love thy first essay,
> And foremost in thy various gallery
> Place it, where sweetest sunlight falls
> Upon thy storied walls."

The scene is one of warmth and brightness, the counter-part of the present reality, only that he is counting the laggard minutes till they reach the appointed hour of tryst; and his mother stands beside him, her hand laid lightly on his head, while she playfully questions him as to where his thoughts were, that he did not hear the opening door and her footfalls on the carpet. She smiles into his eyes lovingly, as she says, " My son, give my dear love to your Margaret, and wish her a Happy New.Year for me."

Another touch of Memory's pencil and the scene is changed. Margaret sits beside him, her truthful eyes turned to him, and her hand in his. He dwells on the varying expressions of her fair face, and reads the earnest thoughts so clearly written upon it. He tells her that the future may not all be bright and cloudless, and she answers, "I have no fear of what the years may bring, while you walk by my side."

.He was by her side no more, as other pictures came: where had her journeyings led her? and how had the years dealt with her? Memory could not solve the mystery of their parted lives. It must remain a mystery, as he "walked desolate day by day." But in the Hereafter it would all be made clear, and in the meantime she was enshrined in the inmost recesses of his heart, as the impersonation of every womanly grace.

Here Fancy, seeing the sober tints which Memory was using, seized her own brush, and drew such a sweet picture of his home, as he had dreamed of it once, with Margaret for its queen, that he could have gazed on the vision forever. But the weary Hours, one by one, laid by their wands, dropping the threads of the magic web they had woven around him, till not one was left. The clock on the mantel struck the death-knell of the Old Year, and distant chimes rung in the New. The vision had vanished, leaving him only the lonely reality of the present.

## CHAPTER XI.

The best laid plans of mice an' men,
Aft gang a-gley.          BURNS.

MR. ALEXANDER THORNE was a shipping merchant, well known in business circles as a successful, honorable man, and his wife was equally well known and influential in the fashionable world. Her dinners and receptions were models of taste and elegance, and their exclusiveness made it well worth while to be among the favored few. Besides her own charms of manner and conversation, she had a beautiful daughter, whose education had caused her much solicitude, and whose *début,* when her education was pronounced finished by her various masters, had occasioned quite a sensation in Mrs. Thorne's circle; as she had, with great wisdom, kept her carefully secluded till the suitable time, and then brought her out in all the freshness of her girlish beauty, never dreaming but that, in due time, her career would be consummated as brilliantly as it had opened. But owing to certain perversities of taste for which, in view of her careful training, she could in no wise account, serious anxieties had recently arisen in her mind.

"Alexander," she said to her husband one morning as they sat alone at breakfast, "do have the kindness to listen to me for a moment."

"My dear, I will listen to you for several moments," he replied, laying aside his paper, and proceeding with his breakfast. "What have you to say to me that is new and interesting, this morning?"

"You may not consider it interesting; indeed, I often marvel that it seems to interest you so little, when to me it is such a vital subject."

"Oh!" Mr. Thorne ejaculated, in a tone that showed him conscious of what the vital subject was.

"It is useless to shut our eyes and try not to admit the fact. Something must be done," and Mrs. Thorne laid her white, shapely hand on the table, by way of emphasis; "something decisive, to divert Claudia's mind from her fool-ish *penchant* for Philip Ventnor."

"If it is only a foolish *penchant,* my dear, I should think it might be left to die a natural death, as such things gen-erally do."

"No," answered Mrs. Thorne; "it will not do to run any risk in this matter. Claudia is a strange girl, and if left to her own unguided impulse, I really believe she would marry that penniless author. She is actually losing her in-terest in society already."

"Mr. Ventnor's being poor is by no means my objection to him. Poverty is nothing against a man of genius, and while I have an abundance, our only child is not likely to suffer, even if she should marry a penniless man. But I couldn't see Claudia marry a man whose principles are un-sound. I am afraid it is true that young Ventnor is too fond of wine."

"And yet you make light of my desire to break up the acquaintance."

"I can't see the thing as seriously as you do, Helen. It seems to me like a mere girlish fancy for a brilliant, talented fellow, and I can't see the necessity of making a tragedy of it. Why, Claudia is but a child yet; she ought not to fall in love for years."

"And, pray, how old must a girl be before she can fall in love? If I remember rightly, I was but eighteen when we became engaged. But, thank heaven, Claudia has a mother who will not see her follow a wayward, girlish fancy, to her own destruction. To think of such beauty and accomplishments being thrown away upon a man without wealth, or position, or name!"

"What do you propose to do? I thought it was pro-verbial that if a girl is opposed in her love-affairs she only gets the more desperate."

"Pray, my dear, give me credit for a little discretion in the management of my child. My plans are laid carefully, and wisely, as you will admit when you see the result."

"Do give me an inkling of your plans," said her husband, inwardly amused.

"I am going to arouse her ambition."

"Ambition? to be an authoress, or Queen of England, or what?"

"To marry wealth and a splendid position," replied Mrs. Thorne; "to win a prize that might well turn any girl's head with envy."

"Do you know any such head-turning individual? I am sure I don't," said her husband.

"Well, I do, and if Claudia possesses one particle of spirit, you will soon see her proudly wearing the honors of the position I refer to."

"Who is it, Helen? I am dying of curiosity, as the ladies say."

"Who should it be, but Mr. Robert Russell, the rich China merchant, with every quality of mind and manner to win a girl's heart, and wealth and position to satisfy her highest ambition."

When Mr. Thorne heard the name of Robert Russell, he so far forgot his good manners as to give a long, low whistle. "Well, I will give you credit for an unlimited amount of enterprise, Helen. Why, I should as soon think of Claudia's wooing a granite statue from its pedestal by the glances of her bright eyes, as to draw that impenetrable man from his shell. How do you expect to bring him within reach of her charms?"

"Oh, fortune favors the brave, you know," answered his wife gayly. "Only do your part as well as I shall mine, and all will be well."

"What is to be my part in this wonderful drama?"

"I am not sure that I can trust you, but it must be done, and if you don't do it, I shall. Philip Ventnor must be informed, before long, that his attentions to Claudia are unwelcome, and that they must cease."

"And that is what you wish me to do?"

"Yes, my dear, if you will?"

"I beg to be excused; I will leave that to you," and Mr. Thorne's hitherto smiling face was decidedly cloudy, as he bade his wife good-morning.

Mrs. Thorne was still sitting behind the coffee-urn, in deep thought, when Claudia came down.

"I think you are taking things quite lazily this morning," she said, as Claudia kissed her, and seated herself at the table.

"I know it, mamma; but I was so sleepy."

"It wasn't so very late when you came home last night. Did you go at once to bed when you went to your room?"

"No, mamma, I did not."

"What was there to keep you up, child?"

"I read a while, mamma," answered Claudia, her cheeks glowing and her lashes drooping.

"What did you find so entertaining as to keep you awake at midnight?" asked Mrs. Thorne.

Claudia hesitated a moment, and then answered, without lifting her eyes, "I was reading Mr. Ventnor's last article."

Mrs. Thorne's eyes flashed. "It was very wrong, Claudia. Society's claims will sufficiently tax your strength, without your taking hours from sleep for things that can be done quite as well in the daytime. I am sure you would be sorry to lose all your freshness before you have been out a year."

"Oh, yes, indeed," answered Claudia, earnestly. Mrs. Thorne's penetration was not at fault in attributing her unwonted warmth on the subject to a thought of Philip Ventnor, but she only said,

"Well, then, don't try your eyes and weary your mind, by reading when you ought to be asleep. I wish you to go out with me this morning. I must call at your aunt's, and see that she and Arabella make no engagement for Thursday."

" What is to be on Thursday, mamma ? "

" I am going to have your uncle and aunt and cousin, and those English gentlemen whom we met thére the other night, here to dinner."

" Any body else, mamma ? "

" Yes ; they know Mr. Russell very well in Canton, and think most highly of him, as indeed all do who know him ; and I shall ask him to meet them."

" Mr. Russell ! " exclaimed Claudia. " You don't mean the man who lives all alone in that large red brick house, like a spell-bound prince ! I should like, of all things, to see him among humans ; but I don't believe the wicked Fairy will let him come. I shouldn't a bit wonder if he is fastened with golden fetters, or changed into some wonderful shape, the instant he steps inside that old house."

" What childish nonsense you are talking, Claudia," said her mother, not caring to show how greatly pleased she was at that same nonsense. " Mr. Russell's sister Clara, now Mrs. Blake, and I, used to exchange visits, and I have had a bowing acquaintance with all the family since I can remember. But Robert has been in mourning for his father ever since he came from China, and of course has not been into society at all. I should have preferred an evening reception," she added, thinking how particularly lovely Claudia looked in evening-dress, " but I see he still wears mourning for his father ; and then, his sister's husband died recently, which of course would make his coming out of the question, except in the quietest way."

Here Mrs. Thorne paused, and looked into Claudia's face, wishing she knew just what cue to take ; but though it was a fair, open face, she had to proceed blindly. " I hope Arabella won't fall in love with this Eastern prince, for I am afraid there would be but little hope for her. He must be proof against womanly charms, or he would have been married before now ; still, Bella is rather pretty, and gentle, and he may chance to be captivated by her ; and if he should, your aunt might well bless me for bringing them

together.  Such a fortune, and such a position, and such
personal attractions, are rare by themselves; but it is only
once in a lifetime that one finds them combined."

Claudia only waited for her mother to finish, to burst into
a merry laugh.  "Oh, mamma, to think that you should be
the good Fairy to bring the enchanted prince and the
enchanting princess together ! "

" What do you mean, Claudia ? "

" Why, it was only the other day that Bella and I were
driving by the castle, and saw the prince dismounting from
a magnificent black charger, looking so reserved and proud,
and withal so handsome, that I said to Bella, ' Don't you
wish you were the fair maiden appointed to break the cruel
enchantment that binds that poor prince ? '  You should
have heard the melancholy tone in which she replied, ' Oh,
Claudie, for three months—ever since I saw him riding that
black horse the first time—he has been my *beau ideal ;* but I
never shall know him.'  And now she will !  And I'll see
that she wears her prettiest dress, and looks her sweetest ; "
and Claudia rested her elbow on the table and her cheek on
her hand, and looked up at her mother, her eyes fairly dancing, over the little matrimonial plot she was laying.

Her mother thought, as she glanced at the graceful,
rounded figure, and the lovely young face, that if Mr. Russell
could see her then, or at any time when her head was not
full of sentimental nonsense about Philip Ventnor, she need
have no fear of his being captivated by the commonplace
Arabellá, instead of her rarely beautiful Claudia.  But she
kept these thoughts to herself, only saying, ' Don't neglect
to do credit to my training, child, in your own toilet and
behavior."

Claudia rose from the table and stood looking into the
fire, until her mother summoned her to come and get ready
for their drive, her face no longer sparkling and gay, but
quiet and grave ; her thoughts no longer of the enchanted
prince and Bella, and her schemes for them, but of Philip
Ventnor.  Must the shadow that had so soon crept over her

life deepen and darken till it shut Philip from her forever, except in dreams?

Mr. Russell accepted Mrs. Thorne's invitation to an informal dinner, out of regard for the friends whom he was invited to meet, little imagining that two heads were plotting against his solitude. And Mrs. Thorne would have been far from satisfied had she known how little place her dinner had in his thoughts, as he entered his house earlier than usual Thursday afternoon.

"Has any one been here?" he asked of Janet, who met him in the hall according to her custom.

"Yes, Mr. Robert; there's a young man been here some minutes. He's in the library."

Two or three mornings before, Mr. Russell's attention had been attracted by a young man who stood near the door as he entered his counting-house. The first passing glance had made him look again, and he saw that his clothes were worn and old-fashioned, but that he had a refined, intellectual face, and that he was looking for something. No doubt there was a kindly interest in Mr. Russell's eyes, for the young man stepped forward, though with some hesitation, and said, "Do you know, sir, of any one who wants a copyist, or bookkeeper, or any thing of the kind?"

"Is it for yourself that you wish the situation?" asked Mr. Russell, thinking the eyes that looked so steadily into his must belong to a true and loyal heart.

"Yes, sir; for myself."

"Come in a moment," said Mr. Russell, leading the way to the office, which was empty.

"Are you a stranger in the city?" he asked.

"Yes; I have not a single acquaintance here, or I would not have troubled you, sir, an entire stranger, in this way;" and a faint tinge of red flushed the pale face.

"Don't think it a trouble. I may be able to help you in your search, and shall be glad to do so. New York is a great, busy place, and there are many, like you, in quest of work."

"I am afraid I have made a mistake in coming to New York," said the young man; "but it seemed the only thing for me to do."

"I would not call it a mistake," said Mr. Russell, "if it seemed the best thing to be done. If your search proves unsuccessful, you can take the next best thing with more satisfaction, for having made this attempt. But now tell me something about yourself," he said, smiling. "I want to know your name, and where you live, and just what you want to do."

"My name is John Heath; my father is a minister, and my home is in Rockdale, in this State. I am ready to do any thing I can do that will earn money. I have had no experience in bookkeeping, but I have been studying it for the past two months, and think I could undertake it. I suppose it would bring better pay than copying."

"Well, we will see what our combined efforts can do," said Mr. Russell, as Mr. Kent and another gentleman entered the office. John rose to go, taking from his well-worn pocketbook two letters, which he handed to Mr. Russell.

"Those are the only recommendations I have," he said; "one is from my old teacher in Rockdale, and the other from one of the professors in —— University; but," he added, "my father knows me better than any body, and you could trust to his giving an impartial account of me."

This was said with a smile that made the manly face almost childlike, and very winning; and Mr. Russell said, "Leave these letters with me, Mr. Heath, till Thursday, and then come to my house—there is my address—at four o'clock, and I will talk with you more about your plans, and tell you if I have heard of any thing for you. Is there any thing I can do for you till then?"

"Thank you, sir, I think there is nothing;" and John Heath went away by many degrees lighter hearted than he had been fifteen minutes before.

It was he who sat gazing with such hungry eyes at the book-lined walls of the library, when Mr. Russell entered.

"You look at my books as if you had an affection for their kind," Mr. Russell said, as they shook hands.

John's eyes passed slowly along the lines of substantial, attractive-looking volumes; and he answered, "I have given them up; at least, for some years to come I expect to have very little to do with them."

"You have had a good deal to do with them thus far, I see from the letters you left with me," said Mr. Russell.

"I have done nothing all my life but study; but now I must work."

"Your father's letter tells me—you see, I acted upon your suggestion," said Mr. Russell—"that your plans have been broken up, and intimates that the change involved a great sacrifice on your part; but he leaves you to tell me more fully about it."

John hesitated a moment, while the workings of his face showed what a sore subject it was to him; and then he said, "Ever since I was fifteen years old I have intended to be a minister, and all my studies have been with a view to that. I was fitted for college when I was eighteen, and had just entered the junior year, when I was obliged to leave."

"Your father has no church now, I believe?"

"No," John replied; "he had been the pastor of the church in Rockdale for thirty years, but had grown old, and was less vigorous than he used to be; so the church decided that they needed a younger man—and father is too broken-down to be called to another church, or to undertake any thing else. But I am ready to work for him and my dear mother; as long as they live they shall never lack a comfort that I can provide; and my younger brother shall have the best chance for an education that I can give him."

"It must, indeed, be a very strait and narrow path that hedges you in from the possibility of carrying out so sacred a purpose," said Mr. Russell, thoughtfully.

"I find it so," replied John. "I know that I can serve my Master in other ways, but I did hope to consecrate my

whole time and every power of my soul to Him, as I think
only a minister can."

"Suppose that now a way opened before you to carry
out your purpose; would you not feel it to be your duty to
do so, even if the way were at first repugnant to your pride,
and sense of independence?"

John looked at Mr. Russell wonderingly, and answered
that, no matter what the way might be, if it were opened for
him, he should not hesitate a moment; but he could not conceive of such a possibility, when he was the sole dependence
of his parents.

"But suppose that one, who is but an older brother, to
whom the Father has intrusted more of this world's goods
than to you, should offer you the means to pursue your
studies and fit yourself for His service, and at the same time
should promise to take a brother's care of your parents, that
you might the sooner enter upon your work: would you dare
to refuse the offer?"

John sat motionless for several minutes, while Mr. Russell waited for his answer. At length he said, in low tones
of deep feeling, "No, sir; I should not dare."

"I knew you would not," answered Mr. Russell. An
hour later, when he suddenly remembered his engagement at
Mrs. Thorne's, he had briefly stated his plans and wishes,
formed since he received Mr. Heath's letter, and arranged to
see John again; and John left the house, hardly knowing
whether he trod on earth or air.

When Mr. Russell entered Mrs. Thorne's drawing-room,
she received him with the perfection of hospitable grace,
assuring him that she esteemed it a great favor that he
should so honor her, under the circumstances. She inquired
with the warmest sympathy after his sister's health, of
whose affliction she had learned with such pain, and then
they joined the group of busy talkers at the other end of the
room, where Mr. Russell was presented to the ladies—to
Mrs. William Thorne, delicate and languid—to Arabella,
with her flaxen hair and blue eyes, looking her sweetest, as

Claudia had said she should—and to Claudia, whose violet eyes, long black lashes and black hair, together with her peachy complexion and delicate features, formed a whole that was as rare as it was beautiful, and did not escape Mr. Russell's quick eye. Mrs. Thorne felt quite at ease as to the impression they had made; Claudia was so self-possessed, and yet so perfectly unconscious of herself, and Arabella so shrinking and self-conscious, when Mr. Russell addressed them.

Claudia meditated the daring act of altering her mother's arrangements so far as to place Bella beside Mr. Russell at dinner; but that was not an easy thing to do, and she found herself in the place she intended for her cousin. However, Bella was just opposite, and for a time Claudia busied herself in trying to look at her through the stranger's eyes. But before long she had yielded to the charm of Mr. Russell's conversation, sustaining her part with a simple grace and spirit that greatly pleased his fastidious taste. Even after the talk became general, she remained perfectly oblivious of the weighty plot her little head had been charged with for the last three days, and listened eagerly to the reminiscences of life in Canton exchanged between the three gentlemen who had met there, and to the talk of travels, books, and men, that followed. But by-and-by she chanced to catch Bella's eyes, fixed upon her so reproachfully, that it all flashed across her mind, and it was only by dint of effort that she refrained from laughing.

She mentally shook her head at herself, saying, "It will never do. I'm sorry I encouraged the child to think of such an absurd thing." She glanced up at her neighbor, and shook her head again as she looked over at Bella. "Oh, dear, no; she is a mere chit of a girl, and he is—I don't know all he is. I think Philip and he could understand and appreciate each other."

When dinner was over, Claudia put her arm within her cousin's, and as they walked across the drawing-room she said, laughingly, "Instead of being princesses that the prince would deign to notice, we are like little mice, trying to play with a lion. He could walk over us and never see us."

The lids of Bella's eyes were actually pink with her efforts to keep back the tears. "I didn't think you would do so, Claudie. You kept talking to him all the time, and never gave him a chance to say a word to me, or even to look at me."

Claudia laughed. "Why, Childie, I believe you are in love already. You shall have him all to yourself the rest of the evening."

"You know very well that we have another engagement this evening with those prosy men, and we shall go very soon, and I may never see him again."

"Oh, dear! what shall I do?" cried Claudia, wringing her hands in pretended distress. "Oh, I know;" and she drew Bella towards the rest of the company, saying:

"Mamma, before Bella goes, I should like to hear the song she has just learned; wouldn't you?"

"Oh, Claudie, I really can't!" cried Bella, blushing.

"Do, my dear," urged Mrs. Thorne, thinking that Claudia would sing afterwards with more effect.

"Sing, my love," said her mother; and so Bella sang her song, which was no other than "*Robert, toi que j'aime,*" and Claudia and Mr. Russell stood by to listen, Claudia feeling much inclined to laugh at the unusual touch of pathos in her cousin's voice, and a little shocked at her own temerity, as she met her mother's grave looks.

When Bella rose from the piano, Claudia would have left her standing beside Mr. Russell; but he asked her to sing, and, without the least hesitation or apology, she seated herself, and sung the first thing that occurred to her, only thinking that she would not mar the effect of Bella's "*Robert,*" by singing any thing of the same style. The sweet, simple ballad she sung charmed every body; but there was no time for any thing more, as her aunt rose, saying that if they were going to the concert, it was fully time for them to start. Mr. Russell remained to hear another song, as Mrs. Thorne entreated. He did not see the pathetic glance from Bella's eyes, as he bowed to her and her mother, and shook hands with the gentlemen; but Claudia did, and she was giving herself a sound scolding for her mischievous match-making, when Mr. Russell said, "Do you sing a little German song, Miss Thorne, called ' *Gut Nacht, Fahr' wohl* ' ? "

Claudia's cheeks took a brighter tint, as she replied: " Oh, yes, I sing it often ; " and she went to the piano.

Mr. Russell wondered that a light-hearted, careless girl, just on the threshold of a life full of sunshine, should be able to throw such intense feeling into the song. Every tone seemed to come straight from the heart of the singer, and fell sweet and tender and thrilling upon the ears of the listeners.

Claudia did not hear the door open, or know that some one had entered the room, and stood behind her at a little distance while she sang the closing strains. Mr. Russell, standing by the piano, had noticed the cold, stately greeting of Mrs. Thorne, and Mr. Thorne's embarrassed, though kindly manner, but all tacitly waited for the song to end. When the last lingering notes had died quite away, Mrs. Thorne came forward and said, " Mr. Ventnor, let me introduce you to Mr. Russell," and Mr. Russell turned—but not before he had caught the flash of joyful surprise that brightened Claudia's face, whose expression, till she heard the name, had been so in keeping with the spirit of her song; yet her greeting was constrained. Not till he had dropped Claudia's hand, did it seem to dawn upon Philip to whom he had been introduced ; and then, with his handsome face all aglow, he grasped Mr. Russell's hand.

" Mr. Russell ! I never had the pleasure of meeting you before, and yet I have a right to claim you as a friend."

Mr. Russell returned the warm grasp, saying, " I have a prior right to claim your friendship, for I have known you through your writings."

The gleam of pleasure that shone in Claudia's eyes was not lost upon him.

A little bit of skilful manœuvring on Mrs. Thorne's part placed Mr. Russell beside Claudia, and Mr. Ventnor beside herself; and though the conversation was general, and never flagged, Mr. Russell was conscious of something uncomfortable in the atmosphere, and was not surprised that Mr. Ventnor's call was short. He merely bowed low to Claudia as he passed her on his way from the room; and Mr. Russell found himself meditating upon all these little signs that the current of this young love did not run smoothly.

The outer door was scarcely closed behind Philip, when Mrs. Thorne said, "What a pity it is that a young man who is as talented as Mr. Ventnor, should ruin his prospects by dissipation."

Mr. Russell was too surprised and shocked to speak. He only glanced involuntarily at Claudia, who sat leaning slightly forward, her hands clasped tightly together, and an expression of sharp pain on her face, in strange contrast with its child-like brightness an hour before.

"I think you state the case too strongly, Helen," said Mr. Thorne. "I am afraid it is true that Mr. Ventnor inherits his father's weakness, but he is very far from being ruined by dissipation."

"It is only a difference of terms; if, as you say, he inherits his father's weakness, there can be no hope for him. His father died a victim to that fatal weakness, and I suppose there is no doubt but that his son is following in his footsteps."

"'No hope' and 'no doubt' are very strong terms, Mrs. Thorne," said Mr. Russell, as he rose to go. "With such safeguards as I am sure Mr. Ventnor possesses, I think there is every reason to hope for his welfare, and to doubt his yielding to the fatal weakness."

He said good-night to Mr. and Mrs. Thorne, and received their warm expressions of grateful pleasure, and then turned to Claudia. Mrs. Thorne drew her own conclusions from the meeting of their eyes, and the clasp of their hands; they were not to her, as they were to Claudia, the simple to-

kens of a brotherly interest in her, and in Philip, though
Claudia could not have told why she felt so much stronger
and safer, just because of her look into those kindly eyes.

That night, as Mr. Russell sat beside the fire in his sanctum, his thoughts dwelt for a time, with quiet satisfaction,
upon the easy task of enabling John Heath to fulfill his
cherished plan of giving himself to Christ's service. Then
they turned to Philip Ventnor, with the solicitude of a strong
and generous nature for a gifted one, tried and in peril; and
the thought of the young heart, whose happiness seemed
linked with Philip's fate, added intensity to the interest that
few are capable of feeling for those to whom they are only
bound by the tie of a common brotherhood.

But how was his interest to avail any thing? He could
not see, as yet, but trusted that time would develope a way.

# CHAPTER XII.

The shade by which my life was crossed,
Which makes a desert in the mind,
Has made me kindly with my kind.    TENNYSON.

"I THINK I will return with you to Rockdale," said Mr. Russell to John Heath, in the course of their next interview. "I am anxious to know your father and mother, and have them regard me as a friend. It is but a few hours from New York, and I can go and come in one day. There are some things that I should like to talk over with them."

John's delight and surprise at this new proof of Mr. Russell's kindness were unbounded.

"I know," he said, "that nothing could give them greater pleasure than to know you, sir."

He spent that evening with Mr. Russell, and the next morning they started for Rockdale; and if Mr. Russell had felt any misgivings as to the wisdom of his project, they would have been dispelled as he gained a clearer insight into John's character. The genuineness of his piety, his earnest love for the work he had chosen, and his lofty views of its sacredness and responsibility, together with his genial, frank nature and vigorous intellect, impressed him more and more, and deepened the interest he had felt in him from the first chance meeting. His plans for him were all arranged and explained with business-like precision, and there was little said of obligation or gratitude; for when one generous spirit confers a great benefit upon another, words are not needed to remove a painful burden of obligation, or to make the appreciation of its value felt. Moreover, John knew that it was a service done for the sake of their Saviour; and while that took nothing from his personal gratitude to his friend, it kept self out of sight, and made it easier for him to look the benefaction calmly in the face.

They reached Rockdale about noon, and a few minutes' walk brought them to the little house in the village where Mr. and Mrs. Heath were staying.  John pointed out, in passing, the church where his father had preached for so many years, and the parsonage where he and his brothers and sisters had been born and brought up.

John's arrival, and with a stranger, was a great surprise, as he had written but once during his absence, and then only to give them a glowing description of his first meeting with Mr. Russell, waiting till he saw them to tell the wonderful thing that had befallen him.  But Mr. Russell's own letter to Mr. Heath had won their hearts, and insured him a warm welcome ; and his coming to Rockdale for no other purpose than to see them, was a proof of interest they could hardly credit.

In the little old-fashioned parlor they sat till dinner-time, talking of things in general, though John's restless manner, and eager, sparkling eyes, marked his impatience to tell his story.  But Mr. Russell had reserved that to do himself, in his own time and way.

Mr. and Mrs. Heath interested him at once.  Their simple, trusting piety, breathing through all they said, and shining in their care-worn faces, was all that was needed to win his confidence and respect ; but their intelligence, native refinement, and warm-heartedness, were equally apparent ; and Mr. Russell looked upon their gray heads and bent figures with a mingling of tenderness and reverence.  Mrs. Heath 'had evidently known much of care and sorrow, but the wrinkles could not hide the sweetness and patience of expression that trouble, gently borne, had given her face ; and her cheerful manner and views, together with all the signs of suffering, carried a lesson that Mr. Russell took to his heart.  Mr. Heath had rather a rugged face, with deep-set, piercing eyes, and his strong, vigorous thoughts, and original way of expressing them, contrasted strangely with his white hair, bent figure, and tremulous tones.  John had previously told Mr. Russell that his father seemed to have grown ten years older since he had been deprived of his pastoral cares.

After dinner, John went out to find his brother Henry, whom he had not seen yet; and then Mr. Russell broke his plan to the minister and his wife, very much as he had first broken it to John himself—leaving them no option but to accept it as the way Providence had opened for their son's usefulness in his chosen path. The deep joy and thankfulness of their hearts were not such as could find vent in words. They listened with tearful eyes to Mr. Russell's expressions of interest in their son, and his confident hope of seeing him one of the most useful laborers in Christ's vineyard. When Mr. Heath spoke, it was to reproach himself for his want of faith. "Here have I been mourning over John's broken hopes, almost ready to question the providence that shut him away from a work for which he seemed peculiarly fitted, forgetting that He who sees the end from the beginning could bring it about, if it was best. I am utterly unworthy of this."

"My dear husband," said Mrs. Heath, in trembling tones, "we don't deserve it, but we will accept it thankfully, and be careful to trust for the future. Oh, John," she added, "to think that we may, after all, live to see our boy a preacher of the gospel!"

Mr. Heath bowed his head, feeling that he could not trust himself to say a word; and after a few moments' silence, Mr. Russell, remembering that he had not very much time before the train left, touched upon his plans for them.

"I suppose you would much prefer remaining in Rockdale. You must have many warm friends here, and it is no small undertaking to make a new home in a strange place."

"We did hope," answered Mrs. Heath, "to live and die here. We have five dear children sleeping in the graveyard, and we thought we might live near them, and be buried beside them. But if God wills it to be otherwise, we will not complain."

"But why should you leave Rockdale? If Mrs. Ford

wishes you to remain with her, I should think you could hardly have a more comfortable home."

"No, it is true we could not," answered Mr. Heath, "but there seem to be obstacles in the way of any such arrangement;" and then Mr. Russell, not waiting for them to refer to the perplexities that had arisen out of the change in John's plans, with all the skill and tact of which he was master, made known his intentions with regard to them and their son Henry; and before the two brothers came in, they had yielded to his persuasions, and promised to treat him as a son. So it was arranged that John should return at once to the University, that the others should remain in Rockdale, and that Henry should study with his present teacher for another year, and then decide whether he would enter college, or go into business.

When Mr. Russell left them, was it any wonder that he carried the blessing of four grateful hearts with him? or that, when John entered upon his studies again, added to his first and highest motive for improving his time and abilities to the utmost, he should have cherished that of proving to his kind friend that his confidence was not misplaced?

Several weeks passed, during which Mr. Russell called two or three times at Mrs. Thorne's, drawn thither by his interest in Claudia, and his enjoyment of her music, and not less by his hope of seeing or hearing something of Philip Ventnor. But he saw him no more, and his name was only mentioned once, and that was when Claudia had left the room for a moment: Mrs. Thorne said, "By the way, have you happened to see or hear any thing of Mr. Ventnor of late?"

"Nothing whatever," answered Mr. Russell. "I had hoped to meet him again before this; but I suppose his home is at Mr. Tapscott's, and, as he lives out of town, I have not known where to find him, or I should have called upon him."

"We hear occasional rumors concerning him that are any thing but creditable. But I think you are mistaken as to his living at his grandfather's. It would be better for him if he did, but I am quite sure he has rooms in town. His visits here are at an end, and we know very little of him, but that little is quite enough."

Claudia came back, and the subject was dropped; but Mr. Russell needed to hear no more to determine him upon finding Mr. Ventnor without delay. He had noticed a change in Claudia since his first visit; her cheek had lost its bloom, her eye its sparkle, and her manner was often quiet and depressed; and again, she would laugh and talk with a wild gayety that was more painful than her sadness. He associated the change with Philip; and when he knew their intercourse to be entirely broken up, he understood it all, and felt that her pain must be increased a thousandfold by the knowledge, which her mother would probably take no pains to keep from her, that Philip was growing reckless and desperate.

As he bade Claudia good-by, he longed to tell her that he was going to seek Philip, and try to help him. He felt sure that the pleading look in her sorrowful eyes was an appeal to him. But he could only give her the silent sympathy of his eye and hand, and go the very next day to ask Mr. Tapscott for Philip's address.

It was not the first time that Mr. Russell had seen Mr. Tapscott since the affair of the note. More than once had he been assured that his kindness had saved him from losing every thing he had in the world; but now it was reiterated with unabated warmth, and Mr. Russell began to fear that it would never be forgotten.

"I came to ask for the address of your grandson, Mr. Philip Ventnor," he said, as soon as Mr. Tapscott gave him a chance.

The old man's face grew very grave, as he replied, " Ah, poor boy! I am afraid there's a bankruptcy pending there that no friendly hand can ward off."

" Don't be hopeless about him, Mr. Tapscott. ' Hope on, hope ever,' is a good maxim for all kinds of troubles. I want to have Mr. Ventnor come and dine with me, in my bachelor's hall. Where shall I find him?"

Mr. Tapscott gave him Philip's address, saying, with a brightened expression, "I am glad of it—glad of it! and so will his poor mother be."

"I find my home rather silent and hum-drum," said Mr. Russell, as he bade Mr. Tapscott good-morning, "and I should like to have Mr. Ventnor's wit and intelligence to enliven it occasionally."

His invitation to Philip to dine with him was politely declined, but with a formality and coldness that rather surprised him, when he recollected Philip's manner at Mr. Thorne's, and he was a little uncertain what to do next.

Two or three evenings after, Mr. Russell had occasion to see a gentleman on business who was in town for a few days; and as they walked together through the hall of the hotel, after their business was over, sounds of revelry came from one of the smaller dining-rooms, as they drew near.

"A party of young men, of whom, I am sorry to say, my nephew is one, are giving a birthday supper to a young author," Mr. Russell's friend explained, "and I suppose there will be a great expenditure of wit and wine before the night is ended."

Just as they came opposite the door, it opened, as if on purpose to disclose to Mr. Russell the flushed face of Philip Ventnor, as he was in the act of holding a glass aloft, and breaking into the first strains of a wild drinking-song. The door closed again, but all through his walk home, and through his solitary vigil by the fire, that vision was before his eyes, that wild strain sounded in his ears like the dirge of a lost spirit; and Philip's good angel might well have rejoiced that night, through his sadness, at having gained such a determined ally.

Immediately after dinner the next evening, Mr. Russell directed his steps to the address Mr. Tapscott had given him. At the door, when he was told that Mr. Ventnor was at home, he hesitated whether to send up his name; but con-

6*

cluded not to run the risk of being refused, and proceeded up the somewhat narrow, ill-lighted stairs, to the "fourth-story back."

"Come in," Philip's voice called in answer to his knock, and he opened the door.

A dim light shone through a blue haze of cigar-smoke, and Philip, who lay on a couch by the fire, turned his head to see who was there. The instant recognition made him spring to his feet, and he stood, in dressing-gown and slippers, with tumbled hair and haggard face, before Mr. Russell. His look of blank amazement gave place to a flush of chagrin, as his visitor advanced towards him, and he reluctantly received the offered hand.

"I hope I need not apologize for coming up unannounced," said Mr. Russell, who had prepared himself for any manner of reception.

"Not at all. Pray sit down, sir," said Philip, attempting to cover his embarrassment with a formal politeness.

"You know we laid claim to each other's friendship some weeks ago, and I believe the claim was mutually admitted. I have no intention of lightly relinquishing my right. I value it too highly."

Philip met his eyes coldly, but made no reply.

"So after trying in vain to lure you to my solitude, I have come to yours," added Mr. Russell.

"You do too serious despite to your elegant solitude by naming it in connection with mine," said Philip, casting his eyes about the little room, where utter disorder prevailed, though there were evident signs of a refined and cultivated taste, in the few choice engravings on the walls, and in the books, papers, and magazines that lay around, adding to the general confusion.

Mr. Russell wondered if the icy cloak in which Philip had wrapped himself would ever melt, and let him see his genial, frank self again. He made no direct reply to Philip, but said, "I had supposed that you lived at your grand-father's, out of town; and when I learned to the contrary, I

hoped you would have a sufficiently fellow-feeling to dine
with me occasionally, in my bachelor's hall, though I know
you must have many demands upon your time."

"I make no visits," answered Philip, looking into the fire.

Mr. Russell, after talking for some time without much
encouragement, happened to mention a new book which lay
upon Philip's table, awaiting a review; and seeing that his
attention was aroused, he skilfully led him to a discussion
of its subject, so that something of the natural warmth and
animation came into his face and manner. The talk lasted
some time, and interested Mr. Russell so much, that when
he rose to go, he had almost lost sight of the icy barrier
that had existed during the first part of the visit, and said,
"I have an old book in my library that I picked up years
ago in an antiquarian bookstore, which treats the subject very
originally and quaintly, and when you return my call, I will
show it to you. I hope I shall have the opportunity soon."

Every ray of warmth left Philip's face; it became cold,
gloomy, and haggard, as before. He stood silent for a moment, and then said, "I believe in plain speaking and frank
dealing, and so I must assure you that I no longer lay any
claim to your friendship, and do not desire it. I fully appreciate, and can never forget, your kindness to my grandfather,
and, through him, to my mother and brother and sisters.
But save in that, we are—strangers, I had almost said ene-
mies. You will lose nothing by it. God knows, no man
need covet my friendship."

Mr. Russell waited a moment, and then said, quietly,
"You cannot wonder that I beg to know what has brought
about this state of feeling."

Philip instantly fixed his flashing eyes on Mr. Russell,
and his color came, and his breath was quick and sharp, as
he said in a suppressed voice, "Suppose you were—not rich,
influential, courted, as you are, but—poor, obscure, dependent
on the daily labor of your brains for your daily bread, your
home a den like this, with nothing in the wide world that
another need covet, save the love of one heart, the winning

of which was the one thing that could make life desirable, and for which you would lay down your life, yes, sacrifice your soul, if such a thing could be; moreover, you felt that the love of that heart was all that could save your soul. And suppose that I, having every thing else that could make life bright and desirable, should covet that one heart, and set myself to win it away from you, bringing my wealth, and influence, and name, to weigh against your devotion: do you think that, after having cast you out and won the heart, or the hand without the heart, if I should come to you with the offer of my friendship, you would accept it? No, you would spurn it, as I do yours!" and Philip made a gesture as if he were casting something he despised under his feet, while his fierce eyes never moved from Mr. Russell's.

For several moments the two stood motionless, looking at each other, while the meaning of Philip's parable gradually dawned upon Mr. Russell's mind, and at length a smile of sorrowful sympathy came into his face.

"Will you bear with me while I give you a parable in return for yours?"

There was something in the gentle request that impressed Philip like a demand for justice, and he involuntarily handed Mr. Russell a chair, and the two sat down.

"Suppose that, instead of being twenty-four or five years' old, you were thirty-seven; and suppose that, long ago, when life lay before you beautiful and glowing, you had met your ideal of womanly loveliness. You gave all the tenderness and devotion of which any human heart was capable, and your love seemed returned in full measure, and for one happy year you called her yours, and looked to have her by your side all through life. But the year came to an end, and found you desolate, with an impenetrable mystery enveloping the blighting of your hopes; for your love was unchanged, death had not taken away your idol, you knew her to be true and steadfast as the hills in her nature, and she had said she loved you. Yet she had withdrawn her hand from yours, and you were alone, with life before you robbed of all its brightness. You felt that you could not live near her as a stranger, so you left your country, and for nine long years you were a lonely exile, bearing in your heart the unfading image of the beloved face, and the perplexing, harrowing, and yet sacredly cherished memory of every token of her truth and loveliness, and of her affection for you. Then you come back to a home, which the death of your father soon makes very cheerless; for your mother left it forever in the first year of your absence, your sister is married, and your brother stayed behind in the foreign land. You go in and out of your lonely, haunted house, memories of loved ones lost your only heart-companions, knowing no more of the dwelling-place of her whom you love than if you were in different worlds. You would be happier to know that she was in heaven, for she could not be more lost to you than she is: and now you are often beset with fears, lest her life may be as joyless and desolate as yours. Then suppose that in the course of months you come from the silence and solitude of your home, with that cherished, ineffaceable memory locked in your heart, to meet a fresh, beautiful nature, that impresses you like the glad sunshine. But you speedily see tokens of a maturity of womanly feeling, and of power to suffer, that deepens your interest. You know so well what it is to walk in shadow, that your heart goes out to those who are threatened with shadows; and that this young life should be so soon clouded, fills you with pain. You see that her fate is linked with one whom you know, whose rarely gifted mind you appreciate; and you gather him and his interests into your heart, resolved that, if a brother's hand can dispel the clouds which seem to threaten these two, it shall be done. You feel that you have the full, sisterly confidence of the one, though no words have been spoken; and you seek him whom you yearn over as if he were indeed your young brother; but he spurns your offered friendship, and charges you with robbing him of the heart you know to be his alone."

Mr. Russell kept his eyes fixed on Philip's, watching his

changing expression, until his face was buried in his arms upon the table; and now a convulsive sob broke from him, and for many minutes he wept like one heart-broken.

Mr. Russell knew well that many griefs were finding vent in those agonizing tears, not the least of which was for his own unworthiness, and he hailed them as a happy omen of better things.

A few words of almost despairing contrition and self-condemnation fell from Philip's lips, to which Mr. Russell replied with kindest sympathy and encouragement, and then left him, commending him to the aid and watch-care of One who has all power to save, and a tenderer than any earthly pity for the erring. But the next morning he gave Janet instructions that the crimson room, with the bed-room opening out of it, should be aired and made ready for a gentleman, who was coming to make a long visit.

"Let the sun shine in, Janet, and have a good fire," was his parting injunction, "and have a particularly good dinner."

And that very night saw Philip, much to his own bewilderment, with his books and other belongings, in possession of the crimson room, and sharing the peace and safety of Mr. Russell's fireside; feeling much as a child may, who, after being long lost, is found and brought home.

# CHAPTER XIII.

Instruction sore long time I bore,
And cramming was in vain.     ANON.

WHEN Mrs. More came to live in the house to which
Chloe introduced herself so unceremoniously, it stood alone
in the midst of wood and prairie lands. Her husband was
an Englishman, but came to America when a young man,
drawn by his enthusiastic admiration for republican institu-
tions, and his desire to carry out his taste for farming, on a
grander scale than he could do at home. The countless acres
of rich farming lands at the West seemed to him the *ultima
thule* of his wishes, and he intended to invest his fortune in
a few hundreds of those acres, and devote his energies to
their perfect cultivation.

His plans were interrupted for two or three years, as,
when he reached New York, he fell in love with the sister
of a gentleman to whom he brought letters of introduction;
and fearing that a delicately brought-up and accomplished
girl would be horrified at the idea of forsaking her home
and friends to follow his fortunes in the wild West, he relinquished his project and went into business in New York,
and the wedding followed in a few months.

Business, and city-life, however, proved utterly distaste-
ful, and he sighed for the fulfilment of his vision of a model
farm, and the free, untrammelled enjoyments of the country.
He could not hide his restlessness from his young wife, who
at length succeeded in convincing him that there was no
place in the wide world so distant or so solitary that she
should dread going to it with him. Then he began to make
his arrangements with an eager delight that fully compensa-
ted her for the sacrifice of leaving her friends; and six
months saw them in possession of a thousand acres of
excellent land, keeping house in a style that would have

made their city friends lift their hands in dismay, but which they enjoyed with all the zest of their young, brave hearts.

Fortunately, Mr. More united untiring energy and perseverance with his enthusiasm for what he loved, so that things steadily progressed. Plans once conceived, and found feasible, were carried out through every discouragement, and in a few years they had built a comfortable, tasteful house, and a large part of the thousand acres was made productive and available.

Either Mr. More's wisdom, or his good fortune, in the choice of his location, was proved by the speed with which railroad stations and little towns sprung up around him; and when a dozen houses, a church, a store, and a blacksmith's shop, had been built within a mile or two of his home, it was called Moresville, in honor of the first settler. It was well understood that there was not to be found, far or near, a more enterprising, intelligent farmer, or a wiser and kinder-hearted man, and that Mrs. More was unequalled as a house-keeper, friend, and neighbor. It was therefore natural that they should exert a wide and strong influence. That they did, was apparent in the air of taste and refinement in the village-homes, in the intelligently-managed farms, in the simple, inexpensive elegance of the church, and the well-ordered village-school.

The passing years led some of their children to distant homes of their own, and others into the silent land; but when they were left alone, they sat down beside their quiet but cheerful hearthstone, to look back over the forty years of their happy life, and wait for the summons to a happier, It came soon to one, and the other was left to wait alone; but she did not murmur, even when the weeks grew to months, and the months to years. Her married children all begged for her presence in their homes; but she felt that it would be like tearing her heartstrings asunder to leave her own, and she set their minds at rest, as far as she could, by inviting the widow and daughter of her husband's cousin,

Mr. Rice, who had been the first pastor of the village-church, to come and live with her.

Mrs. More fully appreciated the failings of both Mrs. Rice and Lucinda, yet she had no fear of having her peace disturbed, either by the somewhat acrid temper of the one, or the sentimentalism of the other, when it seemed best for them to share her home. She had learned, in her long life, to bear with the faults and weaknesses of others, as she would have them bear with hers; and so she could smile at. them, or tenderly regret them, or give suggestions for their conquest, as the case might be.

When the Rices left England, Mr. More's mother had sent with them a young man and his wife, who had been in her household from childhood, to take any places for which they might be fitted in her son's mysterious Western *ménage ;* and Thomas soon became Mr. More's invaluable aid on the farm, and Honora equally invaluable in the kitchen and dairy. They were too well-trained to get upset by any peculiarities they might meet in the native "helps," and so they proved an unfailing reliance through all the vicissitudes of house-keeping in the country. With regard to the changing supplies of other posts in the domestic economy, they might have said, as they doubtless did in spirit, "They may come and they may go, but we go on forever." In course of time Thomas came to understand Mr. More's wishes so well, that he relieved him of care, and spared Mrs. More all anxiety when she was left alone.

Chloe's walking into the quiet routine of the kitchen had occasioned a little excitement; but her being in a somewhat subdued state of mind, owing to her terrible experiences and her unabating regret at having lost "Miss Marg'et," pre-vented her keeping it alive, as she might have done if she had been in her usual spirits.

The special excitement occurred the morning after her arrival, when she was sent up to Miss Lucinda's room to kindle the fire. Miss Lucinda woke to discover Chloe sitting on the floor, looking at her, the whites of her eyes gleaming

in a frightful manner, while her black face and woolly head
gave her so much the appearance of a small goblin to the
sensitive vision of the young lady, that she shrieked frantic-
ally for help, and her mother and Honora came running to
know what was the matter. They found her, with her
double row of curl-papers, lying back on the pillow, her eyes
shut, while her finger pointed at Chloe, who sat in silent
wonder before the stove.

Honora conducted Chloe from the room in disgust,
declaring that Miss Lucinda might make her own fires after
this; and Mrs. Rice remained to deliver to the horrified
Lucinda a lecture on common sense.

Chloe speedily learned to love Mrs. More—whose beauty
she continued to consider as second only to " Miss Marg'et's "
—as well as the kind, busy Honora, who appointed her easy
tasks. These two drew from her, at different times, the
fantastic yet pathetic story of her adventures with Simon
and Nance, at first with the hope of gaining some clue to
her former home. But they soon relinquished that hope, as
her journey had become so exaggerated to her mind, that,
in dwelling upon its horrors, she gave the idea that weeks
had passed from the time she was seized at the gate till she
reached that place of safety. When she was asked how
long it was after her escape from the school-house that the
" ole Missus " pulled her out of the sleigh, she replied, " Oh,
I dunno, Missus. I 'specks it was t'ree days. I was mos'
done deaded, an' dat's de trufe." So she was regarded as a
permanent member of the household, to be made as happy
and good and useful as possible.

Chloe's affection for Mrs. Rice and Lucinda was rather
doubtful. Mrs. Rice had too many outside calls upon her
time and thoughts, to do much more than look at her in
sudden wonder whenever she encountered her, as if she
never could cease to be surprised at seeing her there. But
Lucinda's attention had been concentrated upon her ever
since her recovery from that first shock. The nature of
the interest she manifested may be gathered from a few

of the many lines confided to her beloved journal at the time :

My soul in secret long hath mourned
That one for some high purpose formed,
As so I felt myself to be,
Should miss such lofty destiny.

I would not, dare not, *love* again !
I could not twice endure the pain
Of giving my heart's wealth to One
Who'd cast me off to weep alone.

Ah, no! that's past!   A mission high
I now would have! and I would vie
With lordly ones whose souls are bent
On loosing those in prison pent. *

I've *found* a soul to bring to light!
She's one whose prison's black as night;
But though I cannot make her skin
Less black than now, I can let in

Such hope and joy as knowledge brings,
And cause to grow such strong, free wings,
That she will soar aloft with those
Who would the gates of progress close

From all whose dark-hued brows proclaim
The dye of Afric's burning clime—
Who think but those whose brows are fair
Are worthy of Heaven's light and air.

With beating heart I hail the day
That sent this dark-skinned waif this way;
And future years may tell her story
In lofty strains of swelling glory.

The lover to whom the poem alluded was a myth to everybody except Lucinda herself.  Her family knew that on a certain day she retired to the privacy of her own room, and remained there, wrapped in gloom and a dressing-gown, for some days ; but nobody knew who was the hard-hearted one to whom she sometimes darkly alluded, and nobody knew what caused her suddenly to emerge from her solitude, and tread the paths of every-day life again.  The fact was, that she had conceived the cheering idea of finding a mission, to take the place of her lost love, and nothing could have been more opportune than Chloe's advent. She at once accepted the child's mental and moral elevation as her much-desired destiny, and began to pursue it with a vigor that increased Chloe's bewilderment, and filled Honora's sensible soul with secret derision.

One morning Lucinda appeared at the door of the storeroom, where Honora was inspecting her preserves and pickles. "Where is Chloe, Honora?" she asked, in melancholy tones.

"She is in the back-kitchen, cleaning knives, Miss," answered Honora; "leastways, that's where I left 'er ten minutes ago."

"Honora, I am surprised that she should be cleaning knives, when it is a full half-hour after her appointed time for coming to me!"

"You can 'ardly expect a hignorant woman like me to remember that a little niggro child 'as appointed hours," replied Honora, moving her pots about energetically.

"I do think you should refrain from giving her tasks that will interfere with my plans for her education," answered Lucinda, thinking, as she proceeded to the back-kitchen, how much she had to contend with in her mission of love.

Chloe was scouring away busily, with her head bent over so that she did not see or hear Lucinda, who wore thin kid slippers, till she stood close by and spoke her name.

Chloe started, and stood with her hands dropped at her sides, a knife in one hand and her scourer in the other, looking at Lucinda.

"Chloe, don't you know that it is half-past eleven o'clock? and *eleven* is the hour for your lessons to commence."

"Miss Jenkums tole me to clean dem ar knifes," answered Chloe, dropping her eyes to the toe of her shoe, which she began to dig into the floor.

"Stop, child—stand still," said Lucinda, mildly, for mildness was one of the rules she had adopted in her system;

and Chloe let her toes rest, but began to twist her tongue about.

"Now, don't use your tongue in such a manner, Chloe; you will find plenty of use for it when you come to say your lessons. Why did you not say you had an engagement with me, when Honora set you to do those knives?"

"Dunno, Miss."

"Don't say 'dunno,' child; say, 'I do not know.' How many times must I tell you that before you will remember it?"

"Dunno;" and then, realizing that she had offended again, she began both to dig her toes and twist her tongue.

"Oh, disheartening child! what can I do with you? But finish your work now, and then come to me in the sitting-room."

So Chloe was left to finish her task in peace. For about two minutes she indulged herself in all sorts of antics and contortions, that would have made Lucinda utterly hopeless; then she addressed herself to making the knives shine, while her feet, and her head with its little bobbing tufts of wool, kept time with her hands, and she discoursed to herself in the following fashion: "Oh, laus, laus! I nebber did see de likes of dat ar Miss 'Cinder. 'Pears like I can't do nuffin 'tall. What's dat ar she tole me 'bout de-gagemum long o' her? I declar I dunno—dat ar ain't um—oh, laus! I do dunno, an' dat's de trufe."

In the meantime Lucinda had gone to the sitting-room, and nothing could be more cheerful and comfortable than that room in a winter's day. The prevailing color was a warm crimson; and the furniture, though old-fashioned, was rich and well preserved; and the deep fireplace, with its blazing logs and shining andirons, the stand of geraniums and roses in one of the windows, with the sun resting on them, all helped to make it a most attractive place. Mrs. More, too, in her rocking-chair on one side of the fire, with the vacant chair opposite, added to its quiet charm. But it could not be said that Lucinda did, when she came and stood

near Mrs. More. Her pale-green delaine did not harmonize
with the warm tone of the room, neither did her pale complexion, pale eyes, and lustreless brown hair, which she wore
in curls, with an artificial rosebud arranged to look as if it
were just going to fall out, though in reality it was tied in.

"Aunt More," she said, "I must beg you to give Honora
orders about Chloe. This is the second time that she has
been performing some servile task when I was ready to teach
her."

"I suppose Honora thinks it important that she should
know how to do useful things, as well as how to read and
write," replied Mrs. More, looking up from her book.

"Oh, my dear aunt! is an illiterate woman to decide
what is most important? If the body is first, well and
good; but if the soul, I must have a chance to enlighten it.
It will be difficult at the best."

"I fear so, my dear, for both you and Chloe, as you are
undertaking to do it now," said Mrs. More gently.

"I am sure my plan is the true one," replied Lucinda,
going to the plants and bending her curls over them. She
always fled to Nature when she felt herself unappreciated.

Presently Mrs. Rice came in. She sat down near the fire,
and proceeded to untie her bonnet-strings in gloomy silence.
Mrs. More laid by her book and took her knitting, saying,
"Well, Rachel, what success have you had?" and Lucinda
sat down to listen, with a blossom to smell of.

"Don't ask me! The world is clean given over to greed
and covetousness, and I am ashamed to live in it."

"Why, wouldn't any body give you any thing, ma?"
asked Lucinda.

"I have been this whole blessed morning," said Mrs.
Rice vehemently, "getting in and out of that sleigh, and
have just got nothing worth naming. Every body has plenty
to spend, it's plain to see, but it's on gimcracks for their
houses, and furbelows and fandangoes to pile on themselves.
Come to ask them for money for the missionaries, and they
give little mites that are worse than nothing."

" Christ did not despise the mites, Rachel," said Mrs. More.

" No; but it was the *widows'* mites," replied Mrs. Rice. " That's one thing, and it's another when it comes from rich men and their wives."

" I am sure I didn't know there were any rich people in our church," said Lucinda.

" There are plenty," replied Mrs. Rice, " who live in good houses, and dress their wives and daughters like puppets. There's Mr. Armstrong; he had the face to tell me that he couldn't afford to give me any thing just now. And look at his wife and children of a Sunday ! "

" I think they have very few new things, and I know that Mr. Armstrong gave quite a large sum to the agent when he preached here," said Mrs. More.

" He did, did he ? Well, if that's the way I'm to be treated ! He knew that I was the collector for our church, and what business had he to give his money, except into my hands ? "

" Where else did you go, ma ? " asked Lucinda.

" Go ! I went clear out to Keziah Kinney's, and to every house between there and the village; and poor enough pay I got for my pains. That Mrs. Kinney ! she unblushingly gave me fifty cents ! "

" She is a widow, you know, Rachel."

" Yes, I know that; and I know that she's got a bran-new green satin bonnet, all decked off—and that, if she'd have put the price of those bows and feathers and artificial flowers into my hands, she'd have done better. But, thank goodness, I ain't accountable for any body's sins but my own; " and Mrs. Rice took off her bonnet, with a face full of indignation at every body's sins except her own.

" Well, now ! " she exclaimed, as she turned towards the door, " I never ! Just see that child ! " And Mrs. More and Lucinda turned, and saw Chloe standing behind them, her feet and tongue busy.

" Why didn't you tell me you were there ? " asked

Lucinda, opening the door for her, and following her from the room.

Mrs. Rice looked after them, remarking to Mrs. More, " It beats me, cousin, to think you should keep that creature in the house, when you've no earthly use for her; it just gives Lucinda a notion to waste her time on."

" It is one of my mites, Rachel," answered Mrs. More.

Lucinda's room would have been a very pleasant one, but for the fact that she delighted in a " dim religious light." A " gaudy glare " of sunshine was something she could not abide ; and if a stray gleam ever ventured into her private apartment, it was quickly shut out.

Chloe always felt as if she were going into a dark closet when she entered that room, and the darkness that affected her spirits may have affected her mind ; for certain it is, that as yet she had rather grown uncertain of what she did know, than learned any thing new. Lucinda felt very much aggrieved when she found that Chloe was not utterly benighted—that she knew who made her, and could even say a simple prayer, and knew some of her letters ; and she became so tired of hearing Miss Marg'et quoted on all possible occasions, that she pathetically requested Chloe not to mention the name again.

" Come in, Chlorinda," said Lucinda—for she had decided to give her a more refined name during the process of her mental discipline.

Chlorinda had stopped at the door, but now came forward and took her place before her teacher, who sat in an imposing arm-chair which she had brought from the garret.

" Now let me hear what the last lesson was about."

Chlorinda's toes started to her assistance, but were instantly checked.

" There, stand still, Chlorinda ; don't let your manners run riot while your mind is being educated. Well, what was the lesson about ? "

" Dunno."

" ' Don't know,' you mean. Well, look at this that I

hold in my hand, and listen while I spell it for you as I did yesterday, and then you will tell me what it spells. D-o-g."

Chloe looked at the little tin toy her missionary held up at arm's-length for her inspection, but could not distinguish it clearly in the dim light; so she said "Hoss"—not finding any aid from the letters that had been uttered.

"No, Chlorinda, it is not a *horse;* d-o-g spells dog. Now, what is this I hold in my hand?"

"A apple," answered Chloe, briskly.

"No, Chlorinda, not *a* apple, but *an* apple. When a vowel follows the article, it is *an* instead of *a;* but we will leave that till another time, when we are prepared to take up grammar. An apple, then, is a kind of fruit which grows on a tree. The first apple is mentioned in the Bible, and occasioned the fall of our first parents. Only think, Chlorinda, an apple like this tempted our first parents to sin. Who were our first parents—the father and mother of the whole human race? There, stand still, Chlorinda."

But Chlorinda's eyes had been wandering with her thoughts, and had caught sight of a cotton-wool doll that Lucinda had bought at a fair for a pin-cushion; and utterly oblivious of every thing except her curiosity to know what this first image of humanity that she had ever seen could be, she exclaimed, "Oh, Miss 'Cinder, what's dat ar? Won't you please to le'mme see dat ar little missus?"

Lucinda's surprise at her mission's audacity knew no bounds. "Such disregard of all rules of decorum!" She sat looking at Chloe for some moments in silence, when, having made up her mind what course to pursue, she rose from her chair and produced a handkerchief from a drawer, which she tied over Chlorinda's eyes, telling her very mildly, that if she made any noise she should tie another over her mouth; then she put the cotton-wool doll on the table, and placed Chloe before it.

"Now, Chlorinda, the doll which excited your undue curiosity is right before you, within reach of your hand; this is your punishment for your disrespect to me, and your

7

indulgence of one of the worst foibles of which you could be guilty. Stand there till I take off your bandage."

Lucinda sat down, with a red and gilt volume of Tupper's Proverbial Philosophy to while away the interim in her teaching. While she skimmed lightly over her favorite passages, and Chloe stood opening and shutting her eyes under the bandage, clutching her dress with her hands to keep them from grasping the forbidden object, there came a knock at the door, and Honora's head appeared.

"Miss Lucinda," she said, while her eyes discerned Chloe in her disgrace, "your ma wants you immejately. She is in a desprit 'urry."

Lucinda looked discomposed, but rose and laid her book down, saying, "Chloe, I shall only be gone a moment; I expect you not to move till I come back;" and she left the room.

A moment after, Honora came back and lifted the handkerchief from Chloe's eyes, with a derisive laugh.

"What's the matter, Chloe? What have you been doing so 'orrid?"

The room seemed light compared with the previous darkness, and Chloe's eyes quickly rested on the doll. "It's dat ar; I wanted to take dat little missus;" and Chloe pointed at it, clutching her dress again.

"Well, for goodness sakes, take it, child;" and Honora thrust it into her hands. Chloe examined it in great amazement, but in a moment Lucinda's step was heard on the stairs, and Honora replaced the bandage and the doll, and telling Chloe not to mind, that she should have a doll for herself, left the room as Lucinda entered.

"Have you stood still, Chlorinda? Did you touch any thing?"

Chloe dug her toes and contorted a little, and then answered, "I tetched dat ar, an' dat's de trufe."

"Well, then, you must stand twice as long as you have," answered Lucinda, and she seated herself with her book. "I regret to see you show such a lack of self-control."

# CHAPTER XIV.

The face the most fair to our vision allowed,
Is the face we encounter and lose in the crowd.   OWEN MEREDITH.

"Now clean up them things, an' don't be long about it, neither," Mrs. Kinney said to Betty one morning, pointing to the dishes she had been using; and then she took a panful of doughnuts and another of cookies, one under each arm, and trudged out of the kitchen with them.

Mrs. Kinney, having placed the contents of the pans in two huge stone jars, which she kept in the dark recesses of her bedroom-closet, took off her apron and cross-barred muslin cap, preparatory to improving her appearance, when, suddenly remembering that she had not looked into the parlor since she sent Betty in to fix the fire, she hastened to see if she had dropped any chips on the carpet. As her search was fruitless, there not being a spick or a speck to be found anywhere, she merely put her head inside the kitchen-door to see that Betty was busy.

"You be quick with them things, Betsey Jane; it's 'most time to put on the dinner," and returned to her bedroom to go on with her toilet.

"Sakes alive!" she ejaculated, as she looked in the little glass that hung over the bureau, "ef I ha'n't gone an' been an' let that minx see me without my cap on!" and she put both her hands on her head, as if she thought it might not be too late, even then, to prevent disclosures.

She labored under the delusion that nobody knew that the reddish-black hair, which came to such a sharp point at the top of her forehead, and ended in three little stiff curls on each side, was not as natural to her head as the thick iron-gray locks, the tips of which always showed a little below her cap behind.

"Gracious!" she exclaimed again, still holding her hands

to her head. "That Betsey Jane 'll go an' tell all creation
what she's seen! Whatever—but there! it's no use cryin
over spilt milk, and I'm sure I don't care if she does tell
'em; let her, if she wants to;" and with no other sign of a
disturbed mind than the jerky way in which she handled
whatever she touched, she proceeded to array herself in a
yellowish brown dress, a cap gayly decked with pink satin
bows, and a very large lace collar. If she was satisfied with
the *tout ensemble*, that was enough, even though, being quite
short and scant in the skirt, the gown made her look rather
more bunchy than usual, and the pink ribbons were not quite
suited to her sallow complexion.

Having locked the closet-door and put the key under the
pillow—she changed its hiding-place every time she locked
the door—she took her knitting, and, with the air of a pudgy
princess, shut herself in the parlor, lifted the curtain about
an inch to look out, and then sat down with her feet on the
fender of the Franklin stove, and began to knit.

For about a half-hour Mrs. Kinney sat alone, sometimes
knitting energetically, and sometimes pausing to cast a complacent look upon her surroundings; and they were such as
her soul delighted in. Every thing had an air of severe order
and good preservation,—the striped green and yellow and
black carpet, the very same that she had begun housekeeping with, the six shining mahogany chairs that stood at regular intervals against the wall, and the red and yellow table-
spread and astral lamp, and the tall brass candlesticks and
gay china vases on the mantel. On the wall, with its gayly
flowered paper, hung the portraits of herself and Mr. Kinney, painted by a travelling artist some years before Mr.
Kinney died, which had always been considered "wonderful
good likenesses" by the originals, though their acquaintances
looked in vain, whenever they were permitted to look at all,
for any resemblance. Mrs. Jarley would have been more
likely to recognize them as portraits of some of her wax-
figures.

In the midst of one of her contemplations, the sound of

footsteps in the next room caught her ear; and while yet the look of blank horror was on her face, the door opened, and Mr. Skinner came in, with the pinched, blue appearance of a thin-blooded person after a long cold ride.

"Shut that door!" Mrs. Kinney screamed to Betty, who, having admitted Mr. Skinner, still stood holding the knob, as if she could not bear to tear herself away with only that little bit of satisfaction for her curiosity. She had no doubt, of his being the expected guest, but why any such fuss should be made for him, was a mystery she needed to have solved.

When Betty was gone, Mrs. Kinney took up her knitting, having cast a wrathful glance at her visitor, that made him stop midway between her and the door, and changed the beaming smile with which he had been regarding her to the most sheepishly downcast expression.

"Whatever you come to that back door for's mor'n I know," were the first words with which she greeted him. "Ef you wanted to see Betsey Jane, fer goodness sakes why didn't you stay in the kitchen—not come in here, a-trackin' up my bettermost carpet?"

Mr. Skinner lifted up first one foot and then the other, to see if there was any snow under it; and as there was none, and more especially as a hasty glance around the room had advised him of its grandeur, which was as new to him as if he had not put up there for ten days after New-Year's, he took courage to say, "I—I'm sure I have no wish in life to see any body but you. Oh, look not so distant and forbidding upon your humble servant, my *dear* friend."

"Don't 'my dear' me, if you please, sir;" and Mrs. Kinney tossed her pink bows in the most indignant manner; "it's gen'ally presumed to be proper for pussons to come to the front door when they come a visitin', partic'larly ef they hev designs. But it's all one an' the same to me, I'm sure;" and she knit away in grim disregard of the fact that her guest was still standing.

He took a step towards her, holding his hat with both hands.

"I would ruther have come to the front door, and project-ed myself into your fair presence, but I too wividly recalled your oft-capitulated injunctions to enter at the back door; and, my dear—I would say I did wiolence to my feelin's, and sub-mitted to be brung to this aujence by a menial. Oh, dear ob-ject of my affections, may I ventur' to hope that you will oversee my offence, and restore me back again to favor once more?"

Mrs. Kinney was really very much softened by this fervent appeal, but it would not do to succumb too readily; so she replied, "I don't know's I will. I don't know whatever on the face of the airth you come back here at all fer, to either door. It beats me how these men will stick round. It was jest so with Tobias Kinney," and she shook her pink bows with irresistible effect—at least, it would seem so, for Mr. Skinner at once stooped over and set his hat on the floor, and having possessed himself of a chair, sat down near Mrs. Kin-ney, and with a smile that was meant to be very tender, said, "Oh! do you ask me what I come here for? oh"—

"Oh, go 'long! don't be silly, fer pity's sake"—and the coquettish Mrs. Kinney braced her feet against the stove, and gave her chair a shove back; but her tone was such that Mr. Skinner felt free to follow her.

"Oh! words cannot inform you what egonies of mind I have underwent sence I bid you adoo a week ago to-day. Oh! do not keep me in suspense no longer."

"I ain't a keepin' of you in suspense. What folderols! It beats me what you're a-drivin' at."

Mr. Skinner coughed and rubbed his knees, and was very nearly at his wit's-end, not being in the least able to fathom Mrs. Kinney's perversities; but there was too much at stake for him to give it up without a desperate effort; so, hitching his chair a little nearer, he began: "Oh! recall to your recol-lection our last interview, at which I laid my hand and heart, and all of my possessions at your feet, and what you said, which it was, that you would not give me a concise answer then, but if I would call to-day, you would do it."

"Do what, for the sakes alive?" and Mrs. Kinney looked in pretended mystification at Mr. Skinner, who began to feel utterly hopeless.

"Which it was, that you would tell me whether you would accept 'em—them things I 'numerated."

"Accept of 'em! an' in the name of natur' what be I to do with 'em ef I do accept of 'em?"

Mr. Skinner's chin dropped, and his eyes were fixed on Mrs. Kinney, with the blankest expression for a moment. Then the solution of the difficult problem dawned upon him, and rubbing his knees gently, he replied, "Marry 'em."

This coming to the point was what she had been endeavoring to drive her admirer to do all the time, and yet she dropped her knitting, and fell back in the chair, with every appearance of having been taken entirely by surprise, as much so as if the subject had never been presented to her before.

Another hitch of Mr. Skinner's chair brought him near enough to take one of the hands that hung so limp at each side.

"Oh!" he exclaimed, "best of females, have I been too suddent in my overtoors? Oh! fair Keziah, will you have me?"

"Yes," the fair Keziah replied promptly, and in her naturally distinct tones, but without opening her eyes or moving from her touching posture.

"Oh! when? name the blissful day," exclaimed the ecstatic Mr. Skinner, his eyes taking a turn around the room while he listened for the answer.

"A week from to-day," replied the fairest; and she had just unclosed her eyes to look at Mr. Skinner, who, in his speechless surprise, had dropped her hand, when the door opened, and Benjamin Truffles appeared.

Of course, Mrs. Kinney was herself again at once, and started up, screaming, "You rascal! you villain! you good-for-nothing! you Benjamin Truffles! What be you a-doin' here?"

"I come to see ef you'd borry ma your quiltin' frames," answered Benjamin, whose equanimity was not easily disturbed, and who had been taking a look around the room he was so seldom permitted to enter.

"No, I won't, an' that's the end on't. I hate folks as is allers borryin, an' you can go home an' tell her so. Go 'long with you." And Mrs. Kinney, having laid aside once and for all the touching character in which she had appeared for a short time, lifted her hands as if about to drive intruding pigs from her garden, and ran towards Benjamin, who disappeared from the room. At the same instant the kitchen-door shut softly, and when Mrs. Kinney opened it, Betty was quietly dishing the dinner.

Mr. Skinner stayed to dinner, and enjoyed it very much, notwithstanding that his betrothed was too much out of temper to add the charm of amiable conversation to that of the viands. It was fortunate for him, perhaps, that he was quite independent of that accompaniment to his meals.

When dinner was over, he was told, rather peremptorily, considering the newness of his relations to Mrs. Kinney, to go away and not come back till the wedding-day; and when he was gone, Mrs. Kinney bade her man bring round the sleigh, as she was going to Moresville to do some errands. In her usual mufflings she set forth. Having despatched her smaller affairs, she drove to the minister's house, which was next to the blacksmith's shop, and, making her way carefully to the door, she knocked, and then stood gazing at two other sleighs that were in a line with hers, quite filling the space between the minister's gate and the door of the shop. The one in front of hers was Mrs. More's, and that lady and Mrs. Rice were in it, talking to Henry Newton, who was on the sidewalk. The people in the third sleigh, which stood before the shop, had evidently stopped to have one of the horses shod; for Mr. Newton was busy with his tools, while the gentleman of the party was talking to the ladies in the sleigh.

"It looks like a weddin'," thought Mrs. Kinney, as she

cast an admiring look at the array of teams; and it suddenly
occurred to her that she would give her invitation to Mrs.
More and Mrs. Rice then and there, and save herself time
and trouble. So, saying to the girl, who had by that time
opened the door for her, "You jest wait a minute; I'll be
right back," she descended to the sidewalk, and pushed
Henry Newton away.

"How do you do, Miss More? how do you do, Miss
Rice? Be you both on you well?"

Being assured that they were, she lowered her voice a
little, and pointed to the sleigh before them.

"Who be them folks? They don't belong to Moresville,
that's sartain sure."

"No, of course they don't; I should know who they
were, if they lived anywheres within ten miles," said Mrs.
Rice.

"I'll ask Mr. Newton who they be," said Mrs. Kinney,
lifting her head preparatory to lifting her voice.

"Pray don't, Mrs. Kinney," said Mrs. More, hastily. "It
is not necessary that we should know who they are; and if
it were, we could ask some other time."

"We'll wait till they go," said Mrs. Rice, decidedly; "it
won't be long;" and Mrs. Kinney, having bestowed another
look of scrutiny upon the strangers, turned again to her
acquaintances.

"I thought as how I'd take this 'ere opportunity to speak
to you, as I've got such a power of things to see to this
week, that I couldn't call, mebbe. I expect you to keep it
an awful secret," she added; "I don't want all creation to
know it, 'cause they ain't all goin' to be invited."

"Oh, you are going to give a party, eh?" said Mrs.
Rice.

"No, I ain't; that's to say, it ain't exactly a party; it's
more'n a party—it's a weddin'."

"Oh!" exclaimed Mrs. Rice, her curiosity fully roused.
"Who's going to be married?"

"I be," answered Mrs. Kinney.

7*

"You going to be married?" cried Mrs. Rice, so loud that the lady on the back seat of the other sleigh turned her head, and Mrs. More's feeling of astonishment at the piece of news she had heard, was arrested—it was such a sweet face of which she had a glimpse.

"Yes, to be sure it's me; an' why not?" asked Mrs. Kinney sharply; "an' the weddin's to be a week from to-day, an' I should be pleased to hev you both come; an' bring your darter Lucindy, with my respex," she added to Mrs. Rice, who said she certainly would; she "wouldn't miss the spectacle for the world," as she said afterwards.

Just then their attention was directed to the strangers again, as, the loose shoe being fastened on, and two boys summoned from the shop where they had been entertaining themselves, the gentleman was tucking the buffalo-robe around the lady in the front seat. One of the boys climbed in behind, and snuggled down beside the lady whose face Mrs. More had seen, while the other mounted in front, calling out, "I say, doctor, let me drive; will you?"

"No, no, my dear; come back here to me. You know you can't drive."

The boy obeyed, saying, "Are we going straight home now?"

"Yes, straight home," answered the gentleman, taking his seat; and gathering up the reins, he turned the horses' heads to go the other way, and then Mrs. More had another and better view of the fair face. This time the sweet gray eyes looked full into hers; and when they started for home, after Mrs. Kinney and Mrs. Rice had plied Mr. Newton with questions as to the strangers, none of which he could answer, while half listening to Mrs. Rice's denouncement of "such ridiculous marriages," she still had that face in her mind.

What would she have given to know, when within hearing of her voice, that it was the face of Chloe's Miss Marg'et? and what would Margaret have given to know that those soft dark eyes that met hers, and those silvery curls, belonged to her who had rescued Chloe from cruelty, cold, and hunger—

that ten minutes' fast driving would have brought her to Chloe's refuge? What would she have said, if she had known that the sharp face and bunchy figure that caught her eye for a moment, belonged to the bride-elect of her *ci devant* lover, Mr. Skinner? And what would she have felt, if she had known that the lady with the soft dark eyes and silvery curls was not only Chloe's friend, but Mr. Russell's "kind aunt," to whom he had hastened from the little red school-house on the day, so far away, and yet so near?

Mrs. Kinney, having engaged the minister to perform the important ceremony, went home, and that week was full of business for her and Betty. She did not spend much thought on her wardrobe, as most brides do. She had bought the new green satin bonnet, which had given such umbrage to Mrs. Rice, with a view to " walking out bride in it," and she had her black satin cloak, which was " just as good as new," though she had worn it for ten years and more. Then, her green brocaded silk dress was plenty good enough to be married in, and the yellow bows on her best cap looked white by lamp-light.

But her mind was filled with cakes and pies and jellies, and all the cookeries necessary for the grand occasion; and it was as much as ever she and Betty could do to get every thing ready in time. They succeeded, however, and the momentous hour arrived when the guests began to assemble. Mr. Skinner came rather sooner than he was expected by his spouse-to-be, but she easily put him aside till it was time for them to take their places in the keeping-room.

As the clock struck seven, the guests being arranged in double and triple lines against the wall, Mrs. Kinney rose up, and Mr. Skinner rose up, the minister stepped forward, and in a few moments Keziah Kinney and George Washington Skinner were pronounced husband and wife.

The minister offered his congratulations, and his wife offered hers; and then there was a pause in the festivities, which Mr. Skinner embraced to smile upon his bride. But the beaming look was lost upon her, as she was occupied in

looking daggers at Benjamin Truffles, whose good-natured
face, in the opposite corner, had reminded her of her discom-
fiture on that day week.  When her attention was withdrawn
from him, it had to be bestowed upon Miss Lucinda Rice,
whom the august occasion had impressed, as all such occasions must, after the heart-experiences she had undergone.
She came forward .in Swiss muslin, with nothing to break its
child-like simplicity save a string of pearl beads and the
inevitable white rosebud, and taking the hand of Mrs. Skinner in one of hers, and that of Mr. Skinner in the other, she
looked into their faces by turns, and said, in distinct tones :

> Oh, ye happy, smiling pair,
> Highly favored as ye are,
> May no cloud of sorrow cross,
> May no wave of trouble toss
> The life begun in brightness here ;
> And may ye know, from year to year,
> How blest united hearts indeed,
> And *ne'er* how hearts dissevered bleed.

She dropped the hands simultaneously with the last word,
and retired behind her mother, who was half elated at this
new proof of her daughter's genius, and half contemptuous
at the occasion upon which she had chosen to display it.

Mr. and Mrs. Skinner gazed after her in blank amazement,
while a buzz of conversation began, which grew louder as
the stiff rows broke into groups.   Presently refreshments
were announced by the bride herself, who had slipped out to
oversee Betty, and was from that time, to all appearance, no
more a bride, but the busy, bustling Mrs. Kinney.

Mr. Skinner could not have been surprised at the speedy
reassumption of her own character, after the experiences of
their betrothal day, though in all probability he had given
little thought to that phase of his union with his Keziah. · And
as, " from year to year," he had a settled habitation, from
which his better half never ejected him, however she might
threaten to do it, and having plenty to eat, he felt that he
was " blest indeed," and asked for nothing more.

# CHAPTER XV.

And, for what's past—I will not say in what she did that all was right,
But all's forgiven; and I pray for her heart's welfare, day and night.

OWEN MEREDITH.

AFTER New-Year's day, Margaret persisted in calling her-self well, though Miss Patty remonstrated, and would have been glad to keep her up-stairs in peace and quiet for weeks longer.  One thing the little woman would not consent to, and that was, going home and leaving Margaret to resume her household cares.  Nobody knew where a servant could be found who would not be more trouble than help.  So Miss Patty stayed on, and reigned supreme in the kitchen. Sometimes she would come to the sitting-room door, and, if any body else was there, having caught Margaret's eye, would beckon with her hand; then, when she had her con-valescent in the kitchen, would make her sit down in some warm corner out of the draught, while consulting on some point of domestic economy—more for the sake of enjoying Margaret's presence than that she really felt herself incapa-ble of deciding such questions.

Dr. Doane's visit of a week had lengthened into three, and a part of nearly every day had been spent at the farm-house.  Indeed, it was plain to see that the charm which had kept him so long was there, and not at his host's home, as Mrs. Somers and the children were still away.  Dr. Somers himself was glad to escape from its loneliness, and join the pleasant circle in the sitting-room when he had an hour or two to spare.  He rejoiced to think that the coming of his friend, at what had at first seemed a very inopportune time, had brought a change and variety to the usually quiet life at the farm, and given a real interest to Margaret's convales-cence.

The sleigh-ride to Moresville was to be the grand wind-ing-up of all the good times, as Dr. Doane was to leave, the next morning, for St. Louis. Every minute of the drive was full of enjoyment to Margaret. The beautiful, white, spark-ling snow, stretching away to the blue sky on every side, and the delicate tracery of the leafless trees against the white and blue of snow and sky, and the crisp, frosty air, all gave her exquisite pleasure, while she talked and laughed with the boys so merrily that Dr. Doane turned now and then to look into her bright face and laugh from sympathy, though Fanny managed to keep his eye and ear pretty well occupied.

In the evening Dr. Somers came in, as he had promised to call and take Dr. Doane home.

" Oh ! " was his exclamation as he entered, " you're all safe, are you ? I didn't know but you were all buried up in a snow-drift between here and Moresville ; I thought I'd just look in before I called the neighbors out with pickaxes and shovels. Here, let me look at you," he added, turning Margaret's rocking-chair around, that the light might fall on her face. " Did it kill, or cure ? "

" Oh, doctor, I feel as if I had gained ten pounds since morning."

" Well, I must say you do look fifty per cent. better. I think I'll take you with me on my rounds for a few days, and see if riding with an old man like me will be as beneficial as your ride to-day. What did you do at Moresville ? "

And then Margaret gave a detailed and animated account of their drive, not forgetting their stopping at the black-smith's shop, and seeing the lovely old lady with silvery curls ; while Dr. Doane proceeded with some story he was relating to the boys, and Fanny gracefully reclined upon the sofa, dividing her glances between Dr. Doane's face and the flickering blaze under the stove-door.

" Come, doctor, I can't wait another minute. If you don't come now you'll have to walk," cried Dr. Somers, turn-ing suddenly upon his friend, as if he had been impatiently waiting an indefinite time, when in truth it had only that instant occurred to him to be in a hurry ; and Dr. Doane, who had just finished his story and drawn his chair nearer to Fanny, started up in pretended dismay.

"Oh, don't go," said Jack, seizing his hand; "ain't you coming here any more?"

"I hope so, my dear boy," answered Dr. Doane, laying his hand on Jack's head, and keeping his eyes fixed on him, perhaps afraid to trust them anywhere else.

"I say, Dr. Doane," said George, "why don't you come here and live with Dr. Somers, and ride round with him to see the sick folks? Isn't that what you do in St. Louis?"

"Look out there, Master George!" cried Dr. Somers. "I don't want him. He'd poison all my patients with his new-fangled notions. He'll be back again, boys, never you fear; but whether he will make us twice glad, remains to be seen;" and he gave Dr. Doane a mischievous glance, that actually sent the blood in torrents to his face.

To hide his confusion, he turned to bid good-by to Mr. Crosby, who shook him warmly by the hand, saying, "We shall miss you, doctor. I hope you will pay Dr. Somers another visit before long."

"Thank you, sir; you are very kind. I am sure I shall miss you all more than I can say.—Good-by, Mrs. Sinclair."

"Come, come! you'll never get through, I see plainly," cried Dr. Somers; and Dr. Doane turned to Margaret, who had noted the expression of Fanny's face, as her hand rested an instant in Dr. Doane's.

"Good-by, Miss Crosby. I shall often think of the pleasant times I have had with you all. I little expected, when I left St. Louis, to make such valued additions to my list of friends, for I must count you such."

"I hope you do, indeed," replied Margaret, warmly; "you have made a secure place for yourself in our little circle, and I am only sorry that you must leave it vacant so soon."

"Good-by, my dear boys;" and he threw his arm around each, and returned their affectionate kisses; and with another look at the group, he was gone—leaving a real pain in the hearts he had won by the genial qualities of his mind and heart.

Scarcely a word was spoken during the drive home, and not until the friends were seated by the fire with their cigars, did they fairly break the silence. After a little talk about the trains, and the hour for starting in the morning for Jonesville, Dr. Somers said, " Well, doctor, now tell me what you think of her."

Dr. Doane made a little cloud of smoke that quite hid his face ; and after a moment's pause replied, " I think her very lovely."

" Did I praise her too much ? " cried Dr. Somers.

" No," answered Dr. Doane, quietly ; " she is the loveliest woman I ever met."

" Give me your hand, my dear fellow. I have done you the injustice to fancy you did not appreciate her."

" A man must be blind indeed not to appreciate a character in which there is hardly a blemish."

Dr. Somers sat silent a moment, while he rapidly painted a bright little picture in his own mind, and then he turned to Dr. Doane again.

" You are a queer fellow, doctor, to have kept your own counsel so completely all this time—for of course you are in love ; yet I have not been able to see a trace of it, though I have looked sharp enough to find a needle in a haystack. Did you fall in love at first sight ? " asked the doctor, mercilessly, determined to hear the whole story if he had to draw it piecemeal from his friend's lips.

" I believe so," replied Dr. Doane, consuming his cigar very rapidly in his effort to keep his face in a cloud.

" Whew ! Well, is it all settled ? Have you popped the question ? "

" No."

" No ! And pray why, in the name of all that's reasonable and comfortable, are you going back to St. Louis without doing it ? Why, man, we will put on our coats, and go straight back to Mr. Crosby's again. What does it mean ? "

"I could not satisfy myself that she returned my regard,' answered Dr. Doane.

"Oh! And you could not run the risk of being refused by the woman you estimate as the loveliest you ever met?" said Dr. Somers, looking at his friend with a feeling of indignation rising in his chivalrous heart.

"No, that is an unjust way of putting my case," answered Dr. Doane, clearing away the cloud of smoke, and showing a flushed face; "I shrunk from giving the woman I estimate so highly the pain of refusing me, and I looked in vain for any sure token of the love I yearn for with my whole soul."

"I should think I was unjust," cried Dr. Somers. "I am ashamed of my suspicion. But, my dear Doane, it seems to me that she has shown that she cared for you."

"Oh, yes, I know she does care for me as a friend. She is formed to make friends, but there was no love in the frank, unreserved pleasure she felt in my society. Her sweet blue eyes could look just as irresistibly into other faces as mine, and her smiles are for others as well as for me."

"What! what's that?—blue eyes, did you say? Margaret's eyes are not blue; they are gray—clear, truthful gray!" exclaimed the startled Dr. Somers.

"Margaret's? Of course, I know they are; but—— Somers, is it possible that we are talking at cross purposes? I am not in love with Margaret Crosby, but with her sister, Mrs. Sinclair."

Dr. Somers sprang from his chair, strode up and down the room two or three times, and then stood still before Dr. Doane.

"Do you mean to tell me that you have seen Margaret Crosby and Fanny Sinclair side by side for three weeks, and have deliberately chosen Fanny as the better and lovelier of the two?"

"I cannot say that I did it very deliberately," answered Dr. Doane, rather amused at what he considered Dr. Somers' unreasonable partiality for Margaret, and recalling the fact that, in their talk about the sisters before they met, it was

Margaret whose excellence had been warmly set forth.
" But I certainly should defend my involuntary choice in the
face of the world.  I admire Miss Crosby exceedingly; she is
very lovely indeed, but she has not the peculiar nameless
charm that her sister possesses."

" I should think it was nameless," muttered the disappointed doctor.

" She has such winning softness and dependence, such
graceful gayety at times, and such tender seriousness at
others ; her beauty is so delicate and refined, and she is so
unselfish,—why, doctor, it seems to me that a man must have
a heart of stone not to be won by such a woman."

" Well, commend me to the heart of stone, and deliver
me from being the man to win her, say I," answered Dr.
Somers.

" You are unjust, Somers," said Dr. Doane gravely.
" Your partiality for your favorite makes you unable to see
that her sister has any virtues."

" Well, we will not quarrel about our differences of
opinion," said Dr. Somers, holding out his hand to his friend.
" All I have to say is, that I hope you will be happy.  God
guide you, and give you what will prove a blessing."

The two friends parted for the night, and Dr. Doane
started on his homeward journey in the gray dawn of the
next morning, with a heavy, restless heart.

Margaret's eyes and ears had been busy during those
three weeks; and now her sisterly solicitude, and her quick
intuition, enabled her to unravel the tangled skein of words
and looks and tones, and weave it into a web that was
neither dark nor bright, whose hue would be given by the
sunshine or shadow of coming events.

She had not grown so used to seeing Fanny in her new
character, as to be surprised when it was laid aside as soon
as Dr. Doane was gone, but not the less did her heart ache
to think that what should have been an abiding reality, was
a sort of masquerade array, to be assumed and discarded at
pleasure.

In Margaret's desire to give more time to the boys' lessons and to her father, she still yielded to Miss Patty's persistence in regarding her as unfit to be left to her own devices in the kitchen. But let no one imagine for a moment that Patty was forgetful that charity begins at home. Her sister had a friend with whom she had much more in common than with Patty, inasmuch as she too had the rheumatism, and a querulous, fault-finding temper, who gladly accepted Patty's invitation to stay with her sister; and the two old dames had a fine time together, comparing notes as to which had the most aches and pains, and in backbiting their neighbors.

It was astonishing to see how cheerfully Jotham tackled his team whenever Margaret desired to take a drive with her father and the boys—and that was every day when the weather was fine. He would sometimes remark that "them rides would fetch it," meaning Miss Crosby's strength.

Margaret was far more anxious for her father's health than for her own, for while he was much less silent and absorbed in himself, he looked feebler and had little appetite; and Margaret made every thing tend to his comfort and amusement without seeming to do so.

The time passed happily, with the one shadow of Fanny's listless indifference, until one day, about a month after Dr. Doane's visit, Dr. Somers stopped at the gate and handed Jotham a letter. It was for Fanny, and Margaret, to whom Jotham gave it, could only surmise its source from its having come through Dr. Somers. With a fast-beating heart she carried it to her sister, who sat with her book by the fire, in her wrapper and shawl, as of old. Fanny looked at the handwriting, and a flash of joy lighted up her face, but it changed to a look of annoyance as she glanced at Margaret, and without a word, she put the letter in her pocket. Margaret turned away with a sigh, and soon after Fanny went up-stairs.

Margaret yearned to know if the little web she had woven had taken the rosy dye of happy love, and she had

not long to wait.   At tea-time Fanny appeared, and the first
glance at her unclouded face, and improved toilet, told the
secret, though no reference was made to it until Margaret
and the boys were gone up-stairs in the evening.

Then Fanny said to her father, "I have a letter from Dr.
Doane."

"Have you, child ?" he exclaimed.

"Yes, and it contains a proposal of marriage."

"Of marriage! to you ?"

"Yes, father, even to me," answered Fanny, with some
asperity.   "I suppose it would have pleased you more if it
had been to Margaret ?"

"Oh, no, Fanny, I did not mean that, but you took me so
by surprise.   I never thought of such a thing."

"Very likely not, father, but it is even so, and I have
written my answer; I have accepted him."

"Have you, child ?   Then you love him.   Well, I hope
you will be happy, and make him happy."

Then, as Margaret's step was heard on the stairs, Fanny
rose, and kissing her father lightly, said good-night.

"Are you not going to tell Margaret ?"

"You may do that, father, if you will;" and Mr. Crosby
wondered, little guessing what good reason Fanny had for
not caring to confide her hopes to her sister.

He told Margaret at once of the letter, and they talked
long of Dr. Doane and Fanny and the boys, as Margaret
had never expected to talk with her father ; and when they
parted, at a late hour, Mr. Crosby folded his daughter in his
arms, and called her the comfort of his old age.   She was
thus the better able to bear the impatience of Fanny's manner, as she kissed her, and told her how glad she was for her
new happiness.

The next morning Fanny, no longer listless and languid,
but busy and interested, called Margaret to her room, where
she had opened her drawers and trunks, to discuss their
contents, and see what was available for her *trousseau.*

"You see now, Margaret, the wisdom of keeping my

handsome dresses. What should I do without these silks to be made over? for of course I can have but few new things."

Margaret entered eagerly into Fanny's plans, and said that, with their combined tastes and the help of the Jonesville dressmaker, they could conjure up a very nice wardrobe, one that might satisfy any bride.

"I cannot sew much," Fanny said; "it never did agree with me; but Miss Patty is very handy with her needle, and you fit yourself so nicely—I wonder if you could not fit me better than a country dressmaker?"

"We will manage somehow," said Margaret, cheerfully, and so they did. During the weeks that followed, Margaret's taste and skill, and scissors and needle, were constantly in requisition, while Fanny studied the fashion-books and made suggestions as to the trimmings. But Miss Patty's grave face, as she plied her needle under Margaret's direction and for her sake, gently testified her disapproval of such management, and Mr. Crosby looked on from his sofa with no little solicitude as to its effect upon Margaret.

Dr. Somers courteously offered his congratulations when the engagement was made known to him, and then eschewed the subject, continuing, though ineffectually, to "look after" Margaret.

It was taken for granted that Margaret would explain to George and Jack the cause of all the commotion; and so well did she succeed in gratifying their curiosity, and at the same time in quieting their boyish tongues, that their mother was spared all annoying comments and questions. No doubt they made up for lost time when they were alone with Margaret.

One day, when Fanny had read her letter—every day brought her one—she looked long and soberly at the carpet. At last she said with a sigh, "Dr. Doane speaks as a matter of course of the children's going to St. Louis with us.".

Margaret dropped her sewing, and looked at her in utter amazement. "Did you think of leaving them behind?" she asked.

Fanny colored as she replied, " Of course, I expected to have them with me after a little; but I must say, I dread the idea of taking them at first."

" I supposed, certainly, they would go with you, and have talked to them of it, so that they are quite in the spirit of seeing the great city, and living in Dr. Doane's house," said Margaret, laying away the silk dress she was at work upon, and going to the window to hide her tears.

" I presume it will be a great relief to you to have them gone," said Fanny; and she sighed at the thought of the added cares she would have to assume. Margaret made no re-ply—she could not; and the subject was not again referred to.

The week of the wedding came, and, thanks to Margaret's energy, the pretty trousseau was complete. Nothing was left to do but to lay the last things in the trunks.

Dr. Doane had abundant reason to feel satisfied with his reception by every one, from his bride to Jotham, who had expressed himself in this wise to his mother soon after he learned the news: "I never - had no very pertickler likin' fer Miss Sinclair, an' it's my opine that she'll lead that 'ere nice doctor a pretty dance. But every body to ther taste, an' I wish him joy of his'n. He's a right smart chance of a man, an' I wish, fer his sake, thet he'd a took Miss Crosby. She's wuth a hunderd of her sister."

To the doctor himself he said, "I s'pose you ain't above lettin' a country bunker like me congratilate you ? "

" Thank you, Jotham; I hope I shall have a chance to return your good wishes one of these days."

" I don' know 'bout thet," said Jotham, thrusting his hands deep into his pockets. " I'm rayther skeery of the wimmin folks; but anyhow, I'm obleeged to you all the same, an' wish you joy ag'in."

Dr. Doane was too thoroughly happy to recall his talk with Dr. Somers, and accepted his friend's carefully-worded congratulations as unquestioningly as if he never had reason to doubt his admiration for Fanny.

The marriage-morn dawned at length, and a very lovely

spring morning it was—bright sunshine, soft breezes, and the sweetest of bird-songs were its accompaniments. Early in the day the few guests assembled in the little sitting-room. Fanny came down in her tasteful gray suit—dress, hat, gloves, and boots, all matching in color; and if she had only been as good as she was fair, and as gentle and womanly as she seemed, her bridal would have been worthy the loveliness Nature lavished upon it. The boys stood beside Margaret, who, in her renovated violet-silk, looked as lovely as she really was; and the solemn ceremony was performed that gave Dr. Doane's happiness to the keeping of Fanny Sinclair, and hers to him. Could either look for it unless both could?

A simple breakfast was served, and when that was over it was time for the leavetakings.

The boys were full of eager excitement at the thought of their journey and seeing the city, and were all impatience to be off; but when they were in the carriage, waiting for Dr. Doane and their mother to come, and saw their aunt standing in the doorway smiling at them, George sprang out with a wild cry, Jack followed, and once more they were in her arms, strained to her bosom, and sobbing as if their hearts would break.

"Oh, Aunty!" cried Jack, "come too, do—do come too."

"I won't go, Aunty, unless you do!" exclaimed George, suddenly checking his sobs.

"Yes, you will, my love; and you will be good children, and remember all I have told you. There, go, my darlings, Dr. Doane is calling you," and with one more warm, lingering kiss, she put them from her, and they went back to the carriage, crying bitterly.

A backward look from Fanny, a last glimpse of two little sorrowful faces, a smile and a bow from the happy bridegroom, and they were out of sight. Soon the guests departed, leaving Margaret to put by her urgent tears, calm the wildly-pressing pain in her heart, and talk cheerfully to her father of the events of the day; for he was nearly overcome by the excitement.

# CHAPTER XVI.

What, lose my kind,
When this fast-ebbing breath shall part!
What bands of love and service bind
This being to the world's sad heart?          LOWELL.

"It's a week to-day since the wedding; isn't it?" said Miss Patty, as she came in from the kitchen, and sat down by the basket of mending.

"Yes, a week to-day," answered Margaret, looking ruefully at the basket, which was not piled up with little boys' socks and aprons and things, as on former mending-days, but only contained what might occupy Patty's deft fingers for the hour or so before dinner.

Margaret had been reading to her father for a little while, and laid down her book, just as Patty entered, to stroke his hair, and charm away the pain in his head.

"You will hear from them soon again, my dear," said Patty, putting on her spectacles and threading her needle.

"Yes, I think we shall," Margaret answered; "they must be quite settled in St. Louis by this time."

"And I shouldn't a bit wonder if the boys wish themselves back here," remarked Patty.

"I hope not," said Margaret. "I want them to be contented and happy; and I have no doubt they will be. The attractions of their new home, and Dr. Doane's indulgent kindness, will soon comfort their childish hearts, and turn their thoughts from what they left behind."

"Oh, my dear," cried Patty, "don't think so badly of the poor things! I should count them nothing but little savages, if I thought they could ever choose any home before this, after all your goodness to them."

"You might have kept them, Margaret," said Mr. Crosby. "I am surprised that you did not persuade Dr. Doane to leave them with you."

"I did not feel that it would be best to have them stay, father. Their natural place is with their mother; and I am glad to have so much more time for you, dear father."

"I am a great deal of trouble and care, I know," said Mr. Crosby, with a touch of his old complaining spirit; "but I do not think it will last much longer."

"Take care, father!" said Margaret, tenderly stroking the thin, gray hairs. "I shall be as indignant with you as Miss Patty was with me a minute ago, if you intimate that I would rather do any thing in the world than make you comfortable. Have I behaved as if I wanted to do something else?"

"No, indeed, my dear!" cried Patty, looking up from the stocking she was darning.

"I know you have tried to seem cheerful before me," said Mr. Crosby, "and I feel very grateful."

"Oh, father," exclaimed Margaret, with a pleasant little laugh, "do you really imagine that I have been moping all the time that I have been out of your sight? Why, I thought you knew that we were holding a perfect carnival of cleaning and regulating. And Miss Patty knows that I was not a bit more solemn then, than I am when sitting here by you."

"No, indeed, my dear, you were not; you've been as chirpy as a cricket all the time. I shouldn't say cricket, either," she added, "for I think myself that a cricket makes rather a dolesome sound. I'll say, as those dear little things out there, that hop and sing in spite of the cold;" and she sat a moment, looking at the brave little birds flitting about on the brown branches where the buds were only just swelling, or on the ground, where only here and there a green blade had appeared, lured by the warm glances of the sun, and still held its own, though shivering in the cold rains that had followed.

"I am sure I am glad if you could keep cheerful through the day," said Mr. Crosby, still in a melancholy tone.

"And at night I have only kept awake long enough to

8

give a good-night thought to Fanny and the boys, and to
wonder if you were sleeping quietly. One night I did wish
that Jotham did not need the horses all the time for the
ploughing, or that I were rich, so that I could do even more
for my dear father's health than take him to drive every day.
I have not laid awake to sigh, ' an' dat's de trufe,' as poor
Chloe used to say. I know that you must miss the children,
and Fanny, too," she added, " and Miss Patty and I try to
make up for their loss by being as busy and noisy as we can."

"Yes, indeed, if two busybodies could make up for two
obstrepilous boys "—and Patty finished her sentence with a
laugh.

"The house is all in order now, and Bridget is coming
every day to help in the kitchen ; so you shall not lose sight
of me very long at a time, father ; and I will tell you what I
am going to do—to see if I cannot find somebody's ' hoss and
shay,' as Mr. Skinner would say, that will answer for you and
me to jog around the country with, when the roads get a
little better. We will have the full benefit of the spring
breezes, and watch the fields and woods growing green. If
there is any thing pretty within five miles, we shall be sure to
find it."

"I don't know, child," said Mr. Crosby; "you do not
realize how weak I am."

"I know you are weak now, dear father ; but you will be
strong again, as you will see when we have had a few of our
drives."

Mr. Crosby shook his head despondingly. "I understand
my case better than you do, child. I don't know why I
should care to live. I am of no use to any body, and never
have been."

Margaret's loving remonstrances were interrupted by
Miss Patty, who exclaimed, "My dear, as sure as the world,
here's Mr. Thomas right at the gate!" and Margaret's face
showed how glad she was to hear it.

Mr. Thomas' visits were always blessings, but it seemed
to her that he never came more opportunely than now. He

was almost the only one whom her father ever cared to see, and she hoped that the cheerful presence would dispel his gloom.

"Why, you look as cosy as possible. I did not know but I might find you all deep in the dumps, after my giving away three of the family last week. How do you find yourself, Mr. Crosby, now that the excitement is over?"

Margaret answered for her father, that he was feeling it a little still; the weather had been so dull and cold that he had not been able to rally his strength, as he would when it was clear and bright again. She then asked Mr. Thomas if he knew of any body who had an old vehicle, no matter how nondescript, and a horse to match, which she could hire—their own horses being in such constant use—that she and her father might have the benefit of a drive every day.

"I know of a vehicle that will exactly suit you," Mr. Thomas answered, laughing; "one that I should judge to be at least a hundred years old; it has lost its dashboard, and is altogether as nondescript as you could desire; and I rather think Mr. Davis has a horse to match. That reminds me that I am here for the purpose of asking you, in my sister's name, to come and spend a few days with her—you and your father."

"Me!" exclaimed Mr. Crosby. "I could not possibly go. But Margaret can go without me."

"You know I would not go without you, father," said Margaret, thinking that such a change might be an excellent thing for him.

"Well," said Mr. Thomas, "Jenny told me that she would not let you off, either of you. She has been trying to come and arrange for the visit ever since the wedding, but various things have prevented; and she charged me to say that she should come for you to-morrow, and carry you home with her, whether you would or no."

Miss Patty nodded her head approvingly, declaring that nothing could please her better than to have the house to herself for a little; that she herself would help Mrs. Davis

to take them both away. She then went into the kitchen
to see that the twelve-o'clock dinner was ready for the men,
whom she had espied coming up from the field.

Margaret knew that it must seem a great undertaking to
her father. For five years he had not done more in the way
of visiting than to call on two or three families, and to eat
one Thanksgiving dinner at Dr. Somers'; but she thought
that, by a little gentle persuasion, he might be induced to
yield to her wishes. So it was left that Mrs. Davis should
come; and if they decided in the meantime that they could
not accept her kind invitation, they would at least have the
pleasure of seeing her.

"Well, what do you hear from the bridal party?" asked
Mr. Thomas, as he rose to go.

"I had one short note from Dr. Doane," answered Margaret, "two or three days after they left us, mailed at some
town on the route, and they were having a very pleasant
journey."

"I believe they were not to take a long trip," said Mr.
Thomas.

"No; Dr. Doane could not be away from home now.
They will travel in the summer; and I have half a promise
that the boys shall be left with us while they are gone."

"I have no doubt they will be glad to get back," answered
Mr. Thomas. "Well, Jenny invited Mrs. Thomas and myself
to tea, expressly to meet you to-morrow night; so do not
disappoint us by being absent."

Mr. Crosby resisted Margaret's arguments for a time, but
at last he yielded; and when Mrs. Davis came the next day,
she was both relieved and delighted to find that her invitation had been accepted.

"I feel quite elated with my success," she said to Patty,
as they drove away. "I shall keep them as long as I can."

Patty nodded and smiled after them, and then went back
to her work, as happy as a lark in the thought of Margaret's
pleasure.

The day was lovely, and the sunshine and soft air had

their effect on Mr. Crosby. Margaret's anxious heart grew lighter as she saw how he brightened with every mile of their drive, and how interested he seemed in Mrs. Davis' cheerful talk. They were close by the little red school-house before she knew that they were half-way there: indeed, it had not entered her thoughts that they should pass it. Thus taken by surprise, the flood of memories and associations was almost too much for her; and her friend saw the effect in the colorless cheek and lip, and the startled, quickly-averted eye.

"Poor child!" she thought; "that Sunday must have been a day of sharp conflict and pain, and the illness that followed was the result of an overtasked spirit. A quiet, secluded life does not shield us from such trials."

The pain was conquered in a few moments, and Mrs. Davis looked in vain for any token of it in her face or manner during the visit.

Mr. and Mrs. Thomas came late in the day, delighted to find Margaret and her father there.

"To tell you the truth, Margaret," Mr. Thomas said to her, aside, "I had very little hope of your being able to induce your father to come, but I am very glad that you succeeded. It is a good thing for you both."

"If it only does not prove too much for him," said Margaret, looking anxiously at her father's pale face.

After tea, Mr. Thomas and Margaret had a grand frolic with the children; and when their bedtime came, the grown people gathered in the library, which was the pet room in the house, and the evening passed quickly and pleasantly, even to Mr. Crosby, who forgot his languor and weariness; and Margaret had the satisfaction of hearing her father say, as they parted for the night, that he felt better than he had for some weeks; he was tired, but he thought it was a weariness that would give him sleep.

The next morning Mrs. Davis said that they must take advantage of the uncertain April sunshine; and so, after breakfast, a comfortable, old-fashioned chaise, with the steady old horse which Mrs. Davis drove, came to the door, and

Margaret and her father started for a ride. They had not gone far, when Mr. Crosby interrupted Margaret's cheerful chatter about what they saw, and the loveliness of the day, by laying his hand on her arm, and exclaiming, feebly, "I cannot go on, Margaret; I feel faint."

In great alarm, but seeming perfectly calm, Margaret turned about instantly, urging the horse to his full speed, and they were soon before Mrs. Davis' door again. Margaret looked anxiously towards the house, and in a moment was relieved to see Mrs. Davis, who had caught a glimpse of them from the window, coming hastily out.

"Has any thing happened?"—and then she saw Mr. Crosby leaning against Margaret, with closed eyes and ghastly face; and, not waiting to hear explanations, she hurried back for Mr. Davis, and together the three lifted Mr. Crosby from the carriage and into the house.

A glass of wine, and the chafing of his hands and other little cares, soon restored vitality, but all day he lay on the lounge in the library, hardly moving or speaking, and Margaret sat by, trying to cheer and divert him. At length, towards night, he seemed to sleep, and Margaret left his side and stood by the window, looking out at the softly-falling rain that glittered in the rays of the setting sun, and at the vivid, beautiful rainbow that spanned the wide stretch of land. It seemed to her that all the promises which had been given for the comfort and strength of the tried were embodied for her in that glorious arch.

"Margaret, I want to speak to you," her father said, and she turned quickly from the window and knelt by his side.

"I must go home, child," he said; "do not try to keep me here after to-morrow morning."

"No, of course I will not, father. You shall go whenever you like, and feel able."

"I shall never feel better able than I do now, and I must get home."

Margaret assured him that she would arrange every thing

so that they could take an early start the next day, and she began to feel very impatient for the doctor's arrival.

He came soon after tea; and when Margaret told him that her father was anxious to get home, he said, " Well, by all means take him home.  I think perhaps it is the best place for any body who does not feel well.  I shall not be very busy in the morning, and I'll just drive over and attend to getting you back myself; then I shall know that it is properly done."

Margaret looked her thanks; and while the doctor sat with her father, she went to find Mrs. Davis, and tell her the arrangement.

" My dear, I cannot think of letting you go ! " exclaimed Mrs. Davis.  " Your father's not being so well is the very reason why you must stay."

" You are very kind," Margaret said, " but father feels that he must go, and the doctor thinks it best that he should."

" The doctor ! " cried Mrs. Davis; " why, he is the very one that proposed your coming here and staying ! "

Margaret looked at her friend inquiringly, and Mrs. Davis, after a little pause, said, " I think, dear, that it is only right for you to know that the doctor thinks your father's health is failing.  It cannot be a surprise altogether to you, though you may not have realized (seeing him every day) how much he has failed since last autumn; and I cannot tell you, dear child, how it has troubled me—and all your friends, indeed—to think of your being so far away from us, in that lonely house!  So, one day, when we were talking about it with Dr. Somers, he proposed that I should have you come here for a little visit, and then keep you while——as long as you could be contented.  I cannot bear to think of your going back.  I will just go and see your father and the doctor; " and she started to leave the room.

Margaret had sat motionless, with pale face and tightly-clasped hands, while Mrs. Davis talked to her; but now she caught her friend's hand :

"No, no, don't go.  I know he will not be willing to
stay, and I cannot have him disturbed by persuasions.  You
are so kind—I need not tell you that I appreciate all you
have done and would do, but we will go home.  Miss Patty
will stay with me and I shall have all the help I need;" and
Margaret went back to her father, while Mrs. Davis' kind
heart was wrung with painful sympathy, as she thought of
the trial that awaited her.

The next day, with Dr. Somers' help, Mr. Crosby reached
home safely and comfortably, and the relief was so great to
Margaret that she felt almost hopeful again; but even
in the doctor's cheery, encouraging words to her father,
she clearly discovered a nameless something that kept her
heart awe-stricken and heavy—the more as she saw that
Patty, too, looked at him, as he lay on the sofa, with a little
ominous shake of the head; though when she saw that Margaret's eyes were upon her, she put on a busy air, and began
to tell how things had gone on since they had been away.

"Oh, my dear!" she exclaimed, running to the stand-
drawer and producing a letter, which she held up at arm's-
length; "see what Jotham got from the mail this morning.
I was going to send it over to-night, if you hadn't come
home before I had a chance."

Margaret opened the envelope, and found enclosed in a
letter from Dr. Doane one from George, the sight of whose
boyish handwriting brought the tears to her eyes.

"Father," she said, sitting down by him, "here is a letter from Dr. Doane, in which he tells us of their safe and
happy arrival at home, and says that the boys have behaved
like little gentlemen ever since they left us; besides,—what
do you think! here is one from George, and I will read it to
you; shall I?"

Mr. Crosby assented, and Margaret began:

Dear aunty. you never saw such a big splendid house as this is that we have
come to live to it is as big as our house and the barn and the pig pen and more too
all piled up together and me and Jack have had lots of candy and mother says
we are going to have a guviness to teach us, I don't want to learn now, I drather
walk round and look at the houses.  There are some here biggern this, I just

wish you could see them.  Saintlouy is chuck full of houses and folks.  but I
don't know any boys yet but Jack and he dont go for much cause he is a little
sick and cryes every night for you and doctor Doane gives him some little white
pills for city air.  mother wears hansome dresses all the time after she gets up
mornings and calls us mylove and mydear just like you do, I did cry my own
selph a few times cause I could not kiss you good night but I got some picture
books, and now I am going to ride.  Give my love to granfather. and give him
two kisses for me, and give my love to Jothum. and I send my love to you. o o
o o o those are kisses from your dear

GEORGE.

Mr. Crosby seemed to be a little amused by this epistolary
effort of George, but he soon relapsed into the melancholy
silence of the last day or two.

Margaret had felt, when Fanny and the boys were gone,
that she must have her father nearer her at night; and he
had taken Fanny's room very willingly, keeping his own
room down-stairs for his use during the day; but this night
he was too feeble to climb the stairs, and Margaret rested on
the lounge.  Through the watchful, anxious weeks which
which followed, that arrangement was maintained.

Often, during those weeks, when her voice was cheerful,
and her lips ever ready to smile if her father's eyes met hers,
her heart ached almost beyond endurance, as she looked in
vain for a change from his utterly sad, mournful expression.
She knew he listened eagerly when she read to him from the
Bible; but however cheering and encouraging the passages
she chose, they never caused a gleam of hope or peace to
take the place of those lines of sadness.

One day as she read, she glanced up from the Book, as
she often did, and her heart almost stood still when she saw
great tears forcing themselves from under the closed lids,
and trickling down the wasted cheeks.  There was silence
for a moment, save for that quick, sobbing breath, and then
Mr. Crosby broke it.

"Margaret, what shall I do?"

"Nothing, dear father, Jesus has done every thing."

"Will His sacrifice cover the guilt of a wasted life?"

"Dear father, yes.  It covers every thing.  'The blood
of Jesus Christ cleanseth us from all sin.'"

8*

"I professed to love Him, and I have done nothing for Him—worse than nothing."

"Leave it all with Him, father. He is full of compassion." And then she read again some of the full, free promises of God's love.

This was the first of many brief talks they had; and though Mr. Crosby still mourned over the past, the hopeless look passed away—he could receive unquestioningly the sense of pardon and peace which entered his heart.

The first day of June dawned, bright and cloudless, but it was not so bright as the "perfect day" upon which Mr Crosby entered before its close.

Dr. Doane arrived the night before, and together he and Margaret watched while the spirit took its peaceful flight to that world where, through the loving-kindness of the gracious Redeemer, even the memory of a wasted life cannot mar the exceeding and eternal weight of glory of those who, by faith, enter therein.

# CHAPTER XVII.

I am so worn, so weary, so o'erspent,
To lie with thee in that calm trance were sweet ;
The bitter myrrh of long-remembered pain
May work in me new strength to rise again.    MRS. STOWE.

MARGARET would have been glad to remain quietly at home, after her father's death, but she could not withstand the united entreaties and arguments of her friends, who considered it entirely out of the question that she should stay in her desolate home. Both Mrs. Davis and Mrs. Thomas urged her coming to them for a time, but Dr. Doane would not listen to any plan but her returning with him to St. Louis ; and Dr. Somers favored it so strongly that she at length yielded, and the day but one after the funeral was set for their departure.

Margaret gently but firmly refused to consider Dr. Doane's proposal that the farm should be sold at once, and that her home should be with him and Fanny, and the subject was dropped for the present, though the idea of Margaret's coming back to carry on the farm and lead such a lonely life, was too repugnant to be harbored for a moment. He trusted the matter would adjust itself, when she had been with her sister and the boys for a time, and found that she was as necessary to them as ever.

The few arrangements for Margaret's absence were readily made. Patty gladly remained to care for every thing, Bridget was to come whenever she was needed, and Jotham was to keep the even tenor of the faithful, painstaking way he had lately fallen into, with such help as he required ; and Margaret knew that there was no room for a single anxiety.

The morning of her last day at home—they were to go on the evening train—Margaret drove to the village graveyard, to plant roses and heliotrope beside the newly-made grave ; and there the thought of her father, beyond the

reach of pain and weariness and self-reproach, was overborne
by the sense of her own loss—of the emptiness and dreariness of her life—and desolate tears fell on the flowers, and
on the grave where lay the only one who had needed her in
the wide world.

Patty knew where Margaret had gone, and saw, with an
aching heart, the traces of grief when she returned home;
but, after her usual custom, she looked for the silver lining
to the dark cloud that overshadowed the present; and when,
with Mrs. Somers, and Mrs. Davis, and Mr. Thomas, she
stood watching the carriage that bore the travellers to the
depot, she sent the most fervent wishes and prayers after her
darling.

Margaret had not realized how very weary and worn she
was, until she had nothing to do but sit still and listen to
Dr. Doane, or to watch the gently undulating country, in its
June freshness, and the slowly-fading sunset glow. And after
a while, as darkness crept on and the stars appeared, she was
glad to be made comfortable, and yield to the drowsiness
that came over her. During the long, tedious hours of the
next day, and at midnight, when they reached St. Louis, and
Dr. Doane's house, she seemed in a bewildered dream. They
were apparently unexpected, and Dr. Doane said, as she
stood gazing dreamily around the strange room, "Sit down
here a moment, Margaret, while I see if Fanny is awake, and
will see you to-night."

"Fanny is asleep," he said, coming back soon. "Her
maid says she has been unwell all day, and I do not like
to disturb her. I hope you will not mind waiting till morning."

"Oh no," Margaret answered; "it is so late, no wonder
she did not sit up for us."

Presently a servant came in to show Margaret to her
room.

"Good-night, my poor tired sister," Dr. Doane said, taking her hand, and looking sorrowfully into her face. "I hope
you will sleep, and feel better to-morrow. Scylla, see that no

one disturbs Miss Crosby in the morning, and that the house is kept very quiet."

"Never fear but I shall sleep," Margaret said, with a poor attempt at a smile; "I feel as if I were dreaming already."

The sun was shining when she awoke, and the sense of bewilderment came over her again as she surveyed her luxuriously furnished room, so unlike her little chamber at home. She lay for a while thinking of Fanny, longing yet dreading to see her, and know the effect of their bereavement—of the boys, realizing with a thrill of delight that she should soon have them in her arms, and wondering if they knew she had come; and then rose, thinking that she would dress and go in search of them, though she listened in vain for some noise to betoken that any body was astir in the house.

She was just ready to leave her room, and stood a moment at the window to look out into the wide, pleasant street, when there was a sound of footsteps in the hall, and voices, at first suppressed, but growing louder, until George's was distinct, in angry altercation with a stranger's.

"You just let me alone. I will go in; I say I will!"

The door-knob was seized, but the hand that seized it was evidently snatched away, and the strange voice exclaimed sharply, "You wicked child, you shall not go in. Come away, or I shall myself carry you;" and the scuffling began again.

Margaret had at first hesitated to enter upon the scene of conflict; but now she opened the door, and beheld George dragged along the hall by a woman of slight figure in a black dress. She had nearly overtaken them before the captor or the captive saw her, and then George, who was the first to espy her, with a scream of joy and one frantic struggle, released himself and was in her arms.

"Oh, Aunty! oh Aunty!" he cried, as he clung to her, and she held him close, unconscious of the eyes that were regarding her so steadily. After a minute or two Margaret remembered that they were not alone, and looked up smilingly.

"You must excuse us," she said, as her eyes met the sharp, glittering black ones of the person to whom she was speaking; "but it is a long time since we have seen each other, Georgie and I;" and she put back the boy's tumbled hair, looking lovingly into his face.

"I must only regret"—and the voice and manner, though perfectly polished and very soft, struck Margaret as strangely out of keeping with the cold, hard eyes—"that Mademoiselle should have seen such a most unlovely display of temper on the part of her nephew;" and the black eyes glittered more than ever as they glanced at George, who turned upon her fiercely.

"I'll tell my Aunty what a hateful old thing you are."

"My dear Georgie!" exclaimed Margaret, and her gentle tone subdued him at once.

"*Hélas!* if you were only as good and amiable as your little brother!"

"I am as good as he is! Jack's a little sneak," cried George, roused again by the smooth voice, which seemed to exasperate him beyond endurance.

"I shall inform your mamma, *mon petit*, that you are in disgrace to-day, and must not leave the school-room;" and the French governess, with a formal inclination of her head to Margaret, turned to leave the hall, just as Jack entered. She stooped to kiss him, before he had a chance to see his aunt, saying, "My dear, little boy, you have behaved yourself charmingly this morning, and I am very much pleased with you. Now I have a surprise for my Jacko;" and she took his hand to lead him towards Margaret, who, with her arm around George, had been looking and listening; but one glance was enough to make him break away, and Margaret clasped him to her heart, with an undefined feeling that she must hold him there to keep him from threatening evils.

"Why, Aunty, I didn't know you'd come," he cried. "Did you just get here?"

"No, Jackie, I came last night, long after you were

asleep," answered Margaret, looking into his face and kissing
it again tenderly, as she felt that it was just the same, sweet
and childish, as when she saw it last.

" Well, didn't Georgie go to sleep when I did ? " asked
Jack, evidently wondering how it happened that he was be-
hindhand in the happy discovery of his aunt's arrival.

" I suppose so, dear. I found him here a few minutes
ago."

" I shall tell you how it was, my little Jacko," interposed
Mademoiselle. " Your brother, quite contrary to my wish, left
the nursery whenever he was dressed, while you, *mon cher*,
were still sleeping; and when I come to look for him, I find
him just about to enter the chamber of his aunt, who was so
very tired and needed rest. I am sure you would not have
been so unkind."

" I wouldn't have gone in for any thing," answered Jack,
much elated at this comparison of George's and his virtues.

" My Aunty always gets up early," cried George, growing hot again; " she wanted to see me, I know she did. I
don't care if you do love Jack better than you do me; *she*
don't," and George drew Margaret's arm around his neck,
looking defiance at his governess.

" I suppose the children have no tasks till after breakfast,
and, if you please, I will keep them with me now." Mademoiselle bowed her assent, and Margaret turned away, followed through the hall and down the stairs by the cold
black eyes.

" How did you know that I had come, Georgie ? " she
asked, as they sat down in the pleasant breakfast-room,
where the soft June air came through the open windows,
wafting in the perfume of flowers from the garden.

" Scylla told me," was the reply.

" And who is Scylla ? "

" Scylla ! why, she's our black help, Jack's and mine."

" Oh, Georgie," cried Jack, " ain't you ashamed to call it
' help ?' Maddemoyselle says—"

" I don't care what she says," exclaimed George, fiercely.

"I will say 'help,' if I want to, and she can't make me
not."

"I'll tell—" Jack began, but stopped.

"Do go and tell her, and get me kept in ! I've got to be
kept in anyhow, so you won't make much."

"Aunty," said Jack, "should Georgie say ' help?'
That's what they say on farms, not in the city. Scylla is
our nurse. She waits on Georgie and me, but Georgie
pushes and kicks her sometimes when she wants to dress
him."

"I don't care; I ain't a baby," began George, but Margaret laid her fingers over his lips.

"Don't tell me any more things that Georgie does, unless
they are good things," she said to Jack. Then she looked
at them sadly. "Georgie, Jackie, have you nothing to ask
me about your grandfather ?"

"Mother told us he was dead," said George, in awe-
stricken tones.

"Yes, the telegraph-letter came, and this morning Scylla
put on our mourning," said Jack, admiring his new black
clothes, and long black silk stockings.

"He sent his love and a good-by to you both," Margaret
said, with a feeling of sad disappointment which she checked,
saying that it was but natural. How could they realize what
had happened?

"Mother had Maddemoyselle go out yesterday, and buy
lots of black things," said Jack, "and I went with her in
the carriage."

"She wouldn't let me go," said George.

"No, 'cause you didn't say your French lesson good,"
responded Jack.

"Has grandpa gone to heaven ?" asked George.

"Yes, Georgie, and he is very happy now."

"Has he seen our papa and grandmamma ?—you know
they are both up there," said George, earnestly.

Margaret had no chance to reply, as Dr. Doane came in
just then, and the children ran to meet him.

"How do you find yourself this morning, Margaret?" he said.

"I am very well, and quite rested, thank you;" but Dr. Doane thought that her looks contradicted her words.

"Boys, we must be so good to your Aunty that she will never want to leave us."

"We won't let her go!" cried the boys, as Dr. Doane rang the bell for breakfast.

"I am sorry, but Fanny does not feel able to come down this morning. She has not been well since I left home; and thinks that meeting you will be all she can endure."

"Shall I go to her now?" asked Margaret.

"I think we will have breakfast first," Dr. Doane replied. "Fanny said she would send for you; and you must content yourself with my society till she does."

Mademoiselle appeared as they were seating themselves, and with a "Good-morning, Monsieur," and a polite bow to Margaret, she placed herself between the two boys, and confined her attention to them, apparently absorbed in her duties, unless she was spoken to. There was no sign of any partiality for Jack. She checked George's boisterous way of talking, as softly and gently as she did Jack's propensity to lean his elbows on the table and eat lazily.

When they left the table, she approached Margaret, and said, in the most deferential manner, "Miss Crosby, Madame bid me say to you, when you have finished your breakfast, that she will see you in her chamber. But—pardon!—Madame is not strong. She cannot bear excitement. If Miss Crosby will be very calm—"

Margaret followed Mademoiselle up-stairs, Dr. Doane detaining the boys, who would have gone too. As she entered Fanny's room, she was reminded of fairy-tale descriptions of enchanted palaces—every thing was so bright and luxurious, the fragrance of flowers adding to the charm. Fanny lay on a couch, the soft white drapery of her dress arranged with graceful effect, and raised herself languidly as her sister came near. Margaret knelt by her side, putting her arms around her, and looked eagerly into her face; but only for an instant, as Fanny quickly laid her head back on the cushions, and put her delicate handkerchief to her eyes.

"Pardon, Miss Crosby," said Mademoiselle softly, "but do not excite Madame;" and then she looked at her watch, and left the room.

Margaret still knelt, and there was silence for a moment; then she laid her cheek against Fanny's, and whispered, "Dear father sent his love and a good-by to you, Fanny, and hoped to meet you in heaven."

Fanny gave a hysteric sob, and Margaret arose as the maid came with a cologne-bottle and fan. She bathed her mistress' face and chafed her hands, and then plied the fan.

"I feel better now," Fanny said, faintly, opening her eyes after a minute or two. "I have been really ill, Margaret, for the last week; my nerves will hardly bear any thing. I was ill when Walter left me."

"I was sorry that you could not come, too," said Margaret.

"Oh!" cried Fanny, "I could not have borne that. Even if I had been fit for the journey, I never could have lived through *that*."

Whatever Margaret thought, she made no comment, and presently there was a knock at the door.

"Madame Larisse has come," said the maid who answered the knock.

"Has she? Well, let her come in. It is the dress-maker," she said to Margaret, "come to try on my black dresses. Black is rather becoming to you, but I am afraid I shall look like a very fright in it."

"Ah, Madame!" cried the *modiste*, who had entered in time to hear Fanny's remark. "How you can say such wicked t'ings of yourselve! You look like one angel in white, in black, in every colors;" and she proceeded to open her box, and take out the dresses she had brought home.

"Ah! look Madame!" she cried, spreading one over a chair, and standing off to admire it. "I cannot wait till I see it on. Madame's figure will show it to such an advantage.—Ah, what pleasure to work for you, Madame," she continued, as Fanny, having put on the dress, walked the length of the room to display the effect of the train, with its deep crape folds. "She do me more credit than all my other ladies put together. Such a figure!"

"It does fit me elegantly, Margaret; but oh, dear! doesn't it make me look perfectly ghastly?"

"Eh! what do I hear? So many time have I seen Madame, and always beautiful, I never see her look so like one angel as at this moment. Is it not that it is true?" she said, appealing to Margaret.

"I always thought my sister beautiful," answered Margaret, looking admiringly at Fanny, who certainly might have challenged any body's admiration, as she stood in graceful attitude, her fair hair becomingly arranged, and a delicate color in her cheeks.

"*Mille pardons*, but are you Madame's sister?" asked the *modiste*, laying her hand lightly on Margaret's arm.

"Yes, Madame Larisse; this is my sister, Miss Crosby, and you must try your skill upon her figure. You know what country dressmakers are;" and Fanny looked apologetically at Margaret's plain dress.

Madame Larisse shrugged her shoulders, and cast her eyes up to the ceiling. "*Ah, oui*, it is indeed so; but if your sister will allow me, I shall be only too happy to serve her. Such grace of *contour!*"

"I do hope you will let Madame fit you, Margaret, and have at least one dress that is not outlandish and countrified."

"Well, I have no desire to disgrace you, Fanny," replied Margaret, smiling; "but shall I be likely to see any body now?"

"See any body! Of course you will, child. You will see Walter's family constantly."

So Margaret promised to buy a dress, and let Madame make it, only stipulating that it should not be so imposing as Fanny's, as she would have to wear it at the farm.

When Madame Larisse had departed, Fanny lay down again, as if wearied out with her exertions. "Walter told me," she said, "that you were not going back to the farm, but were to make your home with us."

"I don't know how he dared to tell you that," Margaret answered, looking up at Dr. Doane, who came in at the moment, and shaking her head reprovingly.

"Whatever I have dared to tell was the truth," he replied, bending to kiss Fanny, and sitting down beside her.

"Didn't you tell me, Walter, that Margaret was to stay with us, and not go back to the farm any more?"

"Yes, my love, I did," said the doctor; "but I did not expect you to mention it to her. It's a secret; I told you in strict confidence, and would not have had you repeat it to her, of all people in the world."

Margaret smiled. "You see, Fanny, Dr. Doane knew that I only purposed making you a little visit—that when you start for your travels, I shall start for my home, and be a farmer, for this year at least, and maybe for all my life."

"How can you endure the thought of such a life as that, Margaret!" exclaimed Fanny.

"Do not talk to her about it, Fanny," said Dr. Doane. "She doesn't know her own mind, and we must not encourage her to express it at present. I came up to see when you will have the carriage. I can go with you for a drive this morning."

"I cannot go out this morning," said Fanny, decidedly. "My hat came home last night, the veriest fright. I had to send it back to be altered, and it will not be returned before two o'clock."

Dr. Doane looked disappointed, but brightened up again after a pause. "I should not wonder if I could do my business this morning after all, and go with you this afternoon; and that will be better, for the boys will be through their lessons, and can go too."

Fanny's face changed. "George cannot leave the schoolroom and nursery to-day," she said. .

"Why, what is the matter to-day?" asked Dr. Doane anxiously.

"I don't know," answered Fanny, "I did not inquire into the affair; but Mademoiselle informed me that he had behaved disgracefully this morning, and she hoped you would not interfere with her discipline, as you did the other day."

"Interfere!" said Dr. Doane. "Mademoiselle is rather too presuming."

Fanny colored a little as she replied, that Mademoiselle only meant to do her duty, that it was quite necessary to uphold her authority, and that she was the best judge of when the boys needed punishment.

"I believe I am the cause of Georgie's disgrace this morning," said Margaret, who had listened with painful interest. "Scylla told him that I was here, and his impatience to see me overcame his discretion."

"There, my dear," cried Dr. Doane, much relieved, "I knew there was nothing serious enough to warrant his being kept in close confinement all day."

"You do not know the circumstances, Walter," said Fanny, with undisguised annoyance. "I know from Mademoiselle's manner that George was very rude and ungovernable. The truth is," she added, "that the boys have both been petted and spoiled all their lives. My own ill health has prevented my controlling them as I should have done, and, now that we have some one who understands them, and has the judgment and strength of mind requisite, what folly it would be to interfere with her government."

"I have not seen any remarkable proofs that she does understand them," said Dr. Doane, a little dryly. "I think she seems very severe with George, and very lenient and indulgent with Jack."

"Walter, that just shows how well *you* understand the boys. George is headstrong and fiery-tempered, and not in the least affectionate; while Jack is gentle, loving, and amiable, and it would certainly be very poor proof of dis-

crimination if Mademoiselle were as severe with Jack as she
is with George."

Dr. Doane looked sober and unconvinced, but he dropped
the subject, and left the room soon after, saying, with an
attempt at his naturally cheerful tones, " Well, my dear, then
we will meet at dinner, and have our drive as soon after as
you can be ready."

Margaret was afraid that Fanny might refer to the vexed
question again, and so said that she would go to her room for
awhile, and should consider herself sufficiently at home to
explore the house, if she felt inclined.

" Do just as you please, of course, Margaret, only don't
go into the school-room this morning. You shall go some
time, but not to-day. Mademoiselle expressed the hope that
they should be undisturbed to-day."

Margaret went to her room, so utterly down-hearted and
hopeless, that she felt no inclination to leave it till she was
called to dinner. She looked in vain, through all she had
seen and heard, for one token of improvement, or even possibility for improvement, in her sister. The love of a true,
manly heart, had not developed any tenderness, and the taste
and beauty and devotion that met her at every turn seemed
only to minister to her selfishness and vanity; while their
father's death had, so far as Margaret could see, failed to
arouse one genuine emotion of grief or regret, or one thought
more earnest than that her mourning should be becoming and
suitable. She had for long years been hoping that, through
the discipline of their clouded lives, some pure gold might
come forth from all the dross in Fanny's nature; but the
purifying fires seemed to have wholly failed of their object;
and could she hope that prosperity would do more ? She
thought of him who must soon awake from his dream, to
find his ideal vanished, and a hollow heart in a beautiful
casket in its place—and bitter tears fell for him. And the
boys—what could save them from the effects of such influences as those to which they were subjected ? She was not
hopeless for them. Their young hearts were still guileless

and fresh; but she was filled with keenest solicitude, and felt that she must leave no means untried to rescue them from threatening dangers.

After dinner, at which neither Mademoiselle nor the boys appeared, Margaret and Fanny went up to prepare for their drive. When they met in the hall, Fanny laughed as she surveyed Margaret's plain attire.

"Your outfit looks decidedly skimpy, as the country people say. Walter, I think we must take Margaret on a shopping expedition, before there is a chance of her meeting any body. I don't think I should relish introducing her in such country fixings."

Dr. Doane looked at Margaret's dress, while he drew on his driving-gloves and she smilingly waited for his verdict, and then at Fanny, in her elegant mourning-dress, and long, heavy veil.

"I suppose, being a man, and not having eyes for fine effects in ladies' dresses, that my taste will go for nothing; but I cannot see any thing 'skimpy,' as you say, in our sister's dress. I think she looks altogether what she is, and that is enough to say—is it not, Fanny darling?"

Fanny assented, but not heartily, and they went out to the carriage. When they came home, besides having had a charming ride, which Margaret fully enjoyed, they had ordered a hat and veil, and bought a new dress, which was to be put at once into Madame Larisse's hands.

Dr. Doane was called away soon after their return, and Fanny had visitors, so that Margaret was left to herself. She went to her own room again, wondering when she should see her boys. The twilight was beginning to fall, and she sat busy with her sad thoughts, when quick, light footsteps in the hall caught her ear; and then the door was opened, and shut and locked, and George was in her lap, with his arms tightly around her neck, almost before she knew that it was he.

She soothed and caressed him, for his heart was beating violently, and he was all out of breath. After a little, he lifted his head from her shoulder, and exclaimed, "She couldn't keep me away from you all night, I guess. Hateful, horrid old thing!"

Margaret did not reprove him, but she drew his thoughts away from his troubles, by telling him one of his favorite stories. Then they had one of their talks about being good, and she told him some things about his grandfather. When Scylla came for him to go to bed, he whispered to his Aunty that he had not said his prayers for a whole month, but he should say them always now; and nobody had any trouble with him that night.

# CHAPTER XVIII.

I know that God is good, though evil dwells
Among us, and doth all things holiest share ;
That painful love unsatisfied hath spells
Earned by its smart to soothe its fellow's care.

JEAN INGELOW.

"Isn't that dress finished yet, Margaret? I am afraid you will be late for dinner," said Fanny, coming into her sister's room a few days after her arrival, and finding her busy with her needle.

"I shall be ready in time," answered Margaret. "About ten stitches will finish my dress, and ten minutes will see me arrayed in it."

"To think of any body's being able to sew such weather as this!" said Fanny. "I have not lifted a finger, and have barely kept alive. Rosa has done nothing but fan me and read to me, a few minutes at a time, from the silliest novel she could find."

"The prospect of having something cool to wear has sustained me," replied Margaret; "but it has required no little strength of mind to keep at it, even with such a reward in view."

"The idea of possessing any strength of mind such a day as this! You were foolish not to let Madame make that dress, as well as your black one. She would have given it some style. I am afraid you will look like a representation of rustic simplicity in that unadorned white muslin."

"You forget what an accomplished mantuamaker I am," said Margaret. "Did not I make all your wedding-dresses, and did they not fit to a charm?"

"Oh, for pity's sake, Margaret, don't speak of that!" cried Fanny, casting a hasty glance around, as if she feared that somebody besides herself had heard Margaret's refer-

9

ence to that humiliating fact. "My dresses fitted well
enough; but, dear me! I had to have new ones before I
could go out. They would have answered very well for a
country-bride; but the fact is, we became so accustomed
to plain country things, that we needed to see them side
by side with style and taste to appreciate the difference.
Now you must hurry," she said, as Margaret took off her
thimble, and laid her finished dress on a chair. "Cousin Fred
is the most punctual man in the world, and always expects to
have dinner at the stroke of the clock;" and she left her
to go down to the drawing-room, where Margaret joined her
soon after.

"Why, really, you do look very nice," she said, surveying
Margaret. "I must say that, for a home-made dress, and
such a simple one, that has quite an air, and really becomes
you. I am relieved, for Cousin Fred is such a critic."

"You do not suppose that he will know it is home-
made, do you?" asked Margaret, in a tone of pretended
anxiety.

"Not unless you tell him."

"Oh, not for the world!" exclaimed Margaret.

"And, by the way," said Fanny, rearranging some flowers
on a little stand beside her, "it is not worth while to refer to
the farm, or any thing connected with it, to Cousin Fred, or
any of Walter's friends. We may as well lose sight of the
fact that we have been farmers for five years, when we are
with people who would be apt to regard such a life as vulgar
and uncivilized."

"Are Dr. Doane's friends so very unlike him?" asked
Margaret, quietly, though her cheeks glowed and her eyes
flashed.

"No, no, Margaret," replied Fanny, "I only mean that it
is well to be a little politic. Walter is not in the least so,
and several times, when he has referred to things that happened during his visit, and to Jotham and Miss Patty, and so
on, I have fancied that I noticed a curl of Cousin Fred's
lip, or something in the tone of his voice that made me—

well, feel a little ill at ease; and yet it may have been only my fancy. But I do think we might be somewhat on our guard."

"It is to be hoped, for the credit of Mr. Doane's good sense, that it was a fancy."

",Well, I do not know, Margaret, one must allow for people's education and surroundings. Now the Doane family have been rich and respectable for generations back, and it is only natural that they should not be able to associate good birth and good breeding with poverty and a homely style of living."

"Walter was able to see below the crust of our poverty and homeliness," said Margaret; "have his education and surroundings been different from those of his family?"

"You are very aggravating, Margaret! Of course they have not; but Walter was in love, and did not think of conventionalities; and besides, it is very different to see things, and to hear of them."

"I do not mean to be aggravating, Fanny," said Margaret, "but I have no patience with the foolish, false ideas of respectability one meets in society; and I am afraid I shall feel a constant desire to impress it upon Mr. Frederick Doane's mind that I am a country-woman, and understand farming, and all kinds of housework."

"I should die of mortification if you did," said Fanny; "but I don't believe you will have the desire, when you have seen him and other members of the family. There is Walter's father, who has been out of business for years; you will see how nicely he lives. Then, there is his uncle, Fred's father, with whom Walter studied medicine; he has been a consulting physician for years, and lives elegantly. Fred stays at home with his father and mother winters, and travels summers—he joins us this summer; and there was another uncle still, a bachelor, who was very rich; he died a year or so ago, leaving his fortune to Walter."

"Oh!" said Margaret, eagerly, "then Walter has more than his profession to depend upon?"

"Why, yes, indeed; did you not know that? Dr,
Somers told us he was rich."

"I know; but I thought he had a large practice."

"So he has," answered Fanny, "and the fortune besides.
Why, dear me! he never could support such an establishment
as this by his practice, however good."

Margaret felt relieved, and Fanny went on:

"The house was furnished very much as you see when I
came. I think it does Walter credit, though I have added some
things, and Cousin Fred gave Walter the benefit of his taste."

"I should not have thanked him for that," Margaret remarked.

"Why not?" asked Fanny in surprise. "Don't you like
the house?"

"Yes; but I should think you would have preferred your
husband's unassisted taste."

"Oh, nonsense!" laughed Fanny; "I don't pretend to
any romance or sentiment of that kind. If Cousin Fred's
suggestions improved the appearance of my house, I am sure
I thank him for it; and really, his taste is excellent in every
thing—he has travelled and seen so much. Is it not a piece
of marvellous good fortune," she added, after a pause, "that
I should have been lifted out of a little brown farmhouse in
a desert wild, into such a home as this? People do get their
hearts' desire, sometimes."

"What does Walter think of your making light of sentiment and romance?" asked Margaret.

"I don't suppose he thinks much about it," answered
Fanny, carelessly; "but unless you wish to make Cousin
Fred caustic and cynical to the last degree, do not mention
those words to him. He despises them."

"I should imagine as much," answered Margaret.

"You are making up your mind not to like him, I see,"
said Fanny; "but you cannot help it, and I advise you to
guard your heart; he is famous for his irresistible fascina-
tions, and has never been in love, he says, and never expects
to be."

Margaret made no reply, and just then Mr. Doane was admitted. Fanny received him cordially, and introduced him to Margaret. She bowed, and then turned to Dr. Doane, who entered the room after his cousin, and whom she had not seen since breakfast.

"I need not ask after my sister's health," he said, looking smilingly down into her face, flushed with the excitement of her talk with Fanny, and brightened by the pleasure of seeing him.

"How are you, Fred? And how has my wife been to-day?" he asked, taking Fanny's hands. "Has she missed me as much as she ought?" and the smile with which she answered him seemed perfectly satisfactory.

"You must take a drive immediately after dinner," Dr. Doane said; "it will be the most refreshing thing possible; there is a lovely breeze now."

"Are you not going with us?" asked Fanny.

"No, dear, I cannot. I am sorry to say, I have to take a lonely ride to see a patient two or three miles out of town. I wonder if you would like to go with me, instead of in the carriage?" he added, his eyes seeking Fanny's eagerly.

"Oh, Walter," she said, "don't ask me! You know what a horror I have of going among sick people."

"You need not go in," he said, loth to give up the pleasant idea of having her ride with him.

"I should imagine all sorts of dreadful things while I waited for you," she said; "and, besides, Margaret and Cousin Fred need me to *chaperone* them."

Margaret saw the disappointed look with which Dr. Doane turned towards the dining-room, and felt very sorry for him, and vexed with Fanny.

"Are not the children going to dine with us, Fanny?" the doctor asked, as they sat down to the table.

"Not to-day; they had an early dinner, and went out with Mademoiselle."

"I am sorry for that," returned her husband; "I want to see the little fellows. However, we will have a visit from

them in the evening. Leave word with Scylla when you go
out, Fanny; will you?"

"Yes," Fanny answered, "though I do not know what
Mademoiselle will say."

"It would never do to incur the displeasure of the French
dragon," said Mr. Doane.

Fanny shook her head reprovingly. "You must not call
poor Mademoiselle bad names, Fred. She only complains
that the boys are allowed to speak English so much that it
interferes with their French. But of course, when Walter
wishes it, her judgment must be set aside."

"Thank you, my dear," her husband responded.

When dinner was over, Dr. Doane hurried the ladies
away to prepare for their drive, saying that they must be
back early, or he and the boys would be disconsolate.

"By the way," he said, "I wonder if they have come
home. If they have, I will take Georgie with me."

"Indeed, you must not, Walter," exclaimed Fanny,
quickly; then meeting Mr. Doane's eyes, she added, "Jack
would be so grieved to be left behind! If you could take
them both, it would be another thing." And she followed
Margaret up-stairs.

As they descended the steps to the carriage, a lady in
widow's dress passed, leading a beautiful little girl. The
lady bowed, and smilingly checked the child, who exclaimed,
"O mamma, there's Mr. Doane!" and would have sprung
towards him.

"Why, Margaret," said Fanny, when they were seated in
the carriage, "what is the matter? You look like a ghost."

"Do I?" returned Margaret.

"You certainly did, for a moment. Fred, who was the
lady to whom you bowed just now? Her face struck me as
being familiar, and yet I do not know that I ever saw it
before."

"It was Mrs. Blake," he replied; "and the little lady
who showed such emotion at seeing me was Miss Clara
Blake, one of my sweethearts."

" And who is Mrs. Blake, and where does she live ? " questioned Fanny.

" She lives in —— street. Her husband died last winter, and she lives in the greatest seclusion, which accounts for your not having met her."

" Was Mr. Blake rich ? "

" Oh, yes ; he left her a large fortune, and she had one when he married her. And yet she mourns ! I think theirs must have been the traditional match made in heaven, for the usual tokens of discord and incompatibility were wholly lacking."

" Was Mrs. Blake a St. Louis lady ? "

" She was from New York ; you may have heard of her —she was a Miss Clara Russell."

Mr. Doane's eyes were upon her, and Fanny managed to conceal any emotion she may have experienced, and to answer with tolerable composure, " I—I believe I have heard the name."

" I met Mrs. Blake's brother last winter," continued Mr. Doane, " and judged him a brother worthy of such a sister. It was none of my business, but I did take it upon my-self to wonder why she did not return with him to New York, as he is unmarried, and living alone in the old family home."

By this time Fanny had fully recovered her self-posses-sion, and when a covert glance at Margaret had assured her that she too was—at least outwardly—calm, she carelessly changed the subject, and chatted about ordinary things with Mr. Doane, who the while bestowed brief, inspecting glances upon Margaret's thoughtful face, of which she was quite unconscious.

Mr. Doane had been attracted by his cousin's graceful, fascinating wife, when they first met, and his chagrin at find-ing, after a time, that his boasted penetration had been for once at fault, made him especially wary of the charm her sister's face and manner possessed for him. He watched with actual impatience for some chance lifting of " the veil," as he mentally styled the air of true womanliness which pervaded all she said and did.

At length he suggested that they should turn back, or the doctor might be at home before them.

"Oh, yes, let us go back," said Margaret, eagerly. "I have hardly seen the children since I came."

"Are children more interesting to you than grown people, Miss Crosby?" asked Mr. Doane, with a feeling much akin to pique.

"Some are—Georgie and Jack, for instance—than some grown people."

"Do you mean, than Cousin Fred and me?" asked Fanny, "because it sounded very much like it."

Margaret shook her head in smiling denial.

"You do not think it worth while to prove to the contrary, I see," said Mr. Doane, as he saw the quiet, far-away expression coming back to her eyes.

"How can I prove it?—only tell me!"

"By treating us with some attention," he answered; "by bestowing your regards upon us, instead of the earth and sky, and giving us the benefit of a few of your thoughts."

The injured tone with which this was said amused Margaret, and, in a sudden change of mood which took her and her companions by surprise, she assumed the air of an assiduous, anxious hostess, introducing one topic after another, in a way that made Mr. Doane, at least, sorry when the drive came to an end.

"Do you consider that you have done your duty by us, so that you will feel at liberty to indulge in another fit of abstraction this evening?" he asked, pausing with his hand on the carriage-door.

"I do consider that I have been very good to you, and shall devote myself to the children for the rest of the evening," she replied, laughingly.

"Will you not count me among them?"

"Oh, Fred! have done with your nonsense, and help us out!" exclaimed Fanny.

Margaret was already on the sidewalk, and Fanny was just stepping from the carriage, when their ears were greeted by unwonted sounds coming from the garden, which opened upon the street.

"G'long, g'long off! What for yer come into dis yer' for? De massy! G'long off wid yer poor white trash."

A gruff voice was heard to reply, and then two miserable-looking objects came out, grumbling and complaining. The cook's black face was seen for a moment, and the gate was shut and locked.

The man and woman stood still for a moment, and then the man drew near to Mr. Doane, causing Fanny, who had waited to see the cause of the disturbance, to utter a little scream and run into the house.

"What do you want, fellow?" asked Mr. Doane, who felt as if even to look at such a ragged, unwashed, unkempt object, was contamination.

"So'thin' ter git lodgin' an' vittles," was the surly reply.

"Take that, then, and be off," said Mr. Doane, throwing some money on the ground at a little distance. "Miss Crosby," he cried in amazement as he turned and beheld Margaret standing beside the woman, "what are you doing?"

She took no notice, but continued to talk to the woman, while the man tucked the money away among his rags; and Mr. Doane exclaimed, "In heaven's name, Miss Crosby, what can you have to say to *that?*"

"Leave me a moment," she said, hastily, as the woman made a movement to follow her companion, who had gone a few steps away, and was calling her sharply to come on. Margaret succeeded in detaining her, and Mr. Doane stood by.

"You are very poor," said Margaret, earnestly; "if you will bring her back to me I will give you money, and do all I can to help you."

"I tell you I dunno whar she are. I hain't never seen—"

"Shet up yer head, can't yer!" exclaimed the man, who

9*

had come back to listen. "Be ye her as tuck the nigger gal
off, an' didn't never pay a cent fer't?"

"I am the one who took Chloe from you," answered
Margaret, "and now if you will let me have her again, I will
pay you well."

"She's wuth a heap, ef she be a nigger," said the man,
"an' it'll hef ter be a mighty smart chance as'll git me to
let yer hev' 'er."

"I am sure I can satisfy you," said Margaret, eagerly;
"only bring her to me."

"How much will yer give me down now?" asked the man.

"Miss Crosby," said Mr. Doane, "of course this is all a
mystery to me, but let me suggest that if you wish to recover any thing from these people, you had better allow me
to deal with them," and he added something in a low tone, in
which the word "arrested" may have caught the man's ear,
for he turned shortly away, pulling the woman after him.

"Don't go," cried Margaret, "without telling me something about Chloe, or promising to come again."

"Here, fellow, why don't you answer the lady?" exclaimed Mr. Doane, sternly, as they kept on without a word.

"I'll come agin ter-morry," answered the man's harsh
voice, "an' fotch her along," and the ragged pair disappeared
down the street.

"Pray, satisfy my curiosity without delay, Miss Crosby,"
said Mr. Doane, as they ascended the steps. "Who are those
people, and what have they that you are so anxious to re-
gain?"

"They are Simon and Nancy Stubbs," Margaret replied,
"and it is a little negro-girl that I wish to get possession of."

"I thought I heard something to that effect from the polite lips of Mr. Stubbs," replied Mr. Doane, "but supposed
I must have misunderstood, and that it was a pet spaniel, or
bird, with which they had absconded. The mystery deepens! Are there not plenty of negro-children in St. Louis?
Why should you insist upon poor Mr. Stubbs giving up
what he seems to prize so highly?"

"He gave her up to me first," answered Margaret, "and then took her back."

"Oh, then it is a desire to have your rights—to get the better of Mr. and Mrs. Stubbs, and not that one negro-girl is more to you than another?"

"I prefer Chloe," replied Margaret, as they entered the library, where Dr. Doane sat with the boys in the midst of a very interesting story; but all three started up when they saw Margaret.

"Where is Fanny?" Dr. Doane asked, after a little.

"Have you not seen her?" asked Margaret. "She came in some ten minutes ago."

"She did!" exclaimed the doctor; "and where have you been all this time? We have been expecting you for the last half-hour, but I had not heard the carriage."

Mr. Doane proceeded to give an exaggerated and highly-colored description of their encounter with Simon and Nancy, and when he stated as a climactic fact that the important object in question was a little negro-girl, George and Jack cried, "Oh, it's Chloe, it's Chloe!" and Dr. Doane exclaimed, "Is it possible that those creatures have turned up in St. Louis, and that you really have fallen in with them? Well, wonders will never cease."

"Oh, then, you know all about them, and the black child upon whom they set such a value," said Mr. Doane.

"Yes, I heard the story from the children, and then from Dr. Somers, and a very interesting one it is."

"I shall get the children to tell it to me," said Mr. Doane.

"Oh, yes, we'll tell it to you," cried George; and while the doctor went in search of Fanny—whom he found in a state which he kindly called weariness—Mr. Doane heard how Chloe came to live at the farm; and with the prospect of seeing her on the coming day, Margaret could make merry with the boys and Mr. Doane over her "tricks and her manners."

"You seem very much entertained," Fanny remarked, as she and Dr. Doane came into the room.

"We are talking about Chloe, Fanny," said Margaret "did you know that I have had an interview with Simon and Nancy Stubbs, and have the promise of seeing Chloe to-morrow?"

"Walter mentioned it," replied Fanny; "I hope nobody saw you talking with them?"

"I did," said Mr. Doane. "Can you imagine a greater shock to my sensibilities?"

"Margaret was always queer about those things," said Fanny. "I do not think she would shrink from contact with any degree of poverty, and rags, if she had an idea to carry out."

"I think we have seen that exemplified to-night," Mr. Doane remarked. "Miss Crosby, I dislike to cast the shadow of a doubt over your sanguine expectations, but the number of rags and tags belonging to Mr. and Mrs. Stubbs, and their otherwise unprepossessing appearance, suggest the possibility to my mind that they may conclude not to jeopard their own liberty for the sake of giving Chloe hers."

"I do not think they would suspect me of having any designs upon their liberty," replied Margaret.

"Perhaps not, but you remember the effect my mild interference had upon them, and I may come to assume the shape of an arm of the law to their imaginations. However, I only wished to warn you against counting too surely upon beholding your *protégé* to-morrow."

"I had thought of the same possibility, Margaret," said the doctor.

"Your infatuation about that child is something I never could understand," said Fanny. "I am sure I do not know what you will do with her, if you get her back."

"Take her with me to the farm, of course," answered Margaret.

"That is an interdicted remark, you know very well, Margaret," said Dr. Doane. "You may take her with you on your summer travels, if you think best. After you have seen her, you can judge of her qualifications as lady's maid."

"Is Aunt Margaret going away?" asked George, whose quick ear caught the dreadful suggestion in the midst of an animated conversation with Jack across his aunt's lap. "Is she going, too, when you and mother go?"

"Never mind about that now, my boy," said Dr. Doane.

"Well, I ain't going to stay with that old Mademoiselle," muttered George, adding, in spite of Margaret's checking hand, "if they all go off and leave us with *her*, I'll just up and run away, and so."

"What do you say to having Aunt Margaret sing?" said Dr. Doane. "I have an idea that it would be worth hearing."

"Do you sing?" asked Mr. Doane.

"Yes, she does," cried George; "she used to sing to Jack and me, nights."

"What does she sing, Georgie?" Mr. Doane asked.

"When we'd be going to bed she'd sing, 'Softly now the light of day.' Sing it now, won't you, Aunty?"

"That is our good-night hymn, dear. Nobody would care to hear it but you and Jackie."

"Well, then, sing 'Come to the sunset tree,'" he persisted.

"George," said his mother, "your aunt cannot sing your hymns now. Let somebody else have a chance to propose something."

"I am afraid I shall have to make my own selection, my list is such an old-time one," said Margaret, as she seated herself at the piano.

"Well, Margaret," Dr. Doane said, as she finished her song, "I consider that you have defrauded us; why have you not sung before?"

"'Nobody axed me,' sir," she replied, "and you could not think I would be so bold as to propose it myself."

"Well, we must make up for lost time now," returned the doctor; "let us have something else right away."

So Margaret sang again, and as she ceased, Mademoiselle appeared at the door, smiling and beckoning to the children.

"Pardon," she said, "but I have come to look for my little boys. I could not tell what had become of them."

"Go with Mademoiselle at once," Fanny said. "It is much too late for them to be up, but of course these things are beyond my control now."

Jack started, though reluctantly enough, but George stood pulling himself back and forth by the piano, not in the least heeding Margaret's looks of gentle reproof.

"Why don't you go, George?" asked his mother impatiently.

"I don't want to go with her," he said, crossly. "She's ugly to me; she likes Jack better'n me, she says she does, and I can't be good, or say my prayers or any thing when she's there. I want Aunt Margaret to put me to bed."

"Ah, ah! *mon cœur!*" exclaimed Mademoiselle softly, casting her eyes up to the ceiling.

Fanny looked angry and threw herself back in the chair; Margaret sat still and sad by the piano; Mr. Doane, from a dark corner, watched them all. Dr. Doane went to George, and laid his hand gently on the boy's head.

"Aunt Margaret," he said, "I think if you were to sing your good-night hymn now, it would have a good effect upon this little boy, and he might be able to say his prayers when he goes up with Mademoiselle. Come here, Jack, and Mademoiselle will please sit down for a few minutes."

Margaret sang the hymn, and then Georgie came to kiss her with a subdued manner, and so sorry a little face, that it seemed as if she could not let him go without a word of comfort. Poor little Jack, too—she felt that his easily influenced, pliable nature, needed her care even more than George's, so strong and sturdy, though he had fewer troubles to be soothed away.

Nobody seemed inclined to talk when the boys were gone, and Mr. Doane soon took his leave. For a time his cousin's sober, anxious face was before him, as he thought how slowly but surely the film was falling from his eyes, and his illusion with regard to Fanny was being dispelled. But hope for all came with the thought of Margaret. He had forgotten to doubt the reality of her loveliness, and as he reviewed

the past few hours, he smiled to see how fully he had accepted this fair stranger as his ideal of perfect womanhood, yet
he felt no inclination to cavil at his hasty judgment. "She
cannot be very young," he thought, "but she will never grow
old. She drinks of the fountain of youth, and at seventy
she will be as young in spirit as she is now, no matter what
trials she meets by the way. I do not know the secret, but
I am sure of the fact. Her sweet eyes will never lose their
light; they will always be as clear and true as they are now.
What a voice she has! I never heard one that touched me
so. Her singing of that hymn was like the soft breathing
of a tender benediction. I wish she would sing it *for me;*
I am sure it would ' bring sweet dreams down from the blissful skies.' She has the naturalness of a shepherdess, the
grace and ease of a woman of the world, a warm, true heart,
a bright intellect—heigh-ho! I wish her sister were like
her—no, not like her, for there could not be two such women
in one century, but I wish she were worthy of Walter, poor
fellow! I wonder what Miss Crosby's heart-history has
been. Of course, she has loved. I wonder if she loves still."

In the meantime Margaret, glad of the silence and solitude of her own room, had plenty of food for thought in the
events of the evening. Her life's lesson must have been
poorly learned, she said to herself, if she needed these constant reminders of a happy past; and that she did need them
was proved by the shock they always gave her foolish heart.
She would have known that the face she had seen that day
was akin to Robert Russell—it was so like his—even if she
had not recognized Mrs. Blake, as one to whose heart she had
been taken as a sister, long years ago, because she loved a
brother. Must they meet again? and would she be regarded
bitterly, as having brought a shadow over that brother's life,
or one whom he had put out of his heart as unworthy? As
to Chloe, she reminded herself that there was great reason
to doubt whether she should see her and be able to rescue
her once more, but still she felt hopeful.

# CHAPTER XIX.

At first it seemed a little speck,
　And then it seemed a mist ;
It moved, and moved, and took at last
　A certain shape, I wist—
A speck, a mist, a shape, I wist !
And still it neared and neared.　　COLERIDGE.

A WEEK passed, during which nothing was seen or heard of Simon and Nancy, and Margaret sorrowfully gave up her hope of rescuing Chloe from the terrible life she supposed her to be leading.

In the meantime the weather had become so oppressive, and Fanny seemed so languid and drooping, that an early day had been fixed for their departure from St. Louis. Dr. Doane's plan had been that they should all travel together for a time, and then settle down somewhere, to enjoy country air and scenes. Fanny maintained that nothing could be worse for children than travelling ; it was impossible to keep them under any sort of discipline, and the wisest plan, to her mind, was for Mademoiselle to take the boys to some quiet place, where they could have daily lessons, and not lose all they had gained under her careful tuition.

This proposal made the doctor look very sober, and the dread of having it carried out inclined him to yield readily to Margaret's plan of taking the children to the farm. All her skill and tact did not prevent Fanny's wearing an injured and severely reserved air for a day or two after the question was decided, though in her secret heart she felt that the arrangement was a very satisfactory one, as she candidly owned to herself that she should not in the least relish having any body with her who would divide the devotions of her two cavaliers, as Margaret would surely do. Her only anxiety was removed when Mademoiselle promised faithfully to return to her in the autumn. She asserted that

nothing could compensate for the loss of such an accomplished governess.

Mademoiselle's sensitive heart had been so hurt by
George's tirade against her in the drawing-room, that she
went to Fanny the next morning, and made known with
sorrowful dignity that she must leave her beloved Madame;
she could not subject herself to such humiliation; she should
never be able to look the "docteur" and "Monsieur" in the
face again; she only hoped that Madame would find some
one to fill her place who would be as devoted as she had
been. Fanny was in despair; but she soon found that
Mademoiselle was not implacable, and when George had
been brought to the point of asking her pardon, her wounded heart was healed, and things went on much as usual;
though George confided to Margaret that he was scolded and
shut up in dark closets more than ever, and had altogether
a dreadful time. But Margaret did not encourage him to
talk of his troubles, as she should so soon have him and Jack
rightfully and peaceably to herself.

Not a day passed that did not bring Mr. Doane with
books or flowers, or to take the ladies for a drive or to see
some fine picture. This generally resulted in his spending
the evening, and the evenings were always varied with
music. Margaret discovered that Mr. Doane could play "a
few things," and those few things happened to be passages
from symphonies and sonatas that she used to delight in, but
had not heard for years. He played the flute, too, and, with
her accompaniment on the piano, it proved the source of
exquisite pleasure. Dr. Doane was exceedingly fond of
music, and he enjoyed Margaret's and his cousin's perform-
ances to the full, whenever he was at home, sitting beside
Fanny, who generally reclined upon a sofa.

On Sunday, late in the afternoon, Mr. Doane came, finding Margaret and George in the library.

"Oh, dear!" sighed George, "I didn't want anybody to
come in here. I wish we'd have locked the door."

"Why, Georgie!" exclaimed Margaret; "what a very
rude speech!"

"Well, I know you'll stop reading, and Mademoiselle will come home before Mr. Doane goes away, and I sha'n't have a good time after all. I do wish he hadn't come."

Mr. Doane laughed. "Poor Georgie! it is a hard case, isn't it? But you won't mind my sitting here, if I don't speak or move, and if your aunt goes on reading as if I were really locked out?"

"No; but she won't, I know. Will you, Aunt Margaret?" he asked eagerly.

"She will, Georgie," said Mr. Doane, seating himself opposite Margaret. "She wouldn't like to make me go away, and I shall, unless she reads."

"I think I shall be obliged to," said Margaret, "for I do not like to disappoint Georgie, and I do not care to send you away, either. Mademoiselle invited Jack to go somewhere with her, leaving George to his own devices. So we were having one of our old-fashioned Sunday times."

"Let me have the benefit of one such. It will make up for my not having been to church to-day. You have not been, either, I know."

"Oh, yes, I have; I went this morning."

"What! in spite of the heat? I am amazed at such a display of energy."

"I have so few opportunities to go to church," said Margaret, "that I cannot afford to lose any on account of the weather."

"Is it as a pleasure, or a duty, that you go when the opportunity offers?" asked Mr. Doane.

"There! I just knew you'd talk, and spoil it all," exclaimed George, almost crying.

"Read, Miss Crosby; I won't utter another syllable;" and Mr. Doane shut his lips tightly together, folded his hands, and sat back in his chair with an air of desperate determination, while Margaret opened her book.

"I suppose you have read 'Pilgrim's Progress'?" she said.

Mr. Doane nodded, and she began to read where she had

stopped when he came in. He listened without noting the
words for a time, thinking how pleasant it was to sit in that
cool, shaded room, and hear that sweet, clear voice, and have
such a picture before him; for it was a picture well worth
regarding—Margaret in her white dress, with tea-rosebuds
and heliotrope in her dark hair and at her throat, her face
reflecting the peace and quiet of her heart, with George
beside her, his face full of eager interest in the wonderful
book she read.

But George's questions about the different scenes described, and Margaret's explanations, soon arrested his attention, and he listened as eagerly as George himself.

"Don't you think it's nice?" asked George, turning to
him suddenly, as some little movement reminded him of his
presence.

"Very nice, indeed, Georgie," answered Mr. Doane.

"Do you know what it all means?" George asked.

"I thought I did, Georgie; but I am beginning to doubt
it."

"Well, why don't you ask Aunt Margaret things that you
don't know? She knows 'em all."

"I have been thinking that I should like to ask her
things, but I promised you I would not talk."

"Oh, I'd let you ask questions, if you didn't ask too
many. But don't you know who Christian means?"

"I don't believe I do. Can't you tell me?"

"I should hope so," replied George, disdainfully. "It
means any body that feels that they are very bad and don't
love God—that's living in the City of Destruction. And
when they want to be good, and think they will be—that's
running away from the City of Destruction. And the
Slough of Despond is when they think they can't be good,
and then somebody that *is* good comes and tells them to try
harder, and they do. Then, by-and-by they get to the
Wicket Gate—that's when they ask Jesus to forgive their
sins; but they can't be real happy till they get to the Cross.
See! there it is, in the picture! See Christian's burden—

that's his sins—tumbling off and rolling away down into the
sepulchre.  He knows then that Jesus has forgiven him, and
he keeps being good till he gets to the Celestial City—that's
heaven.  Why! don't you know that Aunt Margaret's a
pilgrim ? and ain't you one, too ? "

"I am very far from being such a pilgrim as that,
Georgie," Mr. Doane replied.

"Well, why don't you be one ?  You're grown-up.  I'm
going to be, when I'm bigger.  I wouldn't not be one then,
for the whole world."

"Does your Aunt Margaret think you are too little to be
one now ? "

"No, she don't; but I do," George answered, hanging
his head an instant.  "Mebbe I'll get to be one this summer;
but I can't while Mademoiselle is 'round.  She makes me so
bad, that when I say my prayers I don't want Jesus to forgive me.  But, Aunty, do people like Mr. Doane live in the
City of Destruction ?  He don't look like Pliable, or Obsti-
nate, or any of these," he added, examining the picture
representing Christian's townspeople talking with the two
" turncoats."

" Can you not find any body that looks respectable and
well-behaved, Georgie?  For I suppose there is no other
place for me in your creed, as long as I do not wear the
pilgrim's dress, and walk in that very strait path."

" Aunt Margaret says that every body lives in the City of
Destruction that isn't a Christian," said George.  "But don't
you know," he cried, as a sudden solution of the difficulty
occurred to him, " that only means that you don't love our
Saviour, and don't try to obey him ?  It doesn't really mean
that you live in a wicked city, and wear ragged clothes."

" I suppose it means that my soul is in rags, and that, if I
were to present myself at the gate of the Celestial City, I
should be turned away as a beggar."

" Is that what it means, Aunt Margaret ? " asked George.

Margaret started at this sudden appeal to her.  She felt
that Mr. Doane was talking to her more than to George, and

knew that he waited for her reply to George's question.  She
hesitated a moment, and then said, " Shall I give you a little
outline of Georgie's creed, and mine ? "

" Pray do," he replied.

" We believe that we all have broken God's law—or, as
Georgie expresses it, live in the City of Destruction—and
could never escape if it were not that Jesus, the divine Son
of God, suffered in our stead, and made it possible for God
to be just, and yet pardon us and treat us as if we had not
violated his law.   When we accept His sacrifice, Jesus' blood
washes away our guilt ; we love Him for His kindness, and
He helps us to keep the very strait and narrow path that
leads to the Celestial City."

" That seems a very simple and logical creed, Miss
Crosby," Mr. Doane said ; " and that it is the one which you
accept and live by, is sufficient to commend its beauty and
desirableness.   But—"

" Do not speak of the ' buts ' now, please," said Margaret, gently, laying her hand on that of George, who, leaning on the arm of her chair, was listening, though only half
comprehending.

Mr. Doane colored a little, but said, with a smile, " I shall
only defer them, then.   I shall lay them before you the first
opportunity I have."

" You've talked a great deal, I think," said George, dolefully.

" You put me up to it," returned Mr. Doane, laughing.
" If you will be quiet now, I will, and we will have a little
more of the ' Pilgrim.' "

So Margaret read till Dr. Doane and Fanny came down.

" Well, Fred," the doctor exclaimed, " I am glad to see
you in such good hands.   You have not been allowed to talk
your French philosophy and German metaphysics to Margaret, I'll be bound."

" When did you come, Fred ? " Fanny asked, looking at
the cosy group—for Mr. Doane had taken his seat again near
Margaret—with a very cloudy face.

"About an hour ago," he replied. "I found your sister and George deep in the adventures of the renowned 'Pilgrim,' and George allowed me, on promise of silence, to sit here and listen; then he engaged me in a theological discussion, so that we have had quite an exciting time."

"Have you really been reading this book to Fred?" asked Dr. Doane, taking it from Margaret. "You found him rather heterodox, did you not?"

"The discussion was between Mr. Doane and George;" she replied, "I did not hear him state his views very definitely."

"His views might be improved,"—and Margaret discerned the real feeling beneath the doctor's light tone. "I don't know of any body who would make a better pilgrim than Fred, if he would but assume the staff and shoon."

"Are the prescribed equipments so uniform, and must every body walk in the same beaten track?" asked Mr. Doane.

"I think there is a vast deal of narrow-mindedness and bigotry in the current views on religious subjects," said Fanny. "I cannot see why one conscientious belief is not as good as another. You can't expect every man's reason to attain the very same result."

"That is why it is so fortunate for us that truth is revealed to us," said Margaret, "and not left to be discovered by any thing so uncertain and finite as our poor human reason. If it makes mistakes in material things, how much more must it in spiritual?"

"Shall we go in to tea, Walter?" asked Fanny. "It was announced some time ago."

"Of course, my dear," replied the doctor, who had been turning the leaves of the book abstractedly; and he led the way with Fanny to the dining-room.

Soon after tea Mademoiselle and Jack came home.

"Hello, Jack!" was George's greeting. "I know you haven't had as good a time as I have. What have you been doing?"

"Oh, nothing much," Jack replied, with a quick look at Mademoiselle, who met it with a bland smile.

"Well, I've been doing something much, and you can't guess what! Aunt Margaret's been reading 'Pilgrim' to me! What do you think of that?"

"Oh, Aunty, read some to me! Do—do!" cried Jack.

"Is it that I shall leave the little boys here, Madame?" asked Mademoiselle.

"No; take them up with you," answered Fanny.

"Come up with us, won't you, Aunt Margaret?" pleaded Jack in a whisper.

"I think your aunt needs to go to church, Jack," Mr. Doane said, in a whisper loud enough for Margaret to hear. "You know, when she gets back to the farm she cannot go, and I think she ought to, now that she can; don't you?"

"I don't see as she needs to go; she's good enough now," said George, who had come to listen. "Let her come with Jack and me."

"No; let her go with me—I know she wants to."

"Did she say she did?"

"No; she has not said so yet, but she is going to."

"How do you know she is?"

"I will ask her, and let you see. Miss Crosby, will you go to church with me to-night?"

"I should like to, very much," she replied; and then she talked to the boys so softly, · that nobody could hear but themselves for a moment, and when she had finished she kissed them, and they said good-night, and went away with Mademoiselle.

"You will have to get ready at once," Mr. Doane said; and Margaret turned to Fanny.

"Would you not like to go? The evening is so lovely."

"Will you go, Fanny?" Dr. Doane asked. "I can go with you to-night, and should like it, of all things."

"I thought you knew that I am not well," Fanny replied; "though that is not worth speaking of. I do not care to go;

but that need not keep you at home. I can call Rosa, or
Mademoiselle, if I feel lonely."

"I don't care to go, Fanny, unless you do," he answered.
"I knew you had felt languid to-day, but I thought it was
the extreme heat."

"Of course, there is always some insignificant cause for
my languor and bad feelings. Why do you wait, Margaret?" she asked, impatiently, as Margaret's eyes rested
sadly upon her for a moment.

"I am sure I can't tell," Margaret answered lightly, and
hurried away.

Mr. Doane tried to be diverting, and to dispel the cloud
that rested over his cousin, and for his sake was kind and
polite to Fanny; but he was glad to escape with Margaret.

They were not, however, destined to go to church that
night. As they went out of the door, they discovered a
woman sitting on the lower step. She did not move as they
came near, and when Margaret stood before her, and spoke,
she answered without lifting her head from the stone post
against which it leaned.

"Why, is this Nancy!" exclaimed Margaret, in amazement.

"I reckon it are," was the reply, in a faint voice.

"Are you sick?" asked Margaret, as Nance slowly lifted
her hand, and pushed back the ragged sun-bonnet that had
partly hidden her face, showing how ghastly and haggard she
looked.

"Oh, drefful sick; I'm 'mos' dead," replied Nance, with a
dismal shake of her head.

"Do you want any thing?" asked Mr. Doane, taking out
his pocket-book; and he added, to Margaret, "We cannot
wait; we shall be late as it is, I am afraid."

"What can I do for you?" asked Margaret gently.
"Do you want to tell me any thing about Chloe, or yourself?"

"Ther' a'n't nothin' ter tell," Nance replied. "I tole yer
I dunno nothin' 'bout the gal, an' no more I don't."

" What did you come here for, then ? " asked Mr. Doane impatiently.

Margaret offered the money that Mr. Doane put into her hand, but Nance only shook her head dismally.

" What can we do for you ? " she asked.

" Oh, I'm awful sick," Nance moaned, " an' I ha'n't got no place ter go to—an' I couldn't never git thar if I hed."

" How did you get here, if you are so ill ? " asked Mr. Doane.

" I jis' crawled along so fur, but I ha'n't got strengt' to go no furder."

" Where is your husband ? " Margaret asked. " Won't he come and take care of you ? "

Nance groaned, and feebly wrung her hands.

" He's gone an' lef' me ; he tuck all we hed 'cept dese yer "—plucking at her rags—" an' went off. Las' night I slep' on de ground. Oh-h ! "

" Is he coming back ? "

" No, he a'n't. He's done clared away down to Kintuck', an' I sha'n't never see him no more ; " and she rocked to and fro, and moaned piteously. " He warn't allers good to me— he'd beat me now an' ag'in, an' 'ud keep more'n his'n share o' the vittles. But I'se lived 'long uv um a good many year, an' it's powerful lonesome 'thout um."

" What made him leave you behind ? " asked Margaret, whose heart was filled with pity for the forlorn creature.

" 'Coz I gin out, an' warn't no use no more ; an' he said he warn't gwine to take care o' me, an' hev to bury me. I wouldn't a' sarved Sime sich a mean trick ; " and she wiped big tears away with her tatters.

Margaret stood regarding her pitifully, and considering, while Mr. Doane waited to hear what plan she had to suggest, knowing well that she would not leave the woman in distress.

" Can she be taken to the hospital to-night ? " she asked, after a pause.

" Yes, unless you like my plan better. I know a poor
10

woman, clean and respectable, whose heart I won by a small
act of humanity, and if I were to ask her to take Mrs. Stubbs
into her shanty, neat as it is, she would do it, and give her
the best of care."

"There could be nothing nicer than that," exclaimed
Margaret eagerly. "It is asking a great deal of the mistress
of the shanty," she added, looking at Nance; "but if you
are sure she would consent—"

"Oh, I've no doubt of it, if she is not ill herself. In
that case it would be out of the question, as she lives alone
with a little grandchild, who couldn't take charge of two
sick women at a time."

"How can we find out about it?" asked Margaret. "Is
she far from here?"

"Not very. If you would not object to the walk, we will
go and make known our wishes, and see what can be done."

"Nancy, will you sit here till we come back?" Margaret
asked. "We are going to find a place where you can have a
nice, comfortable bed, and will come soon and take you to it."

Nance nodded, and Margaret and Mr. Doane hastened
away. The house was a very little one, but it was as neat as
neat could be, and its mistress matched it well. She and her
grandchild were sitting at the door in the moonlight, and
their welcome of Mr. Doane showed how grateful they were
for that "small act of humanity." His proposal was gladly
acceded to, and all Margaret's representations of Nancy's
squalid, ragged condition, and her probable severe illness,
could not daunt the ardor with which they hailed the prospect of doing something to please Mr. Doane.

Margaret waited with them while Mr. Doane went to
bring Nancy, and heard the story of his kindness from Mrs.
Hull; how he had met the child, one day (he knew her,
because she used to go with her father when he was his
father's gardener), and looked so kindly at her, that she made
bold to tell him that her father was dead, and her grandmother was sick, and they had got to leave their house
because they had nothing to pay the rent with. So Mr.

Doane bought the house and gave it to them, and had never let them want for any thing since.

It was not long before the carriage arrived in which Mr. Doane had sent Nancy, and he appeared almost at the same moment. Mrs. Hull looked rather dismayed, when she first saw Nancy emerge slowly and painfully from the carriage with the rough help of the driver, but her horror of dirt and rags did not prevent her showing kindly zeal for the poor creature; and Margaret left her, feeling sure that she would be well cared for.

"If all poor people were like Mrs. Hull," Mr. Doane said, as they walked home, "I should have more pity and sympathy for them."

"I must confess," Margaret replied, "that your object of charity is much more picturesque than mine, and much more interesting; but I am sure none could be more needy than that wretched Nancy."

"Of course, you can count your charities by the score," said Mr. Doane, "while Mrs. Hull and her grandchild are the sole instances of mine. I never made any body else glad or thankful, and if they had been less clean and respectable, I should not have made them so."

"You have been very kind to Nancy, I am sure," said Margaret. "She disproves your harsh judgment of yourself."

"Mrs. Stubbs had very little to do with my motives, I assure you," he replied.

"If you wished to please and oblige me, you have been very successful," said Margaret, earnestly.

They found Dr. Doane alone in the library when they reached home. He asked where they had been to church, and they related their evening's adventure. But though he was interested, and proposed to constitute himself Nancy's physician and to call in the morning, his manner was sad and quiet, and he seemed unable to throw off the depression.

"Will you sing for me before I go, Miss Crosby?" Mr. Doane asked. "It is late, but I feel the need of that soothing influence;" and she went to the piano and sang,

"*Jesus, lover of my soul.*"

"I have heard that before, but never knew how beautiful it was," Mr. Doane said when it was ended.

"It is the sweetest hymn I know," Margaret returned.

"I think you make prayers of the hymns you sing. You put your heart into every word."

"I love them," she replied, "they so often express our needs and longings better than we could ourselves."

"Will you sing one more—one that you think expresses my needs, and ought to express my longings?"

Margaret looked at him wistfully, and there was a tremble in her voice as she sung,

"*Rock of Ages, cleft for me.*"

Mr. Doane made no comment when she ceased, and very soon said good-night.

Fanny did not appear at breakfast the next morning. Dr. Doane, too, was absent, having been called away at a very early hour, and Margaret had breakfast alone with Mademoiselle and the boys. She told the boys of her having seen Nancy again, and what she and Mr. Doane had done for her, Mademoiselle the while thinking what a nice little tale she could make for Madame's entertainment.

Mr. Doane came in the course of the morning, to say that he had stopped at Mrs. Hull's door in passing, to ask after Mrs. Stubbs' health, and had been told that she was very ill, and needed the doctor at once.

"Walter and I were going there directly after breakfast," said Margaret, "but he was called away."

"Why should you go, pray?" exclaimed Mr. Doane, "you surely would not minister to her in the capacity of nurse, and she is by far too benighted to make spiritual advice of any avail."

"I think I ought to go," Margaret replied.

"That is equivalent to saying that you must and will; so I will invite myself to luncheon, and walk there with you afterwards."

Fanny came down to luncheon, and, to Margaret's surprise and relief, was in one of her most balmy, cheerful moods. It was only clouded for a moment, when Margaret, taking it for granted that she knew about Nancy, referred to her incidentally, and seeing her surprise, told the story. She merely shuddered at the idea of such contamination, and wondered that any body should take the trouble to care for such degraded creatures.

"Do you know," she said, suddenly changing the subject, "that Walter has decided to start even earlier than the day fixed? this week Friday? Can you be ready, Fred, and you, Margaret?"

"Oh, yes," Margaret replied. "But I thought Walter could not leave town until next week, and that you couldn't be ready, Fanny?"

"I found that I could expedite my arrangements somewhat," Fanny replied, "and Walter can manage his business so as to leave on Friday. The sooner we get away, the better I shall be pleased."

"Where shall you go first, Fanny?" asked Margaret.

"We—Walter and Fred and I—go to St. Paul's; don't we, Fred? Though I need not appeal to you, for you have declared so often that you had no choice as to our route. That is my idea. I am so anxious to see St. Paul's."

"I should think you would manage to take the farm in your way, and leave your sister and the boys there," Mr. Doane remarked.

"We cannot do that without spoiling our trip," replied Fanny, looking annoyed. "There will be plenty of persons under whose care Walter can place Margaret and the children, without our going quite out of our way."

"I should be very sorry to have you do that," said Margaret. "I should not in the least mind travelling alone with George and Jack."

"If I happened to be going in that direction, would you accept of my escort, Miss Crosby?" asked Mr. Doane.

"Thankfully," replied Margaret.

Fanny looked in perfect amazement at Mr. Doane.

"What has occasioned such a sudden change in your plans, Fred?" she asked.

"My plans have not assumed very definite shape as yet," he replied, "but I have been thinking for some time of going east at once, instead of keeping to my first intention."

Little more was said on the subject, but Fanny's mood was decidedly changed, and when Mr. Doane and Margaret started for Mrs. Hull's, she looked after them with any thing but an amiable expression.

Mr. Doane left Margaret at Mrs. Hull's door, promising to call for her in an hour; and the hour was a very busy one for Margaret. She found Nancy suffering very much, though Dr. Doane had been there, and said that she would be better in a few days—that her illness was caused by the hardships and exposure she had endured. Nobody would have recognized her as she lay in Mrs. Hull's clean, fresh bed, her hair smoothly brushed under a muslin cap, and her face having lost so much of its hard, sullen look in those few hours. Mrs. Hull had slept little, so constantly had the sick woman needed her attention, and Margaret sent her to lie down while she watched by her patient, bathed her aching head, and gave the cooling drinks her parched lips craved. Nancy would now and then open her eyes and gaze at the sweet face with a perplexed look, as if her poor brain were trying to solve the mystery of having such an attendant.

Each day of her stay in St. Louis found Margaret at Mrs. Hull's, and her only regret at going so soon was on Nancy's account. But the worst was over, the doctor said; and Mrs. Hull promised, not only for Mr. Doane's sake, but for Margaret's, to take care of her as long as she needed care. The doctor also mentioned her case to some benevolent ladies, who promised to see that she had work when she should be well again.

When Margaret paid her last visit, on Thursday, Nancy, who took little notice as yet, except to look at Margaret occasionally, heard something that made her raise her head from the pillow and say, in a startled whisper, "Be you gwine away?"

"Yes, Nancy, I am going to-morrow. But you will be taken care of; even after you get well, you will have friends to help you; and you know I have tried to tell you about the kind Father whom you cannot see, but who sees and cares for you."

"Be you gwine 'way off to that place whar you lived?" Nancy whispered.

"Yes; I am going home to the farm, Nancy."

Nancy's head fell back on the pillow, but she did not take her eyes from Margaret. "Ye'll see me agin," she said, emphatically, though her voice was so weak; "I an't gwine to stay yer, whar I can't never see ye—see ef I do!" And when Margaret bade her good-by, she repeated her assertion that she would see her again. Mrs. Hull and her grandchild were well-nigh heart-broken, to take leave of her whom they had already learned to love and to regard almost as an angel. But Mrs. Hull had a secret relief, which was no less than the hope and firm belief that he who had brought the lady to her humble little home, and made it so bright for a few days, would bring her back to brighten a grand and beautiful home of his own for his whole life, and then she should surely have the sweet presence to comfort her very often; for she said to herself, "She isn't one to forget, even such as me."

That afternoon, when Margaret got home, she went to Fanny's room to ask some question about the arrangements for the next morning. Fanny answered her knock with a "Come in," but looked annoyed when she saw Margaret; "I thought it was Mademoiselle. I had sent for her."

She had a little table drawn up beside her couch, which was covered with papers, and two or three large trunks were partly packed, while bed and chairs were filled with the contents of drawers.

"You are busy, Fanny," Margaret said. "I can come again by-and-by."

"No, I am not busy," Fanny replied. "Rosa, gather these papers and put them in my writing-desk, and bring me the key;" and she threw herself back on the cushion.

Margaret looked on while Rosa did as she was bidden, and the desire to have her anxiety relieved gave her courage to say, playfully, "I hope all those formidable-looking bills are receipted, Fanny."

Fanny had been too much annoyed and harassed by her examination to be able to control her irritation and behave discreetly, and she replied impatiently, "They are not receipted, and I'm sure I don't know that they ever will be. If Walter expects me to look after all the troublesome details of housekeeping, and be continually paying this little bill and that little bill, he is greatly mistaken."

"I think Walter mentioned incidentally that he gave you money to meet the current expenses. If he does not give enough, dear, ask him for more. But—I have such a horror of bills."

"So have I," answered Fanny; "and so we will not talk of them."

"You will not leave those unsettled—locked in your drawer, Fanny? Give them to Walter, and let him make every thing right, then you can begin anew when you come home in the fall."

Fanny deigned no reply to this appeal, but called to Rosa, who was in the dressing-room, to come and finish packing; and Margaret went away filled with new forebodings.

Margaret and the boys were to start early in the morning, and Fanny and the doctor later in the day. Mr. Doane's intentions were still unsettled, or known only to himself. He continued to talk of them in such an ambiguous manner that nobody knew what to expect, but the uncertainty was made a certainty when he made his appearance at the depot in the morning, and asked Dr. Doane what messages he should carry to his friends in New York.

"How will you make your peace with Fanny, Fred?" asked the doctor.

"I have just seen her," he replied, "and she has promised to forgive me if I will meet you by-and-by, and I shall aim to accomplish that."

There were tears in Dr. Doane's eyes when he bade Margaret and the children good-by, and in Margaret's too, as she looked back at his sober face when the train left the depot.

She found Mr. Doane a delightful travelling companion, and when he gave her and the boys into Dr. Somers' care at Jonesville, she felt that she should miss her new friend very much, and the pleasure of her return was not a little shadowed by the sense of what she had lost; for it was not likely that they would meet again soon, or probably ever, to resume the pleasant friendly intercourse that had added so much to her enjoyment in St. Louis. He had insisted that he should come for the boys in the fall, whether the doctor would let him or no, and she had assured him that she would not part with them, except to an accredited ambassador. Dr. Somers was delighted to have her back, and his questions as to all she had seen and done since she went away kept her busy answering during their drive from Jonesville, while the boys were in a wild state of excitement at the thought of seeing the farm and Jotham and Miss Patty again.

Margaret's eager eyes discovered the care and taste that had been expended to make the plain little home look attractive to her, and she inwardly blessed every blossom and vine that gave forth their sweet greeting as they drew near.

Jotham was at the gate, and expressed his gratification at seeing her and the boys, in hearty if homely phrase, and Miss Patty flew from the house when she discovered their arrival, sobbing forth her delight, as she clasped Margaret and then the children to her heart. Mr. and Mrs. Davis came that very night; and it happened that Mr. Thomas preached at the little red school-house the next day. Margaret and the boys went, and it surely was some proof to her of strength and grace, that she could meet the memories that place recalled, without losing her peace of heart.

10*

# CHAPTER XX.

I wait for my story—the birds cannot sing it,
  Not one, as he sits on the tree ;
The bells cannot ring it, but long years, O bring it!
  Such as I wish it to be.          JEAN INGELOW.

"I AM glad to find you here. I was afraid you might have left the city," Philip Ventnor said as he entered Mr. Russell's library, where his friend was enjoying the moonlight which streamed in at the window, making the room almost as light as day.

"What occasion had you for such a fear, and where did you think I had gone?" asked Mr. Russell.

"I did not know; I only thought that if you weren't obliged to stay here, you surely would not—it is such a shame to waste these glorious June days and nights in town. Just imagine that moonlight at the seashore, or among the mountains! I wonder how those lovely silvery beams can endure to waste themselves on brick walls and stone pavements, to say nothing of the unappreciative humanity that never thinks whether it is the light of the moon or the street-lamps that shine upon it."

"The moon cannot very well discriminate, and shines on the unappreciative and the appreciative alike; and I believe her influence is often felt when it is not recognized, and where you would never suspect it."

"If the influence is never made manifest, what is the good of it?" asked Philip.

"You mustn't judge of the clod as it lies bare and brown, and seemingly lifeless, under the cold rains and bleak winds of March. Sooner or later it is almost sure to feel

————'a stir of might,
A something within it that reaches and towers ;
And, groping blindly above it for light,
  Climbs to a soul in grass and flowers '—

though you may not be there to see."

"I think it is always March for some poor clods," answered Philip.

"And yet, 'June may be had by the poorest comer.' It isn't always safe," he added, in a lighter tone, "to judge the inner by the outer man. Now, you would hardly imagine that one so material and prosaic as I, could ride on those moonbeams; and yet, they had borne me far enough from the red walls and pavements that you condemn, and from the noise and hubbub of the streets, and it is fair to suppose that a respectable proportion of those who are here in body, send their spirits to enjoy June in the country."

"What keeps you from taking your 'material and prosaic' self there?" asked Philip.

"My aunt, Mrs. More, is coming to make me a visit of a week or two," Mr. Russell replied. "I suppose I should have left town earlier if it had not been for that, but I am not sorry to be detained."

"I never heard you speak of Mrs. More. Is she a sister of your father's?"

"Yes, and she has not been here since long before his death; indeed, I think her last visit was made just after I went to China. She lives at the West, and has been spending some weeks with her children, who are settled in and about Boston."

"I hope you will invite me to come and see her; I have a great liking for old ladies."

"I shall certainly expect you to conceive a great liking for her," Mr. Russell replied. "If old age were always sure to be as lovely and serene as hers, we might well wish for its arrival. It will seem strange enough to her, coming to this old home, and I the only one to welcome her. She will feel the changes as she has never done before, and I could almost have begged her to stay away and to spare her the sight of these empty, deserted rooms."

There was silence for a few minutes, and then Mr. Russell said, "Is your book to come out soon, Philip?"

"I suppose it will be published early in the autumn," he answered.

"How about those 'billows of restlessness?' have they subsided, or borne you to a desired haven?"

"I have been violently tossed about; but the tumult has subsided, for I have resolved to do something as soon as I can find it to do."

"Something more, you mean. Don't cast such unjust imputations upon what you have already done."

"I have scribbled lazily what has earned food and clothes for my useless self, and that is all; and it is very little for an able-bodied, tolerably well-brained man to accomplish. I have been long enough in seeing it, but I trust my eyes are effectually opened now."

"If what you have done has been the result of lazy scribbling," Mr. Russell said, "what would you not accomplish by earnest work with your pen?"

"My pen must help the untried something, but it can't make all the money I need."

"What does your mother say of your intentions with regard to her and your sisters?" Mr. Russell asked.

"I have said nothing to her on the subject," Philip answered. "I thought I would wait until I could disclose something besides intentions; she has too good reasons for distrusting them. And the truth is, I am still utterly in the fog as to what I am to do, there are so few things that come within the range of my capabilities."

"I am glad you discriminate between capabilities and capacities," Mr. Russell replied. "What have you thought of?"

"I could more easily tell you what I have not thought of," answered Philip. "Nothing has escaped my inquisition, from a variety-shop in some small country-village, or district-school, where I could board around and lay up my wages, to a consulship to Kamschatka or Patagonia, or some other foreign part. I find myself contemplating every manner of calling—law, medicine, art, business agencies, offices under government, itinerant peddling, and what not, with a speculative eye; but somehow the right thing—for which

I am fitted, and that is fitted for me—has not turned up yet."

"How would a professorship—of belles-lettres, for instance—strike you?" asked Mr. Russell.

"As the thing of all others to be preferred. But, unfortunately, it is one of the things that seem altogether beyond my reach. No college would choose a young, unknown, inexperienced man to fill such a place."

"As to the inexperience, time would speedily remedy that; the youthfulness might be overlooked; and as to the obscurity, we will not argue that point. Suffice it to say, that, even allowing those three weighty objections, I think you can have a professorship in —— University, if you will accept it."

Philip fairly started from his seat, in his surprise and delight.

"You cannot really mean it! and yet I know you must have good grounds for such an opinion."

"I have very good grounds, Philip," Mr. Russell replied, "although I cannot speak with absolute certainty, until the election has taken place. I should have written you with regard to it, but I thought each day would surely bring you here, and so delayed, when you had a right to know of it as soon as I did. I might have saved you all the fruitless 'contemplations' of the past ten days."

"Do not speak of that," cried Philip. "If I had been enduring untold tortures of mind and body, I should forget them, and be happy now."

Mr. Russell smiled. "You look as confident and sanguine as if you already filled the professional chair, and I were a class of students about to receive your instructions."

Philip colored, but answered earnestly, "I am not ashamed of my confidence, for it is not founded upon my own merits. How could I be doubtful, when you have undertaken my cause?" and he impetuously caught Mr. Russell's hand. "God only knows what I should have been but for you. I wish you could see my heart."

"I do see it, Philip; and what I read there gives me rea. happiness."

Philip's face glowed with pleasure. "Is that really true?" he asked. "I thought I had only been a care and trouble; but to have caused you any happiness, that is almost too much to believe."

"You may believe it fully," Mr. Russell returned. "And now let me tell you on what grounds I base my expectations for you. I have a young friend in —— University, from whom I had a letter the very day after you were here last; and in it he mentioned, incidentally, that the Professor of Belles-Lettres and Modern Languages had resigned, and that he did not think there was any one in view to fill his place. I wrote at once to one of the trustees, with whom I happened to be acquainted, giving your name, and setting forth your qualifications; and I soon received a very favorable answer. I have learned from Mr. Heath, the young friend of whom I spoke, that there are only two or three others under consideration, and their chances are regarded as small; so that I feel quite confident of yours. The election will take place next month, and, if you are the fortunate candidate, you will enter upon your duties in September, I suppose. How will you feel about leaving New York?"

Philip hesitated an instant, looking grave; then answered, that he had no doubt he should find it hard, but he knew very well it was the best thing he could do. He should be more likely to work hard and accomplish something out of New York than in it."

"I saw Claudia this morning," he added, after a little pause.

"Did you?" said Mr. Russell, in surprise.

"It was only for a moment. She was with her father and mother, just taking the train to go north, as I came in from the country."

"Did she see you?" Mr. Russell asked.

"Yes, she saw me; and, like the stupid, blundering fellow that I am, I was just on the point of rushing up to her, when a look in her eyes arrested my insane impulse, and brought me to my senses; and then I saw that her mother's cold eyes were upon me. I suppose they were going away for the summer."

"They are to travel for a time, I believe, and then spend some weeks at the seashore."

"Have you seen her lately?" asked Philip, eagerly.

"I was there a few evenings ago," Mr. Russell replied; but he did not say that he had been invited to dinner, and had received a very polite invitation from Mrs. Thorne to join her party at the seashore.

"I am afraid she is ill," said Philip, "she looked so pale this morning."

"No, she is not ill, though she does look a little pale. But the change will do her good, and she will come back in the fall as fresh and blooming as ever, I have no doubt."

"I do not see why I should have been allowed to darken her bright young life," Philip said, sadly.

"Would she rather have unclouded sunshine than your love, do you think, even though it rests under a shadow for the present?"

"If I only could feel sure that the time would ever come when it would bring to her the peace and happiness she deserves!" exclaimed Philip. "I have wilfully shut my eyes upon my duty to my mother and sisters, feeling that if I recognized that, it would but farther off the bright days for Claudia and me."

"Never fear but they will come," Mr. Russell said, cheerfully. "I have strong faith for you and Claudia; and that you bravely face this duty, does not lessen it. You are both young, and are assured of each other's love, and you can be patient, I know."

"If I could only know that she does not suffer. But her mother is so cold and hard, and so resolute—"

"She loves Claudia, and her father has no sympathy with his wife's ambitious schemes. I think he is a great comfort to Claudia."

" I wonder if her proud mother would utterly look down
upon a Professor of Belles-Lettres. I have no fears but that
Claudia herself would be perfectly satisfied with the position
I could give her as such, and with the income of that position, and my pen."

" I presume she would be happy to live in a cottage and
wear calico, as your wife," replied Mr. Russell, smiling.

" How thankful I am for my undoubting faith in her
love ! " exclaimed Philip. " I never have dreamed of questioning it, since that one chance meeting last spring ; and I
know that she is as well assured of mine. If it had not been
for that one happy hour, how could we have borne the
months of separation before us ? "

" Fortune dealt very kindly with you," Mr. Russell said,
and the sadness in his voice made Philip hate himself for
having talked so freely of what must awaken painful remembrances in his friend's heart.

" I wish I could have my mother and sister with me, if I
get this position and leave New York," he said, by way of
changing the subject. " But that is out of the question, I
know. It would leave my grandparents too desolate, and
they would never consent to it. I presume my grandfather
will rebel against my plans, and call them needless."

" What are your plans ? "

" I thought of taking upon myself the education of the
little girls."

" The very best thing you could do—the simplest and the
wisest."

" Charlie, you know," Philip continued, " has no taste for
study ; he could not be induced to go to school another year,
much less to college, and is waiting impatiently for a vacancy
in grandfather's warehouse. He has such a passion for business, that I think he will succeed, and soon support himself,
besides being able, in time, to relieve grandfather, and perhaps carry on the business himself."

. So they talked on of Philip's plans and prospects till a
late hour. The crimson room, which he had occupied for a

month after Mr. Russell's visit to his "den," was still called Mr. Ventnor's room, and was at his disposal whenever he chose to spend a night in town. At his mother's and grand-parents' entreaty, he had gone home to live, instead of taking a room in the city, when he persisted in leaving Mr. Russell's house; and of late he had been so busy with his book, that he had hardly left the country at all, much to the delight of his family, whose comfort and satisfaction in him seemed to know no bounds.

Mr. Russell said to Philip the next morning, as they sat at breakfast, "I look for my aunt to-morrow morning, and the day after I wish you would come in the afternoon and drive with us, and of course come home to dinner, and spend the night. My aunt is coming from a house full of gay young people, and she will feel the change to one with only a staid old bachelor in it."

Mr. Russell met Mrs. More at the boat the next morning. "You did not come alone, did you?" he asked, when he had returned her affectionate greeting. "I thought James was coming with you."

"So he did," she replied, "but he is looking for Chloe: she has been missing for a half-hour, and I cannot imagine where she is."

"And who is Chloe?" Mr. Russell asked.

"Why, she is a little colored girl that I brought from home," Mrs. More explained. "She is such an erratic little thing, there is no telling what she has done with herself."

Just then her son appeared, and, having shaken hands with his cousin, he said, laughing, "Your attendant has come to light, mother. Follow me, and behold her in a new character."

Mrs. More and Mr. Russell went through the saloon and down the stairs, where the first object that met their eyes was Chloe emerging from the cabin, her hat hanging around her neck by the elastic, leaving her little tufts of wool to bob about unconfined, the cape of her brown linen travelling-dress all crumpled and askew—with a fat, red-faced child of some

two years in her arms, under whose weight she staggered
and gasped. Following her uncertain steps came the mother
of the child, a strapping Irish woman, with two children
tugging at her dress, and her arms filled with bundles and
bags. Most of the passengers had left the boat, but a few
remained, and there was a general laugh at Chloe's expense,
in which Mrs. More joined.

She was about to call to her preoccupied waiting-maid,
but Mr. Russell exclaimed, " Wait, Aunt Clara, and see what
she will do."

So, oblivious of every thing but her weighty charge,
Chloe trudged along, the mother calling, " Get on wid ye,"
" Don't go an' fall over the side, now," and so on. When
they were safely off the plank, Chloe, apparently unable to
hold the child another instant, dropped him on the ground so
suddenly, that he screamed loudly, and the mother raised her
hand to administer a blow by way of punishment for her
want of ceremony in dumping the child; but Chloe sprang-
aside and darted across the plank, nearly running against
Mrs. More and the two gentlemen.

" Chloe ! " Mrs. More exclaimed, " what a looking child
you are ! Put on your hat, and straighten your cape."

As they left the boat, Mr. Russell noticed that Chloe
watched her chance, when the indignant mother, who was
waiting for her baggage to be landed, was busy with the
other children, and thrust a piece of cake from her own
pocket into the hand of the child she had befriended.

" What were you doing to that poor little boy, Chloe ? "
Mr. More asked, when they were seated in the carriage.

Chloe hung her head, and twisted her fingers, and answered, " I warn't a-doin' nuffin with him. His mar beat him
awful, an' said he'd got to walk 'long of hisself; an' I fotched
him, so's he wouldn't haf to."

" That was very good of you, Chloe," said Mrs. More.

" Weren't you sorry you did it, when his mother was
about to beat you ? " asked Mr. More.

Mrs. More said, " Hush, James, my dear ! " while Chloe

looked somewhat surprised, and uttered a faint " No," under her breath.

Every thing was as cheerful and pleasant as Janet knew how to make it for Mrs. More's visit. But her " lead of mind " was to severe order and immaculate neatness, rather than to homelike taste and grace and comfort; and as Mrs. More looked about the rooms, where not a speck of dust could be found, or a chair or book that was not at sharp angles with every other chair and book, without the smallest thing to show the presence of a graceful woman's hand, she sighed to think how different it was once, and how different it might have been now, if—" Ah, well," she thought, " *that* was never to be. But I must hope that Robert will know what it is to have love in his home some time. I wish I could see him as happy as he deserves to be."

" What a blessing it is to have you here, Aunt Clara ! " Mr. Russell said, as they sat in the library that evening. " I have felt for the past few months as if I belonged to another age—as if I had lived on beyond my time; it is so long since I have had any body to take care of me, or to call me by my Christian name. I think I will not let you go away, but will keep you here with me. Now, isn't it too bad for you to live by yourself on a prairie-farm, Clara by herself in St. Louis, and I by myself in New York ? "

" I do think it too bad for Clara not to come and live with you, Robert. She is young, and could more easily break away from old ties than I could. Why, my dear, only think how many years I have lived in that very same house, and how old I am ! "

" It is worth while to be old, to have such soft white curls as yours, Aunt Clara, and such serene, quiet eyes. I should think all the young girls would envy you."

" Foolish boy ! " Mrs. More said ; and she added, " Yes, Clara and her children must come to you—unless you find somebody else whom you can love well enough to bring here."

Mr. Russell answered, lightly, that he was too old and set in his ways for that.

"You are not old, Robert; you are just in the prime of life."

"Look at these gray hairs!" said Mr. Russell, dropping on his knee before her.

"Only here and there one," she replied, laying her hand fondly on his head. "Ah, my dear, how well I remember when the letter came, telling us—your uncle and me—that a boy was born to this house; it seems such a little time ago! We were in our log-cabin then; how happy we were together, your uncle and I, and your dear father and mother, too. No, Robert, I cannot have you live on in this way. It strikes a chill to my heart to think of you alone in this great house."

"Do you think I am such poor company, Aunt Clara? I do get tired of myself sometimes, but not often, and I am by no means unhappy in my solitude."

"I know you are not unhappy, my dear; you have learned too well the secret of contentment for that. But you are not happy and satisfied as you ought to be, and might be. It is not possible. I wish I knew of somebody who was good enough for you," she added, playfully putting the hair back from his forehead. "Your eyes are like your father's, Robert, and I should love you for that, even if I saw you now for the first time, and did not know how well you deserve to be loved."

"How pleasant it is to hear you say such things, Aunt Clara—to feel that you love me because the same blood runs in our veins. But if there is nobody good enough for me, then there is no help for my remaining in single-wretchedness; for you surely would not have me take up with any body that was less perfect than myself."

Mrs. More shook her head a little sadly, for she feared that there were pressing memories underneath that playful tone.

"What a flying visit I made you last winter," Mr. Russell said, after a pause. "It was little better than none at all. Every thing looked so homelike and winsome, that I felt like settling down and spending the rest of my days under your wing—though I must make two exceptions to that 'every thing,' I believe. How are my kinswomen, Mrs. Rice and her daughter—what is her name, she of the drab hair and melancholy visage?"

"Fie, Robert!" exclaimed Mrs. More. "Lucinda would feel very badly if she knew that you could speak of her so, and had forgotten her name. She remembers you with cousinly interest."

"Does she, indeed?" said Mr. Russell. "Well, my remembrance of her is really quite vivid, too, owing to the fact that she never left the room while I was there, not giving me one moment to visit with you alone, and hardly took her pale-blue, mournful orbs from the contemplation of my poor face. I really had sensations of bashfulness under her steady gaze."

"Poor Lucinda!" said Mrs. More, gently; "she is good-natured, and really has some fine traits; but she has been injudiciously brought up, and she has some foolish notions. She undertook to teach Chloe."

"Did she?" said Mr. Russell, laughing. "I'll venture to say that she tried to teach her the dead languages before she knew her letters, and made her learn long, sentimental poems, to say by heart."

"I do not know how she managed, quite, but I thought it was well to bring the child away with me; and, really, she is a very handy little girl, and waits upon me very nicely—when there is nothing to distract her attention."

"Very well put in, I should say, my dear Aunt," Mr. Russell remarked.

"The poor thing came to us in the strangest way," Mrs. More went on. "She walked into Honora's room one cold night last winter, half frozen and half starved, with an incoherent story of long wanderings and sufferings, and of the happy home she had been dragged away from. She never has ceased to this day to refer every now and then to a kind lady whom she calls 'Miss Marg'et,' and loves with her whole simple soul. I never attempted to find out where 'Miss Marg'et' lived, and restore Chloe to her, for it seemed useless; it must have been so very far from us, from her

accounts. But the child lives in the hope of finding her
'Miss Marg'et' some day. You can't grieve her more than
by suggesting a doubt of that."

"Poor child! she has had quite a history, hasn't she ?"

At that moment a door opened slowly in the hall, and
shuffling, irregular steps were heard. Presently Chloe appeared, twisting her tongue, and looking very shy.

"What will you have, Chloe ? Come in," said Mr. Russell, pleasantly.

Chloe came inside the door, and edged herself into the
nearest corner.

"Well, Chloe, what is it ?" asked Mrs. More.

"Is dat ar Massa Russell ?" she asked in a whisper, nodding her head at Mr. Russell.

"Yes, Chloe, I am Mr. Russell," he said, foreseeing that
his aunt was about to send her away.

"Miss 'Cinder tole me to guv um dat ar," she said, sidling
up to him, and handing him a little package tied with white
satin ribbon.

"Why, Chloe, what is that ? Are you sure Miss Lucinda
gave it you for Mr. Russell ?" asked Mrs. More in surprise.

"Yes 'm, she did. She give it to me the mornin' we
come off," answered Chloe, while her eyes furtively admired
the bookcases and bright hangings of the room ; "an' she
tole me I mus' nebber show it to any livin' body 'ceptin'
Massa Russell, an' I fotched it all de way in yer," thrusting
her hand into her pocket, "an' I ain't showed it to nobody."

"Have you looked at it yourself, Chloe ?" asked Mr.
Russell, examining with an amused air the soiled appearance
of the ribbon, and the various folds of the wrapper.

Chloe hung her head almost to her knees, and found great
difficulty in making any answer ; but at last she said, "'Specks
I did, an' dat's de trufe," and darted out of the room.

Mr. Russell and Mrs. More laughed heartily, while
with a great assumption of care and curiosity, Mr. Russell
opened the package, which was found to contain a couple of
verses, mournfully referring to their too brief meeting and

sad parting, besides a very elaborate book-mark, with some mysterious device and appropriate inscription.

When Mrs. More had seen the mark and read the verses, she exclaimed, "Is it possible! Well, I never dreamed that even poor Lucinda could be so foolish."

"Perhaps the fair Lucinda would listen to my suit," exclaimed Mr. Russell. "You didn't think of her, when you said there was nobody good enough for me; did you?"

"Oh, Robert, I wouldn't have believed you could be guilty of such vanity. Can't you receive a simple expression of cousinly regard without making such unbecoming speeches?" At the same time, she could not help feeling very much amused to think that Lucinda's Lost Love was found.

"'I 'specks I did, an' dat's de trufe,'" replied Mr. Russell, as he sat playing with the book-mark. "Is Chloe generally so straightforward?"

"She is very truthful," replied Mrs. More. "I have not known her to tell an untruth since she came to me."

"That is quite remarkable," said Mr. Russell. "I suppose she learned it from 'Miss Marg'et.'"

Mr. More came late in the evening, having been detained down-town by business. "I met a gentleman on the street to-day," he said, in the course of conversation, "who is anxious to see you, Robert—Mr. Doane, from St. Louis."

"Mr. Doane? Oh, yes, I remember him well. I saw him two or three times when I was in St. Louis in the winter, and liked him very much."

"I met him at Clara's, too, before her husband died," Mr. More said.

"I should like to see him again, and know him better," said Mr. Russell. "I will call on him to-morrow."

"I told him I thought you would," said Mr. More, "and he gave me his address for you."

"I will invite him here to dinner. I wish to make it as gay for Aunt Clara as I can, so that she will not be in a hurry to leave me."

# CHAPTER XXI.

Into thy dutiful life of uses,
   Pour the music and weave the flowers;
With the song of birds and bloom of meadow
   Lighten and gladden thy heart and hours.    WHITTIER.

"How fresh and sparkling every thing looks this morning after the rain," said Mr. Russell, turning from the window in the dining-room, where he and his aunt and Philip Ventnor lingered after breakfast.

"Is there any thing in that little square enclosure to be refreshed by a shower?" asked Philip, looking out. "Yes, there's one small tree and a grape-vine."

"Besides grass, and Janet's lady-slippers and rose-bushes," added Mr. Russell. "You ought not to despise small things, Philip. I don't believe Aunt Clara would scorn our poor bits of nature, though she is used to looking out upon the prairies."

"I shouldn't scorn a patch of grass, however small, and I don't think Mr. Ventnor would either. But I am afraid I should feel pent-up and stifled to live in the city."

"Such a pleasant plan has just occurred to me!" exclaimed Mr. Russell. "Philip, are you sure you must go home to-day?"

"Yes, I believe I must; the family will expect me."

"Aunt Clara, do you feel very strong indeed—strong enough to take a long drive into the country?."

"I think I do. You know I ride a great deal at home, so that it does not tire me as it would most persons of my age."

"Well, I have some very particular friends who live about fifteen miles from here, up the river. I have been waiting for an opportunity to pay them a visit; and to-day strikes me as the very one of all others. It is not too warm, the dust is laid, and the country is in its glory. Philip, we'll drop you at your grandfather's gate, if you like a drive and our company better than the railroad."

"Let Mrs. More rest at my grandfather's," said Philip, eagerly. "My mother and grandmother would be delighted to see you both."

"I think it will not be possible, Philip. My friends are only a few miles farther on, and we should hardly have time to rest twice, and reach home before dark."

"My dear, you forget that your St. Louis friend is to dine with you to-day," said Mrs. More.

"Not to-day, Aunt Clara; I invited him for to-morrow."

In the course of an hour the carriage was at the door.

"Chloe, run and tell Janet that we are waiting for her," said Mr. Russell, when his aunt and Philip were seated.

Chloe dashed into the house, and returned a moment after, carrying a basket, followed by Janet with a pail and another basket.

"Hello," said Philip, "it's to be a picnic, is it, and I'm to be left at my grandfather's gate!"

"It isn't a picnic—it's a visit," replied Mr. Russell, "and you can't go. Please to sit on the back seat, beside my aunt. I want to sit opposite, where I can look at her all the time. There! I believe we are all ready. Why, where is Janet going?"

"To give her parting blessing to Chloe, I fancy," said Philip.

Janet took Chloe's unwilling hand, led her up the steps, and put her into the house. When she had done that, and shut the door emphatically upon her, she hurried back to her place beside the coachman, saying, "I humbly beg your pardon, Mr. Robert, but I couldn't leave that child on the sidewalk, an' the house-door open.

"Poor Chloe!" said Mrs. More, deprecatingly; "she doesn't mean to be troublesome, but she certainly is, and I may take the blame to myself for bringing her from home."

"I am very much obliged to you for bringing her," said Mr. Russell; "there she is now—her head, at least, thrust

11

out of the door, to take a farewell look at us. What a com-
ical head it is ! She is out upon the steps now, and is danc
ing a jig. What would Janet say if she could see her ? She
would consider the Russell family irremediably disgraced."

"Why do you take Janet and pails and baskets with
you, Robert?" asked Mrs. More.

"You know your own arrangements best, I suppose," she
added, after looking for a moment into his smiling face; "I
only hope Chloe will not get into mischief."

"Martha will look after her," Mr. Russell replied; "my
anxiety is, lest you should be tired before we get out of the
city. I wish we could annihilate these three or four miles
of pavement, for your sake."

"My mind may grow weary with trying to make this
wonderful reality seem like any thing but a dream. That
is all. Why, my dear, when your uncle and I were married,
and took a house a mile from the Battery, where your grandfather lived, we thought we were going quite out of town.
And when your father wrote us, after we went West, that he
was going to build still further up, we were sure he had
made a mistake, and would regret it. Now to think that
his house is in the heart of the city, with miles and miles of
houses beyond it ! I can hardly credit my senses."

"I think you must feel very much as the king in the fairy
tale did, who woke one morning to find a grand palace, where
there had been an open space the night before," Philip said.

"It does seem like magic," Mrs. More replied. "New
York is a wonderful place, a very rich and gay place, but I
cannot believe people enjoy themselves any more than they
did in the good old times when I was a girl."

"Aunt Clara," said Mr. Russell, "did you ever hear of
an exploit of mine, that came very near being the end of
John and me, when we were boys?"

"Never," exclaimed Mrs. More.

"We were spending the day at grandfather's, and were
sent out to play under the care of the nurse, with many
charges to behave ourselves; notwithstanding which, Jack

and I got into a discussion as to our respective rights to some plaything, and as my fiery, rash temper reached its height just as we came to the water's edge, I gave Jack a push that sent him off the pier."

"Oh, Robert! I can hardly believe it," cried Mrs. More.

"It is true, my dear aunt. In a twinkling I had jumped in after him, and a man, who happened to be close by, followed, and saved us both."

"What must your poor mother and grandmother have felt when you were carried home," Mrs. More exclaimed.

"We were not taken home pale and dripping, as you might suppose, for the brave man who rescued us took us to his house, which was near by, and we were put to bed while our clothes were dried. I believe neither of us felt any bad effects from our cold bath."

"I wonder if any boy ever grew up without just escaping the doing of some deed that would have clouded his whole life?" said Philip.

"Boys will be boys," said Mrs. More. "None were ever more wild and mischievous than mine; yet I have no cause to complain of them now."

"I should think not, Aunt Clara!" said Mr. Russell, smiling at the sweet complacency of her expression.

"Or of my nephews either, Robert," she added, "if one of them did nearly drown his brother and himself too."

It was about noon when they stopped at Mr. Tapscott's to leave Philip.

"I suppose it is vain for me to urge you to come in," he said. "I feel very downcast at being so peremptorily dispensed with, and very envious."

"Console yourself by coming to us in town very soon, Philip."

"Yes, do so, Mr. Ventnor," said Mrs. More. "I should be sorry not to see you again, and my visit is not to be a long one, you know."

Philip expressed his thanks; and as they drove on, Mrs. More said, "Why did you not let Mr. Ventnor come, my

dear ?  Are you not well enough acquainted to take two
strangers, as well as one ? ''

"I am sure of a welcome for you, and indeed for any
friend, but I don't like to presume too much.  I may take
Philip some other time.  Did you ever know any thing
lovelier than this day and this scenery—the air so soft and
full of sweet sounds, the woods so fresh and green, the river
so sparkling ?  Then look at those blue hills away to the
north, and the Palisades, so bold and dark in the midst of
so much brightness.  I sometimes think I should like to buy
or build a little house somewhere on this river—"

"What, and give up the old home, Robert ? "

"No, I shall keep that always.  But I should like some
place where I could come, summer or winter, whenever I felt
like taking 'refuge in the bosom of Nature,' as the pensive
Lucinda expresses it in her poem."

"I think you are quite enough of a recluse now, Robert,
without possessing a hermitage in the country."

Just on the outskirts of one of the pretty villages, a little
back from the main road, the carriage stopped.

"Is this the place, Robert ? " asked Mrs. More, looking
with some surprise at the small cottage, with a little garden
behind and a little yard in front.

"Yes, this is the place.  That large tree shades you
nicely—I will ask you to excuse me, while I go and announce
you and myself."

A little girl, nearly hidden in a calico sun-bonnet, sat on
the doorstep, with a sleepy-looking dog in her arms, which
she had arrayed in one of her own dresses, and whose head
and paws and tail alone were visible.

"Little Mary, how do you do, and how is Ponto to-day ? "
asked Mr. Russell, as he opened the gate.

The child threw back her sun-bonnet, disclosing a face all
crimson, and curls dampened with the exertion of managing
her clumsy plaything.  When she saw Mr. Russell, she pushed
Ponto off her lap, and running with her arms outstretched,
threw them around his neck as he stooped to receive her.

"How is your mother, little one?" he asked.

"She is velly well. She's teaching school to the little child'ens."

"And where is Paul?"

"He's s'ovelling dirt in the garden. I will go yight and tell him you is come."

"I'll go with you," Mr. Russell said, taking her hand; but she espied poor Ponto making frantic efforts to disrobe himself, and gathering him and his draperies up in her arms, she trudged along by Mr. Russell's side, prattling to him very busily.

"Paul, Paul, here's Mr. Yussell," she cried as soon as she saw her brother.

Paul was energetically hoeing corn, but he quickly dropped his hoe, and his hands were clasped in Mr. Russell's, while yet the exclamation of joyful surprise was on his lips.

"I never was so glad in my life," he said fervently.

"I am delighted to see you looking so well, my dear boy. Hoeing corn agrees with you, does it not?"

"Every thing agrees with me here. I am well and strong, and as happy as I can be. I feel as if I am living a week in a day, I have so much to enjoy; and mother and the children are so well too. But come in, Mr. Russell, and let them see you."

"I will go and tell them you is come," said little Mary, trudging away with her dog.

"You are an accomplished gardener, Paul, if this is all your work," said Mr. Russell, looking over the nice, even beds, where the green heads of various vegetables stood in regular rows, with not a weed among them.

"I did most of it, though Edith and Angelica helped. As soon as I was well enough I made the beds and we put in the seeds. You never saw any thing grow so fast as they do. We have had lettuce and radishes already."

"Has it been very hard for you to keep from painting, Paul?"

"I have longed for it sometimes, but I was willing to

wait, after all, for I knew it was better that I should. But don't you think that I may begin your picture soon?"

"I think you may; you look very well, though your cheeks are rather too thin yet. Well, Angelica and Edith! why, what blooming little maidens you have grown to be," he said, as the two children came flying out of the house to meet him, followed by Mrs. Sarelli, while some dozen eyes peered out through the blinds at the visitor.

"I have brought my aunt to see you, Mrs. Sarelli," Mr. Russell said, as they walked towards the front of the house. "I knew you would all love her at first sight, and therefore felt no hesitation about bringing her with me."

"Mrs. Sarelli assured him of the gratification it was to her to receive any friend of his, and Mr. Russell led the way to the carriage, where his aunt awaited them; and by the time they were seated in the little parlor, and Angelica had laid away Mrs. More's hat and shawl, the children had forgotten that she was a stranger, and Mrs. Sarelli felt free to excuse herself and return to her schoolroom for another hour.

"My aunt will spend that time in lying down and getting rested for her visit and her drive home," Mr. Russell said.

In a few minutes Angelica came with a cup of tea and a dainty bit of bread and butter for Mrs. More, and then showed her to Mrs. Sarelli's bedroom, a mere atom of a room, but pretty and tasteful, with its muslin curtains, snowy bed, and home-made toilet-stand.

In the meantime, while Mr. Russell and Paul sat on the doorstep, with little Mary playing at their feet, Janet took her baskets to the kitchen; and by the time school was over, leaving Mrs. Sarelli at liberty, and Mrs. More had risen, refreshed by her nap, a most tempting lunch was ready, of strawberries and cream, bread and butter, cold meats and other good things, and all were summoned to enjoy it.

Afterwards, there was time for a walk to the hill near by, from which Paul's picture for Mr. Russell was to be painted, and then Mrs. More and Mr. Russell bade their friends good by.

"What a lovely family," exclaimed Mrs. More, as the group at the gate were hidden from view by the trees. "Mrs. Sarelli is one of the sweetest women I have ever met, and every one of the children is really beautiful. But where did you become acquainted with them, Robert? You seem to have known them a long time."

"Only since I came home from China, Aunt Clara. But they lived in the city until within two or three months, you know. I saw them quite often there."

"I gathered from your conversation with Paul that he is going to be an artist."

"Yes, he will be an artist, and an eminent one, if he lives. He was so ill last winter that I feared he would never paint again; but he seems quite well now, and I think, with care, he may entirely outgrow his predisposition to consumption. His father was an artist, and taught him all he knows of painting; but he has genius that must be developed, and as soon as he is strong enough, he must study with some first-rate master—perhaps go to Italy, in time."

"Has Mrs. Sarelli any property, or is she entirely dependent upon her school? I should think that would hardly support them."

"She owns the house, and her school pays very well; Paul's pictures, too, will sell readily, and bring good prices, when he begins to paint."

"I have enjoyed this day very much, Robert. I would not have missed it for a great deal."

The carriage was barely out of sight in the morning, when Martha, the housemaid, who had been charged by Janet to keep a sharp eye upon Chloe, found her dancing on the door-steps. Calling her in, she administered a rebuke as much after the manner of the grave Janet as possible, and taking her into the kitchen, set her at such little tasks as she considered her capable of. When she had finished her own labors in that department, she armed herself with broom

and dusters, and said patronizingly to Chloe, "Now you
may come along with me, an' see me sweep an' dust, an'
that's all you can do.  It takes experience to do up such
rooms as them."

Chloe looked on while Martha covered the furniture in
the library, listening in mute admiration while she enlivened
her work with repetitions of Janet's tales of the grand doings there used to be in that house.

"Now, Chloe," said Martha, when the library was in
order, "stay right where you are, an' don't presume to come
acrost the floor an' look in here where I'm agoin'.  It's Mr.
Russell's privit sittin'-room, an' nobody is privileged to come
into't but me an' Janet.  Now, mind, don't you come anigh
the door."

Chloe had great ado to keep her feet from walking
straight into the forbidden room.  She could only restrain
them at the last by sitting down on the floor, and holding
herself back by the leg of the table.

"My sakes alive, Chloe!" cried Martha, when she appeared with her duster, "let loose of that leg.  You'll get it
full of finger-marks.  Come right out of this room, before
you spile every thing there is in it ; " and she hastily caught
her broom and Chloe's hand, and departed to the kitchen.
In all probability, nothing out of the common course of
things would have occurred, but for the fact that Martha,
having occasion to go to the street-door late in the afternoon,
espied an acquaintance passing, and notwithstanding her careful training by the severely unsocial Janet, she so far forgot
herself as to invite her friend into the house.  In the gossip
that followed, Chloe was shut out of the kitchen, and wholly
forgotten.

It did not take her long to appreciate this happy state of
things, and it was natural enough that she should wish to
improve it, which she did by instituting a little exploring
expedition, and that without loss of time, knowing that her
liberty was liable to be cut short at any moment.

She went first to the great, darkened drawing-room, and

took a few turns before the long mirror. This, under other circumstances, would have been unspeakably entertaining, as she had had few opportunities to view herself at full length, and to observe the effect of her characteristic evolutions. But now it had only power to detain her for two or three minutes; and having softly shut the heavy mahogany door, she as softly entered the library. She made the circuit of the room, carefully inspecting every thing, as if each particular article of furniture was the greatest curiosity she had ever seen, or ever hoped to see, until she came to the door leading to the mysterious place where all her longings centered.

"Whar *does* dis yer go to?" she said to herself with an air of surprise. "I'se jes' gwine to open it, and peek in: I ain't gwine in, an' dat's de trufe."

Contrary to her declared intentions, she did go in, and, somehow, the door closed behind her; and after a general survey, she proceeded to examine each thing separately.

"Oh, laus! ain't dis yer beaut'ful!" she exclaimed, under her breath.

It was an old-fashioned desk, of some dark wood, elaborately carved and inlaid; it was open; too, showing the purple velvet with which the writing-table was lined.

"If dat ar ain't mos' beaut'ful!" she repeated; and her courage waxing with her admiration, she speedily mounted a chair, and after twisting the key in the door of the upright part for some time, she succeeded in turning it. An array of little drawers and shelves met her eyes that nearly set her wild with delight. She peered into the drawers one after the other, but found nothing that irresistibly attracted her fingers, until she opened one which contained, besides some dried leaves and faded flowers, a little box. Should she touch the box? Yes, she should, and she did, and looked at the contents—a velvet locket—her eyes growing bigger and bigger as she gazed. In a moment her eager fingers seized the locket, and, without taking her eyes from it, she dropped the box, got slowly down from the chair, and seating herself

upon the floor, rocked back and forth, too absorbed to hear
Martha's anxious call, or the ringing of the bell, or voices
in the hall, and there she sat when Mr. Russell entered.

His first feeling was one of amusement, to see that queer
little object sitting on the floor, and the bewildered look with
which she scrambled to her feet; but the next was one of
extreme vexation, as his eye fell on the open desk and the
open drawer.

"Chloe," he exclaimed sternly, "what have you been
doing?"

Chloe could only hang her head, too much abashed to
speak, or look up or move, only that she still fumbled for her
pocket with her right hand, and Mr. Russell saw that she had
something in it.

"Chloe, come here, and give me whatever you have taken
from my desk."

Then Chloe began to cry piteously, exclaiming, between
her sobs, "Oh, don't take it away! please don't take it
away!"

"Chloe, stop crying instantly, and show me what you
have in your hand."

Chloe, awed by the stern command, slowly and reluctantly extended the locket towards Mr. Russell; but when
her eyes rested upon it again, she renewed her sobs and
entreaties, adding, "Dat ar's my Miss Marg'et, it are. Oh,
Massa Russell, please to gimme it! It's Miss Marg'et, an'
I want it awful bad."

She sobbed on unheeded for some minutes, her hand still
extended.

"Chloe," he said at length—and his voice was so strange
that Chloe took her dress from her eyes to look at him—
"that cannot be your 'Miss Marg'et.' Give me the picture."

"It are—it are Miss Marg'et; I know it are," she cried,
closing her hand again over the locket, and putting it behind
her.

There was another pause, and then Mr. Russell said, "Lay
the picture upon the table, Chloe, and leave the room."

The voice was kind, but Chloe did as she was told.

When Mr. Russell appeared at dinner, his aunt, who had heard a confused account of what had happened from Chloe, looked at him anxiously; but he appeared much as usual, and her loving eyes could detect no sign of pain. In the evening he told her quietly of the discovery Chloe had made, adding, "I know that Mr. Crosby's family are at the West somewhere, and it is not at all improbable that Chloe's 'Miss Marg'et' and Miss Margaret Crosby are identical. Indeed, every thing I have heard of 'Miss Marg'et' helps to convince me of it." There was a long silence, and then Mrs. More, who yearned to know what was in the sealed heart beside her, said, almost in a whisper, "Robert, tell me: if Chloe could direct you to her 'Miss Marg'et,' and you knew that it was your Margaret, would you go to her?"

"I have no Margaret, except in dreams, Aunt Clara. I should have no right to go to her, if she were ever so near. I ought to be thankful that I do not know where she is."

The next morning Mrs. More said to Chloe, before going down-stairs, "Chloe, there are two things that you must remember while you are here. One is, that you are not to go near the room where you went last night; and the other is, that you must not ask for the picture, or even speak of it to any body. I should be very much displeased with you if you did."

"I want to see dat ar ag'in, anyhow," Chloe said, nearly crying.

"Of course it is out of the question, child. It belongs to Mr. Russell, and you must not ask for it, and had better not think about it any more."

Not to think about it was an impossibility; and not to wish that she had taken it away the moment she found it, and had it safely tied around her neck under her dress, was beyond her power; and it was almost more than she could do to keep from dropping on her knees whenever she saw Mr. Russell that day, and begging him to give her 'Miss Marg'et.' At times she was possessed with a sense of the injustice of any body's claiming that picture, and keeping it from her, when she could almost have braved every thing, and gone straight to the forbidden room to seize the coveted treasure.

Her thoughts were diverted, and her curiosity was put upon the alert by the solemn charge she received from Janet, as the dinner was about to be sent up, to stay down-stairs, and keep perfectly quiet. She had been remarkably quiet all day, and, if left to herself, it would probably have never entered her head to forsake the corner where she had been sitting for an hour watching the preparations for dinner.

But Janet's injunction put every thought to flight but the one : how could she escape unobserved from the kitchen, and how could she get up-stairs to see what was going on ?

A little skilful management soon effected the first, and a little more hid her safely behind the door of the butler's pantry, where she had the intense satisfaction of seeing, through the crack, Mrs. More, Mr. Russell, and Mr. Doane, seated at dinner, and Reuben, arrayed in broadcloth and white gloves, waiting upon them. But she soon grew tired of watching the progress of other people's dinner, and there was nothing especially entertaining to her in the conversation. It was a little exciting at first to be in a safe place, and see the staid Reuben pass so close to it, as he went to and fro ; but even that became an old story, and wondering if she should get out as safely as she got in, her eyes fell on so much that called for inspection on the shelves, that she forgot the need of keeping out of sight, and was presently reminded of it by a gentle but admonitory " Chloe ! " from the dining-room. With one glance at the three faces turned towards her, she darted out of the pantry and down-stairs into the front basement, where Janet found her, a few minutes after, having but just missed her from the kitchen. As she was innocently looking from the window, and as Reuben did not take the trouble to mention her exploit in the pantry, she escaped the scolding she had anticipated down-stairs ; and she knew that Mrs. More's reproof would be gentle. Her unexpected safety had a very exhilarating effect upon her spirits, and prepared her to accept any further diversion that offered, without hesitation.

When her dinner was eaten, she returned to the window to watch the children playing in the street, and presently a man with a hand-organ and a girl with a tambourine stopped before the house. The fact that Janet had forbidden her to go out upon the sidewalk may have added zest to her desire to get there as soon as possible ; it certainly did not deter her for an instant. The suppressed energies of many days were speedily finding vent in a wild, fantastic plantation-dance, to the music of the organ and the tambourine, and no little commotion ensued, as all the children gathered around, jumping and shouting. Mr. Russell went to the window to see what was the matter, and Mrs. More and Mr. Doane followed.

"Oh, Robert! what shall I do with the child?" exclaimed Mrs. More, amused, and yet dismayed. "I shall have to keep her shut up the rest of the time I am here."

"There is no harm in her having a dance, Aunt Clara, and entertaining those children, to say nothing of myself. I never saw any thing funnier in my life."

Mr. Doane looked on for a moment, then, turning to Mrs. More, said, "Did you call her Chloe? I think you did, at the table."

"Her name is Chloe," she replied. "She is a good child at heart, but so full of pranks that I can hardly manage her. If I had known that she would develop such wild propensities, I should never have ventured to bring her from home."

"Then she has not lived with you very long?"

"Only since last winter," Mrs. More replied.

"Janet has come to disperse the children and the music, and Chloe's fun is at an end," said Mr. Russell, ringing the bell; when Martha appeared, he told her to send Chloe up.

"What are you going to do, my dear?" asked Mrs. More.

"Only to give the child something to amuse herself with;" and he went into the dining-room, taking with him some old illustrated magazines. Mr. Doane looked after him with a curious expression in his bright blue eyes.

"Janet is rather hard on Chloe," Mr. Russell said, as he came back. "It would be too bad to spoil her dance by punishing her for it."

Mr. Doane replied rather absently to some remark of Mr. Russell's, and said to Mrs. More, "Where did you find Chloe, Mrs. More? I don't wonder that you look surprised at my question, but the truth is, I have heard of one Chloe to whose description this Chloe answers so perfectly, that I am curious to know if they are not one and the same."

Mrs. More glanced at Mr. Russell, but replied, "Chloe came to my house last winter in great distress, and I pitied her, and gave her a home."

"Do you know any thing of her previous history?" asked Mr. Doane—"how she came to be a wanderer, and where she had lived?"

"She was stolen, I believe, and ran away from those who stole her; but I never have had any definite idea as to where her home was."

"Does she mention no names?" asked Mr. Doane.

"She calls her mistress 'Miss Marg'et.'"

The blood rushed to Mr. Doane's face, but he said, with an effort, "I am sure there can be no doubt but that this is the Chloe whose story I heard in St. Louis. She was stolen by a man and woman named Simon and Nancy Stubbs; was she not?"

"Yes, those certainly were the names she used to repeat in such terror—Simon and Nance."

"An accidental meeting with these people occasioned my hearing of Chloe's misfortunes. I wish her friends knew of her safety and comfort."

"In St. Louis did you hear her story, Mr. Doane?" Mrs. More questioned.

"Yes, in St. Louis  The sister of Chloe's mistress is the

wife of my cousin, Dr. Doane, and I met her at my cousin's house."

"Whom did your cousin marry?" asked Mrs. More, the question coming almost in spite of herself.

"He married Mrs. Sinclair, who was a Miss Crosby," Mr. Doane answered. "Do you know the family, Mrs. More?"

"No," she replied, "I do not;" and the involuntary emphasis she gave to the pronoun, together with her equally involuntary glance, carried Mr. Doane's eyes inquiringly to Mr. Russell's face.

"I knew the family some years ago, before I went to China," said Mr. Russell, in answer to the look of inquiry.

"Mr. Crosby is dead," said Mr. Doane; "he died soon after my cousin's marriage."

"Does Miss Crosby live with her sister now?" asked Mrs. More.

"She spent a few weeks there after her father's death, but she has returned home. I believe her plans for the future are not determined upon."

"Is her home near St. Louis?" asked Mrs. More.

"It is quite a distance from St. Louis—nearer to a little place called Jonesville, I believe, than any other town."

"Is it possible!" exclaimed Mrs. More; "only fifteen miles from my home!"

# CHAPTER XXII.

And what is this place not seen,
Where hearts may hide serene?
'Tis a fair, still house well kept,
Which humble thoughts have swept,
And holy prayers made clean.

MRS. BROWNING.

IT was a warm, still, dreamy afternoon in July. The woods skirting the prairies were veiled in a light blue haze; the breeze, that was like a soft whisper from the blue sky, just stirred the leaves and quivered in the grass; the birds sung sleepy little snatches of songs; the hens talked in a lazy undertone to their downy families as they hunted for savory bits; even the distant noise of the reaping and mowing machines, and the call of the men to their teams, were droning sounds. Under the trees in front of the farm-house stood the tea-table, its snowy cover gleaming in contrast with the green grass, and its contents looking very inviting while in the kitchen a demure little figure flitted about, preparing supper for the men, who would soon be in from the field, and the tea-kettle's drowsy hum was in tune with the rest.

Margaret, sitting in the doorway, felt the pleasant languor of the scene, and let her eyes wander from her book over the sunny fields and hazy woods, while her thoughts followed their own sweet will, and they evidently chose the bright paths that day, as there was no hint of a shadow upon the fair face.

The days had passed busily and quickly since Margaret's return to the farm; for, while she had felt her father's death and missed her cares for him anew, almost as a fresh bereavement, she was able to put aside what she called her selfish grief, and devote herself to the improvement and amusement of the boys, and her indoor and outdoor duties, with unfeigned cheerfulness.

A fresh attack of rheumatism had made Miss Patty's sister so cross, that her friend forsook her, making it necessary for Patty to go home as soon as Margaret returned. Bridget continued to do the heavier work, while for the lighter tasks her oldest child, little Biddy, proved quite efficient; so that Margaret had the greater part of the morning for the boys' lessons, and the afternoons for reading and sewing. She seldom saw the boys from dinner till tea-time, for the harvest-field proved even a greater attraction than their aunt's society. It was wonderful how well Jotham obeyed her injunctions to keep them out of danger, and still more wonderful how patiently he submitted to their determination to have a hand in every thing that was done, from the time they left the house for the afternoon's work till they came in at night. Their ragged straw hats and crimson faces were as much a feature of that harvesting as the grass and the grain. Jotham used often to assure them, that, if they ever were obliged to work as hard as they did. then for the fun of it, they would think it " mighty dull business."

Margaret, in her solitude, often thought of some of the pleasant features of her visit to St. Louis. The long, quiet evenings, when the boys, tired out with their play, had gone to bed, and she had not even the diversion of diverting them, oppressed her sometimes, and she would long for a voice to break the profound stillness within and without. She would sometimes try to break it herself by a bit of a song, but it was little relief to hear her own voice, without even an echo to make her feel less solitary.

Yet she was, on the whole, contented, and could think of living on in this quiet way with less shrinking than of setting herself adrift, of having no place she could call her own—no niche in the great world to which she had an unquestioned, recognized right.

Dr. Doane had strongly, almost sternly at the last, urged her selling the farm and coming to live with them in the autumn; he had, at parting, assured her that he should come himself to see that it was done. But she was determined to make the summer as pleasant and profitable to herself and the boys as possible, leaving the future to take care of itself; she had a little hope that Dr. Doane might consent to leave the children with her, at least for the winter. That would make the way clear for her to remain, as the chief objection was her loneliness.

She had heard from the travellers twice, and each time it had been Dr. Doane who wrote. The last letter mentioned a change in their plans. Fanny had met some friends who were going to spend the rest of the summer at Saratoga and Newport, and she had decided to join them. Dr. Doane was to return home after spending a few days with her at the Springs. The tone of the letters was so changed from the happy, satisfied, lover-like letters she had received during the spring, that she felt saddened, and hopeless of the possi-bility of any thing like happiness for the husband and wife.

But none of these anxieties entered into her musings on that especial July day, as she sat in the doorway.

"The things is all ready now, Miss," Biddy said, coming around from the kitchen, and kneeling on the lower step in front of Margaret.

"Well, Jotham will soon be up from the field, Biddy. Suppose you run down and tell George and Jack that tea is ready; but you need not say that we are going to have it under the trees. We'll surprise them."

Biddy ran away to deliver her message, and soon after Dr. Somers drove up to the gate. He accosted Margaret with, "I thought there was something to pay, when I saw that dapper young man from St. Louis helping you from the cars—giving you such looks out of his eyes. Pretty doings, I must say!"

In the meantime he hunted in all his pockets, and by the time Margaret was beside the chaise with outstretched hand and smiling face, he had produced a letter, which he held at arm's-length, with a grim expression of countenance.

"A man's handwriting, you see, and post-marked New

York! I don't believe I'll give it to you, now; you look too pleased about it, and not at all surprised. If you have dared to take a decided step without asking leave of me!"

"No, indeed," laughed Margaret; "I haven't dared, and I never shall dare."

"I never should have known about the Skinner affair if he hadn't told me himself; and I never should have known that you corresponded with this one, if I hadn't happened to have business in Jonesville to-day."

"I do not correspond with Mr. Doane," exclaimed Margaret, still laughing at the doctor's fierce airs.

"Looks like it, doesn't it? I shall keep a sharp lookout, my young lady, and see what comes next. I suppose it'll be the young man himself. Will you promise to read the letter now and here, if I let you have it?"

"If I didn't, it would only be for the sake of showing that I am not to be domineered over to such an unheard-of degree," answered Margaret, receiving the letter and breaking the seal.

As she read the first few lines her face glowed with delight, and she exclaimed, "What do you think, Dr. Somers? Chloe is in New York, safe and happy." Then she read on, adding, with a hearty laugh, "Mr. Doane saw her dancing a jig to the music of a hand-organ and tambourine before——"

"Well, before what?" asked Dr. Somers, looking curiously into Margaret's face, which had flushed, and then grown white as her dress. She turned quickly away, as if to escape the doctor's scrutiny, but came back and said, without raising her eyes, "She is with a Mrs. More, and Mr. Doane saw her at the house where Mrs. More was visiting."

"I'm very glad to hear that the poor child's troubles are over, and glad your mind is set at ease about her," said the doctor, still watching Margaret's face. "But how came she in New York, I wonder? I suppose that man and woman, the Stubbses, took her there."

"No, she has been with Mrs. More most of the time since she left us; she took her to New York."

"Mrs. More? why, it must be Mrs. More, of Moresville
I know her very slightly. I'll take you to see her, and bring
Chloe home any day you like."

"No, no, I would not go there for the world!" exclaimed
Margaret, her face flushing again; then she added, more
quietly, "Mrs. More befriended her when she was suffering,
and I could not ask her to give her back to me now."

"But you might ride over and see Chloe, and hear what
she has to say for herself."

"I cannot go to Moresville," said Margaret, so decidedly
that Dr. Somers said no more about it.

"What! are you going to have a *fête champêtre*, and I
not invited!" he exclaimed, as he espied the tea-table under
the trees.

"The children and I are going to have one," answered
Margaret; "we'd like very much to have you come to it, if
you would."

"I wish I could, but I can't; I've got another call to
make. My wife will expect me home at least an hour before
she sees me. When have you seen Miss Patty? She is not
at all well, and her sister is intolerable."

"I will try to go there to-morrow," replied Margaret;
and Dr. Somers drove away, wondering what there could
have been in the letter. to move Margaret so strangely, and
why she so strongly objected to calling on Mrs. More.

Margaret had no time to think over the strange network
of circumstances which Mr. Doane's letter unfolded, for the
boys came racing into the house the back way, noisily de-
manding some salt; Jotham had said they might salt the
sheep.

"We will have tea first, my dears," said Margaret, "and
then I will go with you to the sheep-lot."

"That'll be jolly!" cried George; "but tea ain't ready,"
he cried again, bursting into the sitting-room; "Biddy, why
don't you set the table?"

"Georgie, I am going to make you feel a little ashamed
of your hasty conclusions. Come here, and see if tea is not

ready." Margaret led the boys to the front door, where they saw the table under the trees.

George did look a little ashamed for an instant, then threw his hat in the air, crying, "Oh my, what fun!" and he and Jack dashed off to their room to make themselves presentable. They soon came down, with nicely-brushed hair and clean faces and linen, bustled out with the chairs, and the three sat down—Georgie opposite Margaret, as he was "next oldest to her," and so entitled to that place of responsibility.

When they were seated, the boys bowed their heads, while Margaret said a simple grace; and, if the birds had sung ever so loud after that, they could not have been heard, for the boys talked so fast and laughed so much.

"Aunt Margaret," said George, "I cut as much as a whole acre of wheat to-day, all myself. I rode on the reaper, and drove the horses, and cut the wheat."

"Drove the horses!" cried Jack.

"Well, didn't I, now?"

"You had hold of the reins, but Mr. Simpkins walked ahead of 'em."

"Well, that's nothing; I cut the wheat, you know I did."

"I shouldn't think you would enjoy that very much," said Margaret. "Doesn't it shake you up pretty well, riding over the rough ground?"

"I guess it does," answered George; "but I don't mind that. I work like every thing down in the field."

"So do I," said Jack. "I was on the wagon while Jotham pitched up ever so many loads to-day, and I laid the bundles straight while he pitched. But what do you think I did once? I thought I'd drive on a little, and I got hold of the wrong rein, and pulled the horses round so that they 'most upset the load. I tell you! wasn't I scairt?"

"If I were a little boy, and almost tipped over a wagon, I am sure I should be frightened, instead of 'scairt,'" Margaret remarked.

"Jotham says 'scairt,'" replied Jack.

"Jotham says a good many things that you had better not say, Jack. But I am afraid you are too venturesome. It would have been a very serious thing if you had upset the load, and yourself with it. It frightens me to think what might have happened."

"I think, myself," said George, in a very grown-up manner, "that Jack is too little to do such things. If I were you, Aunt Margaret, I wouldn't let him."

"Ho!" cried Jack, "you're only two years older'n me—that ain't much."

"What shall I do, Jackie—and you too, Georgie—to make you remember your grammar?"

"I know what Jack ought to have said: 'You are only two years older than I am; that is not much'—only it is, a good deal."

"You might say, 'isn't' instead of 'is not.' But now let me tell you what I heard a little while ago. Dr. Somers brought me a letter from Mr. Doane, which says he has seen Chloe in New York."

"What, our little black Chloe!" cried George, "in New York? How did she get there? Did she go afoot and alone?"

"No; a kind lady who lives in Moresville has been taking care of her all this time, who took her to New York."

"Isn't she coming back to Moresville any more?"

"Oh, yes, I suppose she is there now, or will be in a few days."

"We'll go and get her as soon as ever she gets there, won't we? We can take the horses early in the morning, before Jotham wants them."

"No, Georgie, we are not going to ask Mrs. More for Chloe. I suppose Mr. Doane told her that Chloe had lived here, and if she chooses to give her back to us she will send her. But that is not at all likely; I have no idea that we shall see Chloe again. Biddy answers our purpose very well, don't you think so?"

"Oh, I think she does very well to wash dishes and

things like that, but she can't cut up shines and make fun like Chloe."

"All the better for the 'dishes and things like that,' Georgie, though I should really like to see Chloe again myself. I wonder if she looks and acts as she used to. But if we are going to salt the sheep we must hurry, for it is growing late. Let us take these things into the kitchen, and then we'll go."

"Let Biddy take them in," said George.

"Biddy wants to finish her work so that she can go home for a little while, and we may as well help her. Take these plates and saucers, and you, Jackie, take these things, and I will carry the rest. Don't tumble down, either of you, and break my china. Biddy," she said, as they went in procession into the kitchen, "you can wash these dishes before the men come up from the field, and when you have given them their tea and had your own, you may run home before you do the rest. Tell your mother that if the baby is troublesome, she need not come to-morrow."

"Thank you kindly, Miss," said Biddy, dropping a little curtsey, and Margaret put on her broad-brimmed sun-hat, and she and the boys started for the sheep-lot with a pan of salt.

"Aunt Margaret," said George, "ain't this a heap better than St. Louis? I don't mean ever to go back there, if I can possibly help it."

"You'll have to, though, after a while," said Jack, "when Mademoiselle comes there."

"Don't you say Mademoiselle to me again," exclaimed George, fiercely. "If I do go back, and she's there, I'll make her sorry I've come—see if I don't."

"I don't think we shall see any thing of the kind," said Margaret, laying her hand gently on George's shoulder.

"I want to stay here with Aunt Margaret till I'm big enough to go to China, and get my money, and then I shall come home, and build a house in New York, or 'round here somewhere, I don't know which yet, and Aunt Margaret shall have the biggest and handsomest room in it."

"Ain't you ever going to get married, Aunty?" asked Jack.

"Married!" exclaimed George, scornfully, "of course she won't get married, when she has me to take care of her."

"You are pretty small to take care of any body like Aunt Margaret," said Jack. "I should think she ought to have a grown-up man like Mr. Doane, or such."

"I shall be grown up some day, I guess. Am I always going to be small? Won't you let me take care of you, Aunty?"

"I feel very much flattered by your devotion, Georgie, and if you are of the same mind when you are grown up we will see."

"I must have somebody that's beautiful, like you, in my house, because it will be as grand and fine as any thing you ever saw in all your life. Wait—I'll let down the bars for you," and with an air of boyish gallantry that was quite new to him, and that pleased while it amused Margaret, he took down the bars and stood back for her to pass through.

The children called the sheep, which came in a body from the further side of the lot, and crowded around, eager for the salt which was being thrown on the grass. The boys watched them curiously, singling out the greedy ones for the smaller share, and the meeker ones, who seemed less inclined to push their way and assert themselves, for an extra handful.

"I never saw a 'lamb whose fleece was white as snow,' like the one that Mary took to school, did you, Aunt Margaret?"

"No, Georgie, I cannot say that I ever did."

"I think they are good little things, but I don't think they are very pretty, and they look as silly as any thing when they are all huddled together, with their heads down to keep cool. A funny way to keep cool!"

"Boys," said Margaret, "I see something away in that

corner that looks like a lamb lying on the ground, and I am afraid it is hurt or sick. Run and see about it."

They started off at full speed, and when they reached the corner, they made a brief examination and shouted, " It's a lamb, and its leg is broken."

Margaret hastened across the field, and sure enough, there was a lamb lying on its side, with one of its legs badly hurt. When Margaret stooped over it, it uttered a mournful *Bah !* and looked piteously into her face.

" Isn't it too bad ? " said George. " I know how it feels to get a broken bone, and there ain't any fun in it."

" I don't think the bone is broken," said Margaret; " but I wish we could get the poor thing up to the house."

" Can't we carry him ? " asked Jack.

"Not very well, but Jotham can; and if you run and ask him, Georgie and I will wait here till you come back."

Jack went for Jotham, who, having examined the leg, said it would be all right in a day or two, seeming to think it rather superfluous to take the lamb home; but he did, and Margaret made a soft bed in the woodshed, and bathed and bound up the wound, the lamb lying patient and confiding the while. George and Jack looked on sympathizingly— Jotham with mingled approval and disdain.

" 'Tain't every dumb beast, nor man nor woman neither, as gits sech tendin' as that ere when he's sick," Jotham remarked.

" More's the pity ; don't you think so, Jotham ? "

" Wal, yes, I s'pose kindness is a good sort o' thing, ef you kin git it."

" If we give it, we are pretty sure to get it in return."

" I guess that's true, too," replied Jotham, thoughtfully. " Ef you ain't in much of a hurry," he added, " I'd be pleased to tell you what I've been a cogitatin' on sence you come home."

" I am in no hurry, you can tell me now. Run away, boys ; we can do nothing more for the lamb to-night, except

12

to give it some warm milk by-and-by. I will come to you soon."

Jotham leaned against the door of the woodshed, and began with the air of having every thing he had to say fully digested and prepared.

" I've ben here goin' on a year now, an' I guess you've found me out to be a tol'able honest, decent sort o' feller, hain't you ? "

" Yes, indeed we have, Jotham," replied Margaret, wondering what was coming.

" Wal, an' you hain't found out that I don't know as much as another about farmin' an' lookin' arter things in gen'al ? "

" No, I am very sure I have not found that out."

" An' you're a lone woman now, an' women folks ain't gen'ally 'sposed to kerry on farms on their own hook, an' I hain't no idee that you've got any sech notion ; an' ef you hain't, an' think as how I'm honest, an' know what's what about a farm, what's to pervent my takin' this place on shares, an' makin' the most on't ?  You could live on here the same's you hev', or you could go to your folks in St. Louis, an' whichever you did, you'd know that nothin' was bein' wasted or goin' to rack."

This proposition took Margaret wholly by surprise, as the plan had never suggested itself, and her first impulse was to decline even to consider it. But as she thought it over rapidly, it seemed as if it might be a practicable and wise arrangement. So she replied that she could not give him a decided answer then, but would consider it and let him know in a few days.

" This is a very vallible piece o' land," Jotham said, " an' though I say it that oughtn't, you mout look a long ways an' not find a man as would do as well by you as me ; an' I don't calkilate to live on wages much longer ; " and he added with a little embarrassment of manner, " There *may* be a Mrs. Jotham Wright one o' these days, an' she'll want more'n wages to live on."

" Oh, indeed," exclaimed Margaret, smiling, " so you are thinking of getting married."

"Wal, yes, I s'pose I am a thinkin' on't. I hain't seen the lucky gal yet, though, that I'd give my hand to," and Jotham assumed the look of one who had his wits about him, and was not likely to be duped.

"Well, Jotham," Margaret said, "I have no doubt we can make some satisfactory arrangement. I am very sure I shouldn't like to lose your services, and I shall not, of course, wish you to do what would be against your own interests."

Jotham nodded acquiescingly, and thrusting his hands into his pockets, walked away to the barn.

Margaret stood in the door of the woodshed, looking, listening, and musing. The sun had set, leaving a crimson and golden glory on a few clouds lying low in the west. The breeze had freshened, and the trees waved gently at its touch; the birds flew about busily, filling the air with their blithe evening songs. How strange to think that a year before, all that she looked upon had seemed as far removed from the world and her old life, as if it had been in another sphere; now how near that world and her past seemed. She almost felt as if the chasm were being bridged over by separate links—that her past and present would soon stand face to face.

The gold and crimson faded from the sky, the bird-songs died away as the birds sought their leafy coverts for the night, and the stars began to appear in the darkening blue, before Margaret entered the house. She found the boys asleep on the floor in the sitting-room, and had no little difficulty in rousing them and getting them up-stairs to bed.

When she came down, Biddy had returned and was busy at her deferred duties. Margaret, having made a visit of inspection to the pantry, given the lamb its milk, and seen that it was comfortable for the night, lighted the lamp in the sitting-room and sat down with her book. There were flowers on the mantel and on the table; these she gathered near her, feeling that their sweet presence made her less alone; then with a little effort of will she bent her thoughts upon her reading, and the evening did not seem long.

# CHAPTER XXIII.

He came . . . .
Well, how he came, I will relate to you,
And if your hearts should burn, why, hearts must burn.

MRS. BROWNING.

"SHALL you get in all the wheat to-day?" Margaret asked of Jotham the next morning, as she poured the rich yellow cream he had brought her from the milk-room into the churn, while Biddy stood by ready to ply the dasher.

"'Tain't likely, when I've got to take one of the hosses an go to mill," answered Jotham in an unamiable tone.

"If you can do without the horse, so that it will save time, I will go to the mill myself," said Margaret.

"We could do without the hoss well enough fer a couple of hours; ther'd be another hand at the bundling—of course it ud save time, an' it ud be time well saved, for Tim Simpkins can't come arter to-day; an' what's more, we're a-goin' to hev rain afore another twenty-four hours."

"Bring the wagon to the door before you go to your work, then. I will start as soon as I can, so as to get home before the heat of the day."

Jotham, pulling his hat, which had been on the back of his head, to its proper place, left the kitchen, and Biddy took her place at the churn.

"Now, Biddy," said Margaret, "see if you can bring the butter so that I can take it out before I go. I don't believe I could trust you to do that, your hands are so little. There will not be much for you to do while I am gone, for I shall be back in time to attend to the dinner."

After a while Margaret went into the sitting-room, where the boys sat by the table with their books before them; but just then they happened to be engaged in an animated discussion about something not at all relevant to their lessons.

"Have you looked into your books, children, or have you

been chattering like two little magpies ever since I left you?" asked their aunt.

"I have looked into a book," said George. "I 'most know my geography."

"So do I; but it's awful hard!" said Jack.

"I wonder if you could spend time this morning to go to the mill?"

"To the mill!" cried the boys, dashing their books down, and nearly upsetting the table in their delight.

"Is Jotham going?"

"No; I am going to save his time, because it is going to rain, and he is anxious to get the wheat in to-day. I thought I would just speak to you about it; but perhaps you would rather stay at home and study."

"Stay at home and study!" cried George. "I hope we ain't quite so silly as that. I'll drive."

"Not all the time—shall he, Aunty?" exclaimed Jack.

"I may have to drive all the time myself," said Margaret. "I surely should, if I were to find that it was hard for you and Georgie to come to an agreement about it."

"Well, then, Jack can drive one way, and I will the other; but I'm the oldest, and ought to say whether I rather do it going, or coming."

"What do you think about that, Jackie?" asked Margaret.

"I think the youngest ought to choose."

"Suppose, then, that one little boy thinks he has rights because he is the older, and the other because he is the younger; what is to be done? How can it be decided?"

The boys considered a moment. "I guess you'd have to say," replied George.

"I should say that little boys who were generous and polite would not talk about their rights, and which was the older and younger, but would be ready to yield to each other in little things. Now, I want you to study until I am ready, which will be in less than half an hour."

The boys opened their geographies with a great show of

industry, and, as far as in them lay with such a pleasure close
at hand, kept their eyes and thoughts from wandering, until
Margaret summoned them.

"You may drive, if you want to very bad, Jack," said
George.

"No, you may. I'd just as lief drive coming home."

So George and his aunt sat on the front seat, and Jack
on the bag of wheat behind. Margaret heartily rejoiced in
the "bit of poor housekeeping" that had brought about the
rare luxury of a ride in harvest-time. She joined in the boys'
busy talk, while her senses feasted upon the beauties of the
morning—the sunshine, the soft, fragrant air, the deep blue
of the sky, the rich midsummer coloring of the fields and
far-reaching prairie-lands, and the hum of insects and singing
of birds. She did not long, as she often had, for the bolder
and more varied effects of hill and valley; the very monotony
of the scene seemed to suit the spirit of the day, and her
mood was in harmony with all.

They jogged on at a comfortable pace along the smooth,
level road, till they came in good time to the mill, which was
just off the main road, and stood picturesquely by the side
of the quiet stream ; below the mill the stream was lined on
both banks by trees, that in some places interlaced their
branches above it.

"Good morning, Miss Crosby," said the miller, coming to
the door. "What can I do for you this morning ? It's an
unexpected honor to have you come to my mill."

"I am afraid it speaks little for our thrift, that we are
obliged to bring a grist during harvesting."

"Not at all—not at all. Such things will happen to the
thriftiest of folks. Them are your sister's boys, ain't they ?
They've been here now and then with Jotham; I took quite
a shine to 'em."

"They are very good children," said Margaret, looking
after them as they jumped from the wagon and ran to the brook.

"Will you wait for the wheat to be ground, Miss Crosby ?" asked the miller, lifting the bag to his shoulder.

"Oh, yes, we must wait; it will be more economical of
time than to come for it.  Will it take long?"

"Well, there's a grist a-grinding now, but yours shall
come next.  It won't be so very long."

Leaving the horse in the shade, Margaret followed the
boys, who had gone below the dam, and were already bare-
footed, and proceeding to roll up their trousers preparatory
to wading.  She was a little inclined to forbid it, but concluded that, as the water was low, scarcely covering the
larger stones in its bed, there was no necessity for spoiling
their sport.  Finding a shady nook and a comfortable seat,
she sat down to watch them, and enjoy the pretty scene and
the pleasant noise of the water and the mill.

The boys built miniature dams, sailed impromptu boats,
imagining all sorts of situations and dilemmas, of which they
kept Margaret informed by shouts, looking for her nod and
smile of appreciation of danger or impossibility.  It was
a pity there was no one by, with an eye for the picturesque,
to take in the whole—the brown mill, the clear, gently-flow-
ing stream, with the busy, noisy boys in it, the rough log
bridge, and Margaret sitting at the water's edge in the shade,
her hat held carelessly in her hand, her bright, smiling eyes
resting now on the boys and now upon her pleasant surroundings, while flecks of sunlight sifted through the softly quivering leaves, and fell on her hair and dress and face.  She
appreciated all the beauties of the scene except herself.

By-and-by the miller came to say that the wheat was
ground; and Margaret, hardly less reluctant to leave her
nook than the boys were their play, rose and walked toward
the mill.

"Don't let's go, Aunty," cried George.  "I'd like to
stay here all day."

"So would I," replied Margaret, "but we cannot; Biddy
wouldn't know what to do about dinner.  We shall be late
as it is."

"I'd rather make catarac's and sail-boats than eat dinner,
any day."

" You mean just now, Georgie ; but you will not say so by
twelve o'clock. So much hard work will make you hungry.
Besides, you will want to help Jotham this afternoon, and I
must go to Miss Patty's ; so put on your shoes and stockings
now."

Jack sat down on the grass to do as he was bidden, while
Margaret walked on to speak to the miller. When they
came to the wagon, George was perched on the front seat,
holding the reins and looking as innocent and unconscious as
possible.

" Look at George, Aunt Margaret ! " cried Jack. " He
wants to drive home, too."

" Oh ! did I drive here ? Why, so I did," exclaimed
George, climbing into the back of the wagon, where he sat
down on the bags of wheat and shorts.

" Why, Georgie, what do I see ? " exclaimed Margaret.
" Your bare feet ! Why did you not put on your shoes and
stockings, as I told you ? "

" I thought I'd just like to see how it would seem to go
barefoot," answered George, arranging himself with his back
to the seat and his feet stretched out before him, that he
might have the full benefit of his experiment. " I wonder
what Mademoiselle would say if she could see me now ? "

Margaret could not help laughing as she looked at George,
and pictured the horrors of his polite, precise French governess. Having laughed, she concluded to let George have
his way ; and without further remark, except that it was for
this once only, she took her place, and they started for
home.

" I am afraid it will rain before night," she said, for
clouds had gathered in the west, and fleecy ones floated
across the sky.

" Won't it spoil the wheat if it does ? " asked George.

" No doubt it would be better for the wheat if it were all
stacked before the rain came."

" Well, then, why doesn't the rain wait till it is all
stacked ? "

"Perhaps it will; but if it does not, it will be all right, you know."

"How do I know it? What if we shouldn't have flour enough to make all the bread we want; would that be all right?"

"It certainly would be, Georgie, if it was because the rain came in time to prevent it—if it was no fault of ours; because God sends the rain, and He knows when it ought to come. That is one thing I should like to have you and Jackie learn now, and remember all your lives—not to complain at what our heavenly Father does. Be careful to do the best you can yourselves; then, whatever comes, it will be right, and for your good. Do you understand what I mean?"

"Yes, I know," said George eagerly, kneeling on the bags, and putting his head between Margaret and Jack; "you mean that we ought to work hard to get the wheat in, and then, if the rain comes before we can, and spoils it, so that we have to go without flour, we ought not to feel cross because God made it rain."

"Yes, Georgie, that is just what I meant."

Jotham met them at the gate when they arrived, looking decidedly out of sorts.

"Have you had any dinner yet, Jotham?" asked Margaret.

"Ef that 'ere Biddy hed hed her way, we'd a gone hungry back to work, an' it's no thanks to her that we hed a mouthful."

"I thought we could trust you not to go hungry," said Margaret, laughing, as Biddy's flushed, worried face appeared at the kitchen-door.

"No, ther' warn't no danger o' that, as long's ther' was taters an' meat in the house, an' I knew enough to cook 'em."

"We'll be down bime-by!" shouted George, as Jotham drove towards the barn.

"Nobody wants you," called Jotham, too put out to become good-natured at all suddenly.

12*

"We're coming, anyhow," was the answer.

George ran into the house, and under pretence of helping Biddy, kept her so tossed about in her mind until dinner was ready, that she could think of nothing until it was
fairly over, when she came to say, "Oh, Miss! I forgot to
tell yez that there was a gintleman to see yez while ye was
away."

"A gentleman, Biddy? Was it Dr. Somers, or Mr.
Davis?"

"No, Miss; nayther o' thim."

"Was it Mr. Thomas, the gentleman who took tea here
the other day?"

"No, Miss, it wasn't him, nayther. I niver seed him
afore."

"Can you tell me how he looked, Biddy? Had he dark
hair, and was he tall?" asked Margaret, thinking that it
must be Dr. Doane.

"I shouldn't a bit wonder if he had that same," said
Biddy, brightening. "He was a raal purty gintleman, an'
come a horseback."

"Did he not tell you his name, Biddy?"

"Tell me his name, is it?" said Biddy. "I belave he
told me some name, but it's clane gone out o' me head in-
tirely. He said he'd come ag'in the night, though, afther
tay, and thin he can tell ye his name himsel';" and Biddy
looked fairly radiant at this happy thought.

Margaret said that, if he was coming back again, it was
all right, and prepared for her walk to Miss Patty's, with the
pleasant little excitement of an anticipation. She wondered
that Dr. Doane had not waited for her return, but supposed
that, on his way to St. Louis, he had stopped for the day,
and had improved the time of her own and the children's
absence to call on Doctor and Mrs. Somers. She gave Biddy
directions about tea in case she should be detained, and told
the boys that they might amuse themselves, or come for her,
if she had not returned when they were tired of working
with Jotham.

"I guess we shall be too busy for that," said George who was arrayed for the field.

"Very well; only don't get into mischief, or trouble Jotham. I shall be back to tea, unless Miss Patty needs me."

It was a half-mile to Miss Patty's house, by the short cut across the meadows and through the woods; but though the afternoon sun was warm, Margaret enjoyed the walk, and arrived at her destination with bright eyes and cheeks. No doubt she seemed like a sunbeam as she entered the sitting-room, where Miss Patty sat in a rocking-chair, looking so pale and ill that Margaret was startled into an exclamation of dismay; but the pale face lighted up when her eyes opened and rested on her visitor.

"My dear, how glad I am that you're come at last! I thought you never would," Miss Patty said, in tones not at all like her usual blithe ones.

Margaret smoothed back the gray hair, saying, "I didn't know that you were not well, till Dr. Somers told me, last night. I should have come to you this morning only that I had to go to the mill. But, dear Miss Patty, I had no thought of your being so ill."

"It isn't much, my dear. Sister has been so bad with her pains, and the weather was so warm, I got tired out, that's all."

"And you have had nobody to take care of you," said Margaret, sorrowfully. "To see you sitting in this straight-backed chair, all by yourself! I can't forgive myself for not having come before, but I shall do my best to make you comfortable now."

"The sight of you is comfort, my dear," said Miss Patty, as Margaret left the room.

She soon returned with comforters, pillows, and sheets, with which she made the lounge into a most inviting little bed, whereon she placed Miss Patty; then she brushed her hair and stroked her temples, talking to her in a soothing tone, till she fell into a quiet sleep. It was a less pleasant duty to look after the wants of the sister, who was glad to have some one to whom she could pour forth her complaints, but could hardly be coaxed into any thing like good humor by gentle attentions. Without the tempting little dinner which Margaret prepared, every thing else would have failed. That proved the conquering stroke; and when Miss Patty awoke, Margaret came to her with pleasant accounts of her sister's cheerful frame of mind, which were a balm to her heart.

"My dear," she said, "I didn't ask you before I went to sleep, did I—no, I was too weak and dull to think of it—if you had a gentleman visitor this morning?"

"A gentleman called at the house while I was away. But how did you know about it, Miss Patty? I cannot imagine."

"Why, my dear, he stopped here to ask the way to your house—to Mr. Crosby's farm, as he said—and I told him as well as I could, though my mind misgave me afterwards, for fear I didn't make it clear."

"You did make it plain; but was not it Dr. Doane? It couldn't have been—he would not have needed to ask the way, and then, you would have known him."

"Oh, yes, to be sure I should," said Miss Patty, raising her head to look into Margaret's face. "Don't *you* know who it was?"

"I am not sure. Biddy forgot his name; but as it was not Dr. Doane, I think it must have been his cousin, Mr. Frederick Doane."

"That is the gentleman who came with you from St. Louis, isn't it?"

Margaret assented. Patty shut her eyes tight, but in spite of that, the tears stole from beneath the lids, and betrayed her. And while Margaret saw them with pitying wonder, Patty opened her eyes and smiled a little sad smile.

"I can't help it, my dear," she said, "though I am not going to be selfish, and grudge your being happy. There isn't any body in the wide world that deserves it more than you do. But when I saw that fine gentleman this morning,

though I've been expecting him ever since you came from St.
Louis, and he with you, I was so wicked and selfish that I
could almost have told him the wrong road, so that he
couldn't find my dear, and take her away from me.  But I
didn't; and when she goes, I shall give her my heart's best
blessing.  You didn't see him?" she added, with an anxious
look.  "Isn't he coming again?"

"Yes; he told Biddy that he should come again to-
night," said Margaret, smiling at her friend's inconsistency.

"I'm glad of that," exclaimed Miss Patty, fervently.

"But, my dear Miss Patty," said Margaret, "what could
have put such an idea into your head?  I am not going
away.  I hope to spend all my life on the farm, and nobody
will ever come to take me away, as you are imagining.  So
don't trouble yourself about my leaving you."

Patty shook her head incredulously, and Margaret added,
"You must believe what I say, for it is true;" and she
entered upon an account of their going to the mill, and of her
news of Chloe, which latter item interested Miss Patty in-
tensely.

"I am going to stay to tea, Miss Patty," Margaret said,
"and if there is any thing you would especially like, tell me,
and I will see what I can do."

"Any thing in the world that you make will taste good,"
said Patty.

"You are very easily pleased," said Margaret, going to
the kitchen, but stopping on her way to ask Patty's sister if
she would join the tea-party.

"Oh, la! I never could get in there, and back, with my
lame feet," was the reply.

"I dare say you will do quite as well to keep quiet,"
answered Margaret.  In a little while she had a dainty supper ready, which she placed on a stand by Patty's couch, and
had the pleasure of seeing Patty drink her tea and eat her
toast and jelly with an evident relish.

When the tea-things were put away, and Miss Patty and
her sister made ready for the night, Margaret started on her

homeward walk. The sun had just set, and the first rosy
glow had faded from the earth; but the white clouds that
had been drifting across the sky, and the masses that had
gathered like mountains of snow above the horizon, were
transfigured into unimaginable splendors.

"A shower now—when I am safely in the house—
would complete the beauties of this lavish summer's day,"
Margaret thought; "yet I cannot wish for it. I shouldn't see
Mr. Doane, or my mysterious visitor, whoever he may be, if
it rained."

She walked quickly when she came to the woods, catching glimpses of the changeful splendors of the heavens, wishing that she had had time to go home by the road, and hoping
that the glory would not fade till she could gain one more
full view of it. But when she reached the edge of the wood,
she stood still to look, not at the clouds, but at something
that moved slowly along in dark relief against the sky; and
she continued to look, until the dark object stopped at her own
gate. A moment after, a man's figure moved slowly up the path
to the door. So her visitor had arrived before her, after all.

With the idea still in her mind that it could be no other
than Mr. Doane, she started forward and lifted her hat to
wave it in order to attract his attention, when he turned fully
around, bringing his face into relief against the dark back-
ground of the open door. She drew back a little into the
shelter of the trees, and sat down, because her strength was
gone, and there she sat looking, with dilated eyes, until the
figure entered the house. Then she buried her face in her
hands, trembling violently. But it was only for a few moments. When she raised her head, her face was strangely
beautiful in its calm self-possession, with only a tremor of
the lips and lashes, that would soon cease, to show that a
tender, tenacious woman's heart had been suddenly and
deeply stirred. The struggle had been brief, but sharp; and
the spirit had proved equal to the emergency. The heart
might quail and shiver, but the spirit would keep loyal and
trusty guard; no eye should behold the weakness.

She left the deepening shadow of the trees, and took her quiet way across the meadow with an added touch of stateliness in the unfailing grace of her bearing—noting that the splendor had departed from the clouds, leaving only their edges crimsoned, and that the slender crescent moon rested on one of the crimson fringes.

Biddy came out upon the steps, evidently looking for her; she waved her hat, and Biddy turned back quickly, but it was some time before any one else appeared—not until Margaret had left the meadow and was crossing the road; then Robert Russell, who had waited her coming, walked down the path, her fair face and white dress gleaming before him like a spirit's. It was a spirit-like smile that flitted over her face as she passed through the gate which he held open for her; but when her calm eyes met his eyes, when her warm human hand rested in his hand, and her sweet, low voice fell on his ear in simple words of welcome, he felt her to be, not a spirit, but a woman, high-souled, true-hearted, the very one he had loved; yet the echo of his own words came to him, " I have no Margaret, save in my dreams."

" I am sorry to have kept you waiting to-night," she said, as they walked side by side towards the house. " I ought to have been at home, when I knew you were to repeat your visit. Am I right in thinking that you were here this morning ? "

" Yes ; I called while you were absent, and left my name with the little girl who came to the door."

" Biddy forgot your name. And you inquired the way, this morning, of the friend at whose house I have been this afternoon, but her information was quite as indefinite as Biddy's. So your visit has been a pleasant little mystery."

" You have had a long walk, if you have not rested since you left your friend's house, and must be tired," Mr. Russell said, as he brought a chair for Margaret, and another for himself, and placed them in the little vine-sheltered porch.

" The walk through the woods and across the fields is much shorter than by the road," said Margaret.

" And much pleasanter, I have no doubt," replied Mr.

Russell. "I rode over from Moresville this morning, and, not finding you at home, made my friend Mrs. Davis a visit. But I did not like to return without seeing you, and giving you tidings of your *protégé*, Chloe. Perhaps you already know," he added, "that she is with my aunt, Mrs. More."

"Yes; I heard yesterday, to my delight, that Chloe had fallen into such kind hands."

"But she is faithful to her first friend; she seems to consider her return to 'Miss Marg'et' merely a question of time."

If Mr. Russell could have known the thrill with which Margaret heard him utter her name, even in Chloe's dialect, or if she had known the reverent tenderness with which it was spoken—

"I am quite contented about Chloe," Margaret said, "now that I know she is safe and happy. I was only troubled about her while I thought her a little homeless wanderer."

"I think my aunt will hardly be satisfied not to restore her to you. She returned from New York only yesterday, and notwithstanding her fatigue, she was inclined to drive over with Chloe; but I persuaded her to let me come to-day in her stead."

Margaret was saved the necessity of replying, by the appearance of the boys, who came through the kitchen into the sitting-room with lagging, weary steps. George threw himself on the sofa with an "Oh, dear me, if I ain't tired!" that was like a groan. Jack, espying his aunt on the door-step, dropped down beside her, laying his head, ragged straw hat and all, in her lap.

"Well, Jackie," she said, taking off the hat, and pushing the damp hair from his forehead, "you have had a very long day of it. Did you get all the wheat in?"

"Are you there, Aunty?" called George from the sofa. "Yes, we did get every bit of it in; but if we didn't have to work hard for it, then I don't know."

"Did you come in for your supper, or have you been too busy to be hungry since dinner?"

"Oh, my, no! We couldn't have stood it all this time. We didn't stop to fix up much, though; we just took off our hats and washed our faces, and *pitched in.*"

"Georgie!" Margaret exclaimed; while Jack, lifting his head to look into her face, saw Mr. Russell for the first time. He got up after a brief inspection of the stranger, and, going to George, whispered something that made him start to his feet.

"Georgie, come here," said Margaret. George came, looking decidedly ashamed. "This is my nephew, George Sinclair, Mr. Russell; and this is his brother John."

"You seem to have had a long and hard day's work," Mr. Russell said, as he took the hand of each; but his eyes lingered on George's face, its expression having changed from that of mortification to one of eager, curious inquiry.

At any other time George would have satisfied his curiosity by a straightforward question; but, still feeling somewhat disgraced and self-conscious, he withdrew his hand from Mr. Russell's, and, in a whisper, asked the question of his aunt, "Is that the Davises' Mr. Russell?"

"George has heard of you before, Mr. Russell," Margaret said, smiling; "his friends and your friends, Charlie and Nellie Davis, have made your name quite a familiar one to him and Jack."

"Indeed! then I need not have waited for a formal introduction, for I'm not afraid but that Charlie and Nellie have given good accounts of me. They are my stanch friends, I believe."

"Did you like to live in China, Mr. Russell?" asked George—too much charmed at having a chance to talk with his ideal, to stop for any preliminaries.

"Not very much, George; I like America better. But why do you wish to know?"

"Because I'm going there when I'm a man—as soon as I'm big enough to cross the ocean, I guess. I'm going to live there till I get rich; and I'd like to know if it's a nice place?'

"Well, to tell you the truth, it is not a nice place. If I were you, I would not leave my own country."

"Oh, but you see I must. I made up my mind to long ago."

"How long ago?" asked Mr. Russell, much amused at George's emphatic manner.

"I made it up last winter, one Sunday, when we were at Mr. Davis'. They told us that you went to China, and got ever so much money. I'm going, and when I get home I shall build a beautiful house, and Aunt Margaret will live with me; she's going to take care of me—no, I'm going to take care of her. I shall be old enough then."

"I wonder if it was the Sunday that I was at Mr. Davis' house. Do you know, George?" asked Mr. Russell.

"Yes, sir, it was," exclaimed George. "I know, 'cause we went to meeting in the red school-house, and then went home with Mr. and Mrs. Davis to dinner, and they talked about you half the time. Didn't you see us at meeting?"

"No, Georgie, I did not. But I have often thought of that day."

"It was a wonderful day for George and Jack," said Margaret. "They had so little variety then, that it seemed a great event to go several miles to meeting. Since they have lived in St. Louis they are less easily enchanted."

"Are you going to Charlie Davis's again, Mr. Russell?" asked George.

"Yes, I expect to spend the night there, Georgie. Can I take any message for you?"

"I wish you'd please tell Charlie and Nellie that we want them to come here, now the hurry of wheat is over."

"I will tell them so, with pleasure," Mr. Russell replied, and rising, turned to Margaret. "My aunt sent her regards to you, and charged me to say that as soon as she is sufficiently rested for so long a drive, she will call upon you."

"She is very kind; I shall be happy to see her," answered Margaret.

"Sha'n't you come here any more, Mr. Russell?" asked George.

"I hoped to come again,"—looking towards Margaret.

"We shall be glad to see you," said Margaret.

A quiet good-by was said, and Mr. Russell mounted his horse and rode away, casting but one look at the white fig- ure in the doorway. If he had looked again he would not have seen it, though an eager ear listened to catch the last sound of his horse's hoofs as it died away on the evening air.

"Come, my dears, it is time for such busy little farmers to be in bed. You will hardly be rested by morning."

They went up-stairs, and when they were in bed, George exclaimed, "I never was so ashamed in all my life as to have Mr. Russell hear me say 'pitched in.' Aunt Margaret, wasn't it dreadful?"

"The dreadful part of it was that you said it at all, Georgie," replied Margaret, "not that Mr. Russell heard it, though that was quite bad enough. But do you think you will be likely to forget, and say it again, or any thing like it?"

"No, indeed, I guess not! I want to be just like Mr. Russell when I'm a man. I think he's splendid. What is his aunt coming here for?"

Margaret did not care to excite them by telling the facts about Mrs. More and Chloe; besides, she longed to be alone. So, saying that she would answer their questions in the morning, she left them.

Seated by the window, looking out into the night, un-mindful of the occasional flashes of lightning and the distant thunder, she lived over again that strange, dream-like meet-ing; and thoughts and feelings—a changeful, restless, weary-ing throng—pressed upon her.

But as the storm gathered strength, until the heavens and earth were made glorious by the incessant lightning, and the thunder pealed in terrible majesty, the tumult was stilled; and when, far on in the night, the storm had spent itself and the stars came out, the elements themselves were not more peaceful than her spirit.

# CHAPTER XXIV.

A heavy heart, Beloved, have I borne
From year to year, until I saw thy face.

I find thee: I am safe and strong and glad.     MRS. BROWNING.

AT the last moment, Mrs. More's son, who was to have accompanied her home, found it impossible to do so, and Mr. Russell proposed to take his place as her escort. Nothing could have pleased her more than such an arrangement—inasmuch as her son was to visit her later in the season—for the wish of her heart was that Robert and Margaret should meet; and she said to herself that if once Robert were in Moresville, it could be easily brought about. It might not result in any thing—again it might.

If Margaret had changed, and grown unlovely, which was not at all likely, it would be well to find it out, for then Robert would cease to care for her. On the other hand, who could tell but that she had been caring for him through all these years? She never had known just why the engagement was broken. But if she were worthy of being loved through nine years of separation, she must surely have felt what she professed to feel, and any one who had once loved Robert could never cease to love him; there must have been some misunderstanding, which a meeting might do away with, even now.

Of all these thoughts she said not a word to her nephew. She did not even venture to ask him to go with her when she proposed to drive over, the day after their arrival. Her little guileless plot was to see for herself, under pretence of restoring Chloe; feeling sure that her woman's instinct would tell her whether Margaret had forgotten the past, as well as whether she were worthy of the heart that had been so faithful to her. She had already persuaded Mr. Russell to spend two or three weeks with her, which he was the more ready to do as Mrs. Rice and her daughter were absent on a visit; with only his aunt's gentle presence, the house possessed an inexpressible charm for him.

She thought she did not betray her surprise and pleasure when Mr. Russell said, "You are too tired, Aunt Clara, to take such a long drive so soon after your journey. Let me go to-day and tell Miss Crosby that you will come, when you are rested, and bring Chloe with you."

She did not know that her eyes sparkled, that her face glowed with delight at this unexpected furtherance of her plan, clearly betraying what had been half guessed before.

"How glad she will be to hear about Chloe," she said, "and how surprised, too."

"I doubt if she will be surprised," returned Mr. Russell. "It would be strange if she had not heard of her whereabouts, through Mr. Doane, either directly or indirectly, before this time."

Somehow, Mrs. More did not care to hear Mr. Doane's name in connection with Margaret's.

Mr. Russell gave her a bright smile in return for her wistful look as he rode away, but her thoughts followed him. She almost regretted having urged him not to return that night, so much did she long to know whether his visit had made him sad or glad.

It would have made her very sorrowful to have seen his face, and felt the burden of his thoughts, as he left Margaret in the deepening twilight.

It was not that he had found Margaret changed. Time had only ripened her girlish loveliness into mature womanly graces; her life's discipline of mind and heart had chiselled its holy effects in delicate, intangible touches upon her fair face; and she had received him kindly, leaving him at liberty to repeat his visit.

But while he sat in her presence, she had seemed farther from him than when thousands of miles lay between them; for he felt that if the memory of the past had not wholly died out in her heart, she could not, taken at unawares as he sup-

posed, have received him as an acquaintance of to-day, with
such calm, unfaltering, unremembering eyes. He asked him·
self what he had expected. Had he not known for many
years that she *never* loved him? and had he looked for tokens
of that which never existed? He was forced to acknowledge
that, deep down in his secret heart, there had been a hope
that an unseen tie bound them together all these years, whose
existence might be revealed when they should meet; while
he had said to himself, "Her life must have been a sorely
tried one; now she is alone—not friendless, but her father is
dead and her sister married. I must see her and *know* that
she is happy."

She was clearly happy; her trials had left no dark, blighting shadow behind; she had proved her power to dwell in
unfading sunshine, to brighten and adorn circumstances,
however homely and matter-of-fact they might be. There-
fore he need have "no fear for what the future might bring"
to her, though he walked not by her side. But for himself,
his unacknowledged hope had been as a glimpse of unspeakable brightness, which, shut from his sight, had left him in
utter night, darker than he had ever known; for the love of
all those years seemed concentrated into that hour. He felt
that he should hardly dare to see her again, lest the deep
yearning of his heart for her love might make itself heard in
spite of himself, only to distress and trouble her. Time
would soothe his pain, as it had done before, and he might
be able to think of her calmly, as of some saintly vision that
had been sent to bear a lesson of heavenly import, whose full
meaning he could never learn in this life.

Absorbed in such thoughts, he arrived at Mrs. Davis's,
and the children, who had been allowed to sit up just long
enough to see him and bid him good night, came to the door.

"Oh, Mr. Russell, come in quick! Ain't you afraid of
the thunder and lightning?"

"Not a bit, Charlie," replied Mr. Russell, "are you?"

"Yes, I am, when it thunders very loud. Did you see
George and Jack?"

" Yes, I saw them, and they sent you an invitation by me to come and see them, now that the hurry of getting in the wheat is over."

" Getting in the wheat! What difference does that make about going there, I should like to know ? "

" You would think it made a great deal, if you had seen them come in from the field as I did, looking like two little hard-working farmers. They had been out all the afternoon, I believe."

" I don't see what fun there can be in that," said Charlie ; " such hot weather, too."

" They did not seem to think it was for fun. I presume, if you were to ask them about it, they would tell you they were obliged to help because it was going to rain."

" Well, I'm glad we weren't there to-day, 'cause George always makes us do what he says, and go where he wants us to. He's first-rate to play with, though ; we always have good times when we go there, or they come here. But isn't their Aunt Margaret nice ? "

" Very," replied Mr. Russell.

" There, children, now you must say good-night," said Mrs. Davis, making her appearance at that moment. When the children were gone, she and Mr. Russell seated themselves by the library-window to watch the coming storm.

" I am curious, as well as Charlie," Mrs. Davis said, " to know what you think of our favorite. It is so long since you knew her, that perhaps you may not be able to judge ; but do you think she looks and seems as she used to ? "

" I think she does," replied Mr. Russell, " though it could hardly be possible for any one to have several years'·experience of life and remain wholly unchanged."

" Her life has indeed been a trying one, at least since we have known her. I know very little of her life previous to their coming to the farm, for Margaret never talks of herself, and no one could imagine, from what she says, that she had ever known or aspired to any thing more easy and elegant than looking after the farm, and taking care of her father

and sister and her sister's children. But, from chance remarks
of Mr. Crosby's and Mrs. Sinclair's, I have gathered that
they once lived very handsomely, and that it was a great
trial for them to come West and settle on a farm."

"It must have been a very great trial," said Mr. Russell.
"It all occurred while I was in China; I never have heard
any particulars."

"You did not even know where they were living, did you,
until now?"

"I only knew that they were somewhere in the West."

"Wasn't it generally known among their friends in New
York where they were?"

"I think not, generally."

"It seems strange," said Mrs. Davis, "that a family of
any position could drop out of it and leave no gap behind—
be so easily lost sight of. Yet I believe I can understand it.
Mr. Crosby was a man of not much force, probably absorbed
in business, with little influence outside of it; and Mrs. Sinclair must have been rather a devotee of fashion, who would
not make herself felt very much, except in the sphere where
people soon forget. But I can't see how Margaret should so
easily drop, unnoticed, out of any circle."

"Miss Crosby, I think, never cared much for society. Her
interests were more within her home."

"I have often wished," said Mrs. Davis, "that Margaret
would tell me something about her mother. I never heard
her refer to her but once, and then it was with such an evident effort that I didn't like to ask any questions, or introduce
the subject again. But I have always had the impression that
Mrs. Crosby was a very lovely woman, and that Margaret
resembles her."

"She was very admirable, I know," replied Mr. Russell,
"though she died before I became acquainted with the
family."

There was a little pause, while they both watched the
lightning play among the clouds, and listened to the thunder; and then Mrs. Davis said, "It was very strange that

you should have just missed each other the Sunday that you were here. Did I tell you that Margaret and the boys came home with us from the school-house to dinner ?"

"Yes, you mentioned it."

"I should think you would have seen each other there. But I suppose, not having met for so many years, and not in the least expecting to meet then, you might almost have looked into each other's faces and not have known it."

Mr. Russell made no reply, and Mrs. Davis went on : "I really was quite disconsolate that you could not come home with us, too. I had a feeling, as I told Mrs. Sinclair, afterwards, that you would be kindred spirits—you think alike on so many subjects—little imagining that you had ever been acquainted. Poor Margaret ! that day was the beginning of a series of troubles for her."

"What were you saying ?" asked Mr. Russell, as Mrs. Davis, having been interrupted by a loud peal of thunder, did not at once resume her remarks.

"Oh, yes, about Margaret's troubles. She was ill that day ; she came home with us looking like a ghost, and was very ill for two or three weeks; that very day Chloe was stolen, and it was a source of great pain and anxiety, she had become so interested in the poor little thing. Then came her sister's marriage—not that this was a trial, except that it took the boys from her, and she missed them so sadly ; but she had every thing to do to get Mrs. Sinclair ready for her marriage, she was so inefficient herself. Her father's last illness followed, during which she hardly left his side, and then his death, which Margaret felt very much. I supposed, of course, that she would give up the farm, and go to St. Louis, to live with her sister. But she seems very anxious to remain where she is, and I am selfish enough to hope she may ; we should miss her so dreadfully, though I am afraid she will be very lonely."

"I hear your voice in a very continuous flow, Jenny, but I can't see you in this pitchy darkness," said Mr. Davis,

standing in the library-door. " Oh, there you are," he added,
as a flash made the room as light as day.

" Really," said Mrs. Davis, " I have been so busy talking,
that I haven't thought of lamps. Please ask Ann to bring
them, Charles; though it has been pleasant without, don't
you think so, Mr. Russell ? "

" I do, indeed," replied Mr. Russell.

When Mr. Davis came back, Mrs. Davis said, " I have
been talking to Mr. Russell all this time of our Margaret—of
all she has done and borne."

" It is a fruitful subject for you, my dear," returned Mr.
Davis; " I hope Mr. Russell will not soon tire of it, for I am
sure you will not soon finish your tale."

" For shame, Charles, to intimate that I could tire any
body with my conversation, whatever the subject, but
especially when it is Margaret. I was just speaking of the
Sunday that she was taken sick; it was such a strange sickness—nervous exhaustion, I think the doctor called it. You
remember, dear, how terribly pale she looked when the
service was over; I had to speak to her two or three times
before she seemed to notice; and that was only the beginning. But perhaps I am in danger of growing tiresome; so
I will leave you and Mr. Russell to choose your own topics,
while I go and see if the children are frightened by the
storm. It is getting really fearful, isn't it ? " She went
away with a complacent smile on her lips, saying to herself,
" Now, if those things do belong together on the same chain,
why, then——Nellie, dear, is the storm keeping you awake ? "

When the children, comforted by her presence, had
fallen asleep, she went down-stairs.

" I came expressly to send Mr. Russell to bed," she said.
" After so much riding, you must be perfectly tired out."

" Not so bad as that," said Mr. Russell; " though I am
quite ready to obey your commands."

" Do you know, I have been thinking how strange it is
that Mrs. More and we have never visited," said Mrs. Davis.

" I am sure that is easily accounted for, Jenny," said her

husband; "we have always been very busy people, with
little time for visiting."

"And my aunt has never visited much out of Moresville.
She would be glad to have you for neighbors. I have heard
her say as much."

"Well, you said that she was coming over to bring Chloe
to Miss Crosby; and I want you to promise me that you will
bring her here, without fail. If you came after a few days,
it would be moonlight, and you could drive home in the evening."

"I may safely promise, for my aunt, that she will at least
call upon you; and for myself, I shall be most happy to come
with her."

"Well, I shall look for you."

In the solitude of his room, Mr. Russell reasoned with
the new hope that had sprung into life in his heart. What
was there in the fact that Margaret had been taken ill that
day, that he should connect it with his having been at the
school-house when she was there? He did not see her face;
why should he suppose she saw his? He remembered that
he had sung; but could he dream that she recognized his
voice? If she did, what presumptuous folly to imagine
that she could have been so moved then, and so calm to-day,
when equally taken by surprise.

But where were the inevitable, fixed conclusions he had
so lately accepted? All his reasoning did not bring back the
dreariness and gloom that had possessed him during his ride,
or shut out the sweet hope that seemed to grow stronger
with every argument he used to subdue it, till at length he
yielded to its influence; and when the storm was past, and
peace had fallen from the skies, he had said, "I will not see
her until she knows that, as I loved her once, I love her now
—have loved her through all these years, and shall love her
to the end. I will write, and tell her my story—perhaps this
delicious dream, from which I cannot and would not awake,
may come true, and the mystery of our parting be dispelled."

The morning after the storm sparkled with sunshine and

freshness; rain-drops glistened on every leaf and twig, and the birds vied with each other in singing their loudest, sweetest songs. Nature had come forth glorious and exultant from the fiery and watery ordeal of the past night, and Mr. Russell's heart was in tune with her gladness.

"You must not hurry away," Mrs. Davis said, as they stood at the door, after breakfast; "I am going to take you somewhere with me this morning. I have an errand to do, three or four miles from here, in the opposite direction from Moresville, and you will see something new in the way of prairie-scenery."

Mr. Russell was impatient to be where he could pen his story to Margaret, but having no reason to give Mrs. Davis for haste, waited for the drive.

"I suppose you recognize the little school-house?" said Mrs. Davis, as they approached it.

"Oh, yes, I recognized it at once."

"I should like to see the meeting between Chloe and Margaret," Mrs. Davis said, presently, when they had passed the school-house; "and, by the way, I was thinking, last night, of a little thing that might have shown me that you and the Crosbys were not strangers. When I called to see Margaret, while she was sick, we were speaking of that Sunday—down-stairs, before I had seen Margaret. I chanced to mention your name, and I noticed something very peculiar in Mrs. Sinclair's look and manner, which of course meant that it was not unknown to her. Nothing was said, naturally enough, as we were too absorbed in poor Margaret; and it wasn't important, either, only you know that we who live in the country think more of little things, like coincidences and discoveries, than you who live in cities, and have so much more to occupy your minds."

"Even we who live in cities are sometimes interested in such little things," returned Mr. Russell; and Mrs. Davis, feeling that she had brought out every point that could help him to a conclusion, if he ought to arrive at one, without seeming to have an end in view, settled it in her own mind that she had said enough ; she would wait now, and see what came of it all, if any thing.

When they reached home, it was dinner-time ; of course, Mr. Russell could not go then, and Mr. Thomas came as they were leaving the table, so that it was the middle of the afternoon before he could start on his homeward ride.

It was a little out of his way to go by Miss Patty's, but he thought he would like to see the place where a friend of Margaret's lived. There was no one in sight when he approached the little house. Miss Patty had sat at the window when he stopped the day before to ask the way, but now the curtains were drawn. The door stood a little open, and he wondered if Margaret had passed within it that day.

Whether she had or not, there she was, in the woods on the other side of the road. He could not see her clearly, for the woods lay a little distance from the road ; leafy branches, too, intervened, and then she was sitting with her face from him. But he needed only the glimpse of the dress and figure to tell him that it was Margaret, and with an impulse he did not attempt to resist, he dismounted, fastened his horse to the fence, and walked towards her.

His step on the soft grass was noiseless, and he came within a little distance of Margaret without her becoming conscious of his approach. He stood there as motionless as she, looking at her with tenderly questioning eyes and longing, hungry heart, noting the drooping head, the delicate contour of the cheek and throat, and the hands lying listlessly on her lap. As he looked, a tear fell upon them, and then another.

"Margaret!"

The utterance was involuntary. He would not have chosen to startle her so, but it was done, and she stood before him, tears still trembling on her lashes, her eyes fixed on his, while her color came and went with every wild throb of her heart.

What had become of the barrier of mystery and years

that had seemed so hopelessly impassable but a little time ago?
Had those tears dissolved it, or had it been gradually removed
by unseen hands, so that now they stood heart to heart?

"Margaret!" Mr. Russell said again. What his eyes
had not told of his story, that one word must have told; for
when he came to her and held out his hands, hers were laid
within them. They were clasped convulsively; quivering
lips that could not speak were pressed to them; again eyes
filled with deepest love and tenderest chidings sought hers.

"Oh, Robert!" broke from Margaret then, "Why did
you leave me?"

"My beloved," he said, drawing her within his arms,
"why did you let me leave you? But we will not think of
that now; let us forget that we ever parted." With only
the leaves to whisper to each other of the wonder they
beheld, and the gentle, caressing breeze to listen, the happy
lovers sat long in the shadow of the trees.

Margaret, seeing the deepening shade, said they must not
linger—the boys would not know what had become of her;
and they had gone nearly through the woods towards the
farm-house, when Mr. Russell suddenly stopped, looking smilingly down into Margaret's face, as she leaned upon his arm.

"I don't know whether I shall ever be able to bear in
mind the commonplaces of life again," he said, as he started
back with her in the direction from which they had come.
"I left my horse tied to the fence opposite your friend's
house," he explained, in answer to her wondering exclamation; "but whether he is there still, remains to be seen."

"Oh, he is there, without a doubt," replied Margaret,
"unless he has untied his own bridle, and walked away on an
investigating tour."

A sweet, eloquent silence fell between them as they
passed the place of their meeting, and their walk home was
a quiet one; few words were spoken, but the fulness of
happiness that each felt would have been deemed an impossibility to either a few hours before.

They went home by the road, Mr. Russell leading the

horse, and the boys came to meet them, having been on the watch at the gate.

"Where've you been, Aunt Margaret?" asked Jack.

"Why, Mr. Russell, is that you?" cried George. "I didn't know you were coming again so soon."

"I did not either, George. I am as much surprised as you are; but I hope you are glad to see me."

"I guess I am! If you're going to stay to tea, I'll lead your horse to Jotham to take care of."

"Your aunt has invited me, and I am going to stay to tea," replied Mr. Russell. "Shall I deliver the bridle to this doughty squire?" he asked of Margaret.

"Yes, you may; but, Georgie dear, remember your adventure last winter, and don't attempt to mount this horse."

"I just wish Mr. Russell would put me on his back, and walk behind me while I ride to the barn," said George, with a shade of apology in his manner for asking so much.

Mr. Russell said of course he would. Margaret said that, as he was to be so well employed, she would leave him, and attend to Biddy. So, while Mr. Russell gave George, and Jack too—though George demurred a little at sharing his pleasure—their first riding-lesson, up and down the road and out to the barn, Margaret busied herself about the tea, which was soon ready, and was all that the most critical eye and fastidious taste could desire.

As they were about to take their seats at the table, George exclaimed, "Mr. Russell, you may have my place. You are next best to Aunt Margaret, and ought to sit opposite to her."

"Thank you for allowing me the honor, Georgie," said Mr. Russell, taking the seat, with a look at Margaret that made her cheeks glow; then, as they bowed their heads, he said, in tones that thrilled her heart, "For all Thy wonderful mercies, O Lord, make us truly thankful."

The conversation was chiefly between Mr. Russell and the boys during tea, though Margaret showed no lack of interest. Every smile of hers, and every glance of her eyes, found its way to Mr. Russell's heart, but mingled with the joy it carried, was a feeling of pain that her heart should have been so long shadowed and bereaved, as well as his own.

The eyes that sought Margaret's so constantly left her nothing to wish in the language they spoke; and perhaps it was as well that it did seem not altogether real—something more like a blissful dream than a reality—that her night was past, and the morning of her joy had come.

"Aunt Margaret," said George, as they sat in the porch when tea was over, "what do you think I heard Jotham tell a man to-day?—that he was going to work the farm with shares! What does that mean? I asked him, and he said I wouldn't know any more if he told me."

"I suppose he meant *on* shares," replied Margaret, avoiding Mr. Russell's eye.

"What's that?—on shares."

"Never mind now, Georgie; I will tell you some other time."

"Don't you own the farm every bit, and sha'n't you tell Jotham what to do any more?"

"Yes," said Margaret.

"Well, then, what does Jotham talk as if he was going to have every thing his own way for?"

"Jotham wants to do the work of the farm, and take his pay in wheat and oats, and such things."

"Did you tell him he could?"

"Yes, George, I did."

"When?" asked Mr. Russell.

Her eyes met his against her will, as she answered, "To-day."

"I must start for Moresville immediately," he said, his eyes, with the smile in them, still holding Margaret's; "I shall not reach there now in time to save my aunt some anxiety on my account."

"Georgie, will you run to the barn and ask Jotham to bring Mr. Russell's horse?" asked Margaret.

"Yes, I will, if he'll promise to come again," replied George.

"I surely will, Georgie. That is a very safe condition," said Mr. Russell.

"I never liked any body in all my life as well as I do Mr. Russell," said George, as he and Jack ran towards the barn.

"You don't like him better'n you do Dr. Doane and Mr. Doane, do you?" asked Jack.

"Yes, I do—heaps! They're nice and good, and all that, but they don't begin to come up to Mr. Russell."

"And better'n Aunt Margaret, too?"

"No—o! of course I don't," said George, looking fiercely at Jack as they reached the barn.

"Well, you said so. You said you never liked any body—"

"Well, you might know I didn't mean Aunt Margaret. I wonder if Mr. Russell would like to have Aunt Margaret in his house. I'd let him, if he did. Jotham, Mr. Russell wants his horse."

"What do you think of seeing Chloe on Monday?" asked Mr. Russell, when the boys came back, leaving Jotham to follow with the horse.

"Oh my! won't it be fun!" cried Jack.

"I wonder if she'll do like this?" and George gave a very good representation of Chloe's characteristic antics.

"I have seen her behave very much like that," said Mr. Russell, laughing. "I am curious, too, to see how she will bear the joy of seeing her 'Miss Marg'et.' Good-by, George; good-by, Jack."

He took Margaret's hand, and with a warm, lingering clasp, and a long look into her eyes, left her. But this time, as far as he could see, as he rode slowly away, he looked for the white figure in the door, knowing that loving eyes were following him.

13*

# CHAPTER XXV.

Now God be thanked for years enwrought
With love which softens yet;
Now God be thanked for every thought
Which is so tender it has caught
Earth's burden of regret.      MRS. BROWNING.

A FAIRER Sabbath morning never dawned than that upon which Margaret opened her eyes to wonder anew at the great happiness which had come to her the day before. Storms and gloom without could not have marred the brightness of the day for her, but as the sun shone and the sky was blue, she rejoiced in it, and rejoiced in its being Sunday, so that she need have little to do with work-a-day things. Her happiness was in keeping with the spirit of the holy day, for with the child-like trust that had never faltered through all her trials, she recognized her Father's hand, and received the blessing with deep thankfulness, never thinking to ask why it had been delayed so long.

The thought of those years of heart-loneliness did not cast one shadow over the fulness of her content. She could not regret them, or covet their possession to add to the bright ones that might be in store for her; for had not God taken them for His own kind and wise purposes? With the sunny temper of a gentle child, she gathered her present joys to her heart, and left the past and the future unquestioned.

The one grief that came in the midst of her gladness had been the part her sister had acted.

"Then tell me," Mr. Russell said, when he heard from her lips that her love had never wavered, "why did you so often refuse to see me, disregard my notes of inquiry, and pass my poor letter by without a word of notice? It surely bore the marks of sincerity."

She looked at him wonderingly. "I never refused a visit or disregarded a note of yours, Robert. That letter—how

could I notice it? It admitted of no answer. It was simply
a farewell, and when I received it you were already on your
way to China."

"I mean the long letter, on the fate of which my going
to China depended, Margaret; the one in which I laid bare
my heart to you, and entreated for an explanation of the
change in our relations to each other. Did not that admit
of a little notice?"

"I never received such a letter," answered Margaret,
almost stunned at the thought that so small a thing as the
miscarriage of a letter could have made the history of those
nine years.

"What do you say, Margaret?" Mr. Russell exclaimed;
"that you never received it?"

"It is true that I never did."

"I cannot comprehend it," said Mr. Russell. "I remember as if it were yesterday. I called at the door myself, and
had just delivered the letter to the servant, with a charge to
give it at once to you, when your sister, passing through the
hall, saw me and came to the door. I only waited to tell n y
errand—that I had left a note for you; she said she would
see that you received it without delay. What is it, Margaret?" he asked, anxiously, for Margaret's face had grown
white as her dress, and her eyes, which had been fixed on
his, were turned quickly away, but not too soon for him to
see the anguish in their expression.

She tried hard to think that it was a cruel suspicion, the
conviction that came to her with such a shock, sharpened by
the vivid recurrence of many things long past; but whether
it were or not, it was not to be uttered, even to satisfy him
who sat waiting to know the cause of her emotion. When
she could trust herself to speak, she turned to him. "Robert, as I told you, I never received the letter. But we are
happy now, and the years we have spent apart have not been
lost years, to either of us; shall we not let the causes of our
parting rest, with all the pains it cost, and make much of our
meeting? Only, you shall tell me all the letter contained."

"It shall be so," Mr. Russell replied, reverently regard
ing the veil she had chosen to throw over the mystery, feeling that even in his secret thoughts he would not seek to
draw it aside; though his quick perceptions had not failed
to catch a glimpse of the truth.

Margaret resolutely put away the pain which the unexpected and humiliating disclosure of her sister's falseness
caused. Even that should not mar the gladness of the re-
union, and Mr. Russell must have looked in vain for one shade
of sadness in the sweet eyes or the tenderly smiling lips.

The agony of tears and supplications which mingled with
her thanksgiving that night, God only knew. Long and
fierce was the struggle with the scorn and indignation which
filled her soul, before she could think of her sister with pitying forgiveness, and lay the whole burden of her grief where
she had laid all the other burdens of her life.

The reward of her conquest and her faith came with the
perfect peace, the unclouded joy of that Sabbath morning.

"Aunt Margaret," said George, as she bent over the
newly blossomed, dewy flowers, under the sitting-room window, "aren't you sorry that we can't go to church to-day?
I'd like to go just for the ride, and I guess you'd like to go
for the sake of the sermon and things."

"It would be very nice to go, Georgie, but I can't feel
sorry for any thing to-day. I am satisfied with every thing.
I'll tell you what we will do, to make this lovely Sunday as
good for ourselves and others as it ought to be. We will
have our Bible-lessons and stories this morning, and this
afternoon we will go and see Miss Patty, and take her some
flowers and read to her. What do you think?"

"I think that will do," replied George; "though I don't
know but what Jack and I'd rather stay in the woods while
you are at Miss Patty's. I don't care so very much for sitting down long at a time with sick old ladies."

"Old ladies might find it very dull to sit with little boys
long at a time; yet Miss Patty would stay with you night
and day, if you were sick and needed her."

"Well," said George, after a little pause, "I don't see that she'd need me and Jack, if she had you."

"No, I don't know that she would. But supposing that she had nobody but you, or that it would give her pleasure to have you stay with her; I hope you would not object because she was old and sick?"

"No, I wouldn't, Aunty," answered George, emphatically. "Do you suppose that Chloe will stay here when she comes to-morrow?" he asked presently.

"Not if Mrs. More cares to keep her."

"I shouldn't a bit wonder if she'd rather live here, and I hope she will; it's such fun to have her 'round. Don't you believe Jack and I can stay here, Aunty? Do you think we'll have to go back to St. Louis in the winter?"

"I cannot tell much about next winter, Georgie," replied Margaret, and the heart of the rose she had fastened in her dress was not brighter than her cheeks. "It is a good way off yet; but I doubt if Dr. Doane would care to spare you so long."

"Oh, dear me! I think it would be perfectly dreadful to have to go away from you, and go back to St. Louis," exclaimed George.

"Why, Georgie," said Margaret, taking his cloudy face between her hands, "what a foolish little boy, to trouble yourself about next winter, when the sun shines and the birds are singing, and it's Sunday, and we are going to have such a happy time! There," she cried, kissing each rosy cheek, "run away and call Jack now, and say to Jotham that as soon as he is ready, he can come to the sitting-room—or, no; we will sit under the trees, it is so shady and pleasant there."

"All right, Aunty," responded George, the clouds all gone; and he bounded away in search of Jack and Jotham.

The table, chairs, and books were taken out under the trees, and before Jotham appeared, the boys had said their verses, and Biddy received her simple lesson. Margaret found some difficulty in adapting her topics and teachings to the several tastes and capacities of her listeners, but the morning passed so quickly and pleasantly that they were all surprised when noon came.

After a simple lunch, Jotham and Biddy went to their homes, and Margaret and the boys set out for Miss Patty's with the flowers.

For once the boys found Margaret an abstracted and unsatisfactory companion. They had their talk and their little discussions to themselves; a "Yes" or "No, dear," was all they could gain from her during their walk. It was not to be wondered at, either, with such a halo of unimagined happiness encircling her, with the whispering leaves and zephyrs repeating over and over for her the wonderful things they had heard the day before, that she lost sight of the little figures, now here, now there, and had no ear for their prattle.

When Miss Patty saw them coming, as she sat by the window, she laid down her Bible, and came to the door to welcome them.

"Come in, my dears, out of the sun. How glad I am to see you! How tired you must be, walking this warm day!"

"Tired!" cried Margaret; "oh, not a bit, Miss Patty. It is just warm enough to be delightful."

"Well, my dear, I must say that you don't look tired, or any thing but what is good and happy," said Miss Patty, looking admiringly at Margaret, as she seated herself and took off her broad-brimmed hat.

"Now tell me about yourself, Miss Patty," said Margaret. "How have you been since Friday?"

"Oh, there is little to tell about me, my dear. I was a little speck disappointed not to see you yesterday, but I knew you had some good reason for not coming."

"I am glad you did not miss me any more than a little speck," said Margaret, waylaying a question she thought she saw in Miss Patty's eyes. "How is your sister to-day?"

"She's pretty comfortable for her. I've been reading to her, and she's just gone into her bedroom to lie down."

"Well, I came to read to you, Miss Patty. I brought a

little book called 'The Patience of Hope,' that I think you
will like very much.   Georgie, where are the flowers?"

George started up from his examination of the pictures
in Miss Patty's old-fashioned Bible.   "Well, there! if I
didn't leave them on that stump in the woods, where I laid
them for a minute!  I'll go get 'em;" and he ran out of
the house.

"I am afraid they will be withered," said Margaret.
"Georgie is not the most careful little man in the world."

"I should like to see even a withered leaf from your
yard," said Miss Patty.   "It seems two ages since I was
there, my dear; and I'm going to watch for Dr. Somers to-
morrow, and get him to take me over."

"Wait till Tuesday, Miss Patty, and I will come myself
and bring you."

"Thank you, my dear; that will be beautiful."

In a few minutes George came back, holding up not
only the wilted bouquet, but a glove—a gentleman's riding-
glove.

"See what I found in the woods!" he cried.   "It's Mr.
Russell's, I know it is, but how ever it got there, is what I
can't see."

"Whose did you say it was, George?" asked Miss
Patty.

"Mr. Russell's.  Don't you know Mr. Russell?—no, of
course you don't, because he never was at our house till yesterday and the day before.  But he's coming again to-morrow, and you'd better ask Aunt Margaret to show him to
you, for he's just the splendidest man!"

"He was there yesterday and the day before, and coming
again to-morrow," repeated Miss Patty slowly, her eyes on
Margaret.   "Mr. Russell?   I thought it was Mr. Doane."

"I thought so too, until I saw him," returned Margaret,
feeling almost sorry that she had put herself in the way of
her friend's affectionate curiosity.   "I could think of no one
else.   But it was, as Georgie says, Mr. Russell, a gentleman
I used to know long ago in New York.   He came with

tidings of Chloe; for, strangely enough, the lady at Moresville who has been caring for her is Mr. Russell's aunt."

"Well, I never!" exclaimed Miss Patty.

"What I should like to know," said George, who had
been consulting with Jack about the glove, and trying it on,
"is, how this came to be in the woods, when you and Mr.
Russell went home by the road. Aunty, do you see?"

"Yes, Georgie," said Margaret, half vexed and half
amused that her cheeks should burn and her eyes falter before the questions of her little boys and her simple-hearted
old friend, "I know just how it came there. On my way to
see Miss Patty yesterday, I sat down for a few minutes, and
Mr. Russell, who was riding by, saw me, and came into the
woods where I was. As he had a horse to lead, we went
home by the road. Do you see now how the glove came to
be in the woods?"

"Yes, Aunty."

"Well, then, I will read to Miss Patty."

"Do, my dear; but how will the little boys amuse themselves?"

"Haven't you got some more picture-books besides the
Bible?" asked Jack.

"Yes, indeed," replied Miss Patty. "There's Fox's
'Lives of the Martyrs,' and 'Pilgrim's Progress,' and Bun-
yan's 'Holy War,' and more yet. They're all in that little
cupboard, and you may ransack it to your hearts' content."

"What fun!" cried the boys. They soon became absorbed in the ancient contents of the cupboard, and Margaret
began to read to Miss Patty, who was soon absorbed in the
comforting contents of the little book.

When Margaret stopped reading, Miss Patty said, "I
want to hear you sing. I haven't heard that dear, good old
hymn, 'How firm a foundation,' for the longest time, except
as I sing it to myself. Can you sing it?"

Margaret said "yes," thinking how impossible it would
have been two days ago. She found it rather more difficult
than she expected to keep her voice from trembling, and the

happy tears from filling her eyes ; but Miss Patty thought
she had never heard any thing so sweet in all her life.

"What a short afternoon," she said, when, soon after tea,
Margaret and the boys were starting for home. "How good
you were to come."

She called Margaret back from the gate, to whisper, "My
dear, are you going to let the farm to Jotham on shares, as
you spoke of Friday ? "

"I told him I would, yesterday."

"Shall you stay there yourself, my dear ? "

"I told Jotham I should, yesterday ; but—"

"You may change your mind! Well, God bless you,
whatever you do, my child ; and do forgive me for being so
inquisitive."

"You shall ask me any thing you like," replied Margaret,
kissing her affectionately. She went away, thinking sorrowfully of how forlorn Miss Patty's life must be, as age and infirmities increased, and how sadly she would miss her when
she was gone.

"It was right there that I found Mr. Russell's glove,"
said George.

Margaret smiled as he pointed to the place where she had
received the lost sweetness back into her life.

The three sat in the doorway, reading and talking, till
the daylight had quite faded. Biddy came home then, and
she and the boys went to bed, leaving Margaret to a quiet
evening by herself, as she thought. But she had hardly
seated herself, before she heard the gate open. Slow, heavy
steps came up the walk, and there, in the door, with the
lamplight falling full upon her face, stood a woman in a
calico dress and sun-bonnet and dusty shoes. It was Nancy
Stubbs. Margaret, recognizing her at once, started to her
feet in amazement.

"Ye didn't 'spect ter see me, did yer ? " said Nance, sink-
ing down on the step wearily.

"No, indeed, I did not, Nancy," said Margaret, going to
her. "Where did you come from, and how did you get here ? "

"I come from St. Louis by car, an' I got as fur as Jones-ville last night, an' walked over yer' this arternoon."

"Are you quite well again? You do not look very strong yet."

"I been't as strong's I mout be, but I'm tol'able peert, an' I'll git up my strengt' now, I reckon. Ye didn't know's I meant it when I tole yer ye'd see me ag'in, did yer?"

"I knew you meant it at the time, Nancy; but thought you would find friends in St. Louis, and be contented to live there."

Nance shook her head. "No, Miss, I couldn't do't. Yer was the fust as ever spoke a kind wo'd to me sence Sime an' me lef' ole Virginny, an' I'd a been dead in the street ef it hedn't a been fer ye; an' was I gwine ter live thar 'thout ever seein' yer face ag'in? I couldn't a done it," she said, wiping her eyes with the cape of her sun-bonnet. "I jes arnt wot 'ud buy me a decent gownd an' pay fer a ride in the car, an' then I come. An' ef ye'll jes lemme stay, I'll work my fingers ter the bone fer ye, I will so."

She had risen, and stood with her brown, bony hands clasped, anxiously awaiting her sentence; but Margaret saw that she was weak and faint.

"You are too tired to stand," she said; "come in and sit down. Have you had any supper?"

"I hain't hed nothin' sence mornin', but ain't yer gwine ter tell me whedder I'se got ter go off? I can't eat till I know thet."

"No, you need not go away," said Margaret, putting out of her thoughts every objection and contingency, "you shall stay here, and I will help you to be useful and happy. Now you will come in and have some supper."

Margaret led the way to the kitchen, and speedily placed bread and milk and cold meat before Nance.

"I dunno how ter thank ye as I'd orter," Nance said, wiping away grateful tears, when Margaret showed her the comfortable bed she had prepared for her. "Ye'd a right to treat me orful, arter Sime an' me takin' Chlo off—an' jes' see

the way ye've done by me! Ef ye'll lemme now, I'll tell yer
all I know 'bout Chlo."

"No, never mind, Nancy; I know that Chloe ran away
from you, and I am sure you will be glad to hear that she
went to a kind lady who has taken care of her ever since.
She will be here to-morrow."

"Well," said Nance, shaking her head, "I be right glad
Chlo's been took care on; but she'll hate the sight o' me
worse'n pisin."

"Not when she knows that you would not harm her now
for the world," said Margaret.

"I'd like ter know how poor ole Sime is," thought Nance,
as Margaret left her. "I wish he cud fall in with the likes
o' *her*, mebby ther'd be a chance fer him as well's me."

Margaret's thoughts were too busy with the arrival of
her unlooked-for visitor, and the St. Louis memories it suggested, and with the sweet anticipations of the morrow, to
let her eyes close very soon. But she was up with the sun,
and busy with the preparations for her guests.

Nancy would have been glad to do every thing herself,
and every thing at once, but it was evident that a great
deal of patient teaching was needed before she could really
be of use.

Margaret did not shrink from the task. She thought of
undertaking it the more gladly because the happy idea had
occurred to her of training Nancy thoroughly for Miss
Patty, feeling sure that she might become just what her
friend would need, as age and her sister's infirmities increased.

Chloe's persecutors had so long been the *bêtes noirs* of the
boys' imaginations, that Margaret took care to tell them of
Nancy's advent, to guard them against any thoughtless
demonstration. It was quite a disappointment to them to
find their aunt's description verified when they hurried to
the kitchen and beheld only a plain woman in a clean calico
dress churning.

"Why, Aunt Margaret," said George, afterwards, "if

that's Nancy Stubbs, I guess Chloe needn't be afraid of her
*She* won't bite."

"I am going to manage so that Chloe need not see Nancy
until we have told her how changed she is. I will send
Nancy with a note, asking Miss Patty to let her stay there
to-day, and wash or help as she can. I don't think she will
be a trouble to Miss Patty even if she has nothing for her
to do."

"Let George and me go and show her the way," said
Jack.

"And not see Mr. Russell and Chloe!" cried George.

"They will not be here before noon," said Margaret;
"you would be back before they came." So the three
started off directly after breakfast.

"I'm glad I ain't gwine to be yer when Chlo comes,"
Nance had said; "she'd be scairt to death to see me. But
jes tell her thet I wo'dn't do her a mean trick now fer
nothin.'"

How carefully Margaret surveyed her arrangements,
when the last touches had been given. She might well feel
satisfied, for nothing could be more tasteful and attractive
than the sitting-room and the bed-room adjoining, which she
had prepared for Mrs. More if she should need to rest. Since
her return from St. Louis the sitting-room had been newly
painted and papered, and the straw matting, to which
Margaret had treated herself for the summer, the full muslin curtains, and the pretty chintz covering of the lounge
and rocking-chairs, gave it a dainty air of freshness. Books,
pictures, and flowers completed the charm. The woodbine
which grew so luxuriantly over each window, stirred by the
soft summer-breeze, let in many a stray sunbeam to dance
about the room, seeming to say, "I am glad to be here; it is
a place I love."

Margaret went to dress, thinking that she should have to
wait a little for her visitors. But just as she had taken the
final look at herself in the glass—she did not see herself as
others must see her, so very lovely in her fresh white dress

and violet ribbons—Mr. Russell was helping his aunt from
an old-fashioned carriage at the gate, and there, on the gate-
post, sat Chloe, drumming with her heels, as if she had
never left it; only that she had on her brown linen dress,
and a hat—not on her head, to be sure, but swung wildly
about as she sat and drummed.

The scene was so like an illusion to Margaret, as to make
her forget, for an instant, that she ought to go down and
receive her guests. But when Mr. Russell offered his arm to
his aunt, she turned from the window, and, with a flutter at
her heart, went down-stairs, entering the sitting-room as
they reached the open door.

Her eyes met Mr. Russell's, and the look in them and the
smile he gave held her spell-bound for a moment; but with
one answering smile she approached Mrs. More, who was regarding her with gentle scrutiny.

Mrs. More held out her hand, and drawing Margaret to
her, kissed her, saying, "My dear child! Take her, Robert,
I see she deserves to be as happy as you will surely make
her."

She gave the hand she held into Mr. Russell's keeping,
and went to the door to look for Chloe. Chloe had disappeared from the gate-post; she was nowhere in sight, and
Mrs. More interested herself in the flowers, that looked so
well cared-for, until Margaret came to her. "Don't stand,
Mrs. More. I am afraid you are very tired; it is a long
drive from Moresville."

"My aunt maintains," said Mr. Russell, "that riding over
prairie-roads is scarcely more tiresome than sitting still in the
house. But you will think her a very good traveller, when
I tell you that she drove with me over the up-hill and down-
dale roads along the Hudson for fifteen miles and back,
without being very tired."

"But the day was so beautiful, and there was so much to
see, and I enjoyed my visit with Robert's friends so much—
all those things helped to prevent my feeling weary."

"My aunt does not mean to imply that those pleasant

preventives are wanting to-day, Margaret," said Mr. Russell.

"Margaret knows that I do not, without your telling her
so, Robert," replied Mrs. More, following Margaret into the
bed-room.

"My dear child!" she said, folding her arms about Margaret, "I cannot tell you how much I have felt for you; to
think of those years of separation! But the kind Father has
comforted you, and you are happy at last."

Margaret smiled through her tears—tears that were not
quite free from sadness, for Mrs. More's tenderness seemed
so like her mother's. Perhaps Mrs. More divined her feelings,
for she kissed her again, saying, "I love Robert as if he were
my own child, and I have already taken you, too, into my
heart. I will not ask you to come to me as you would to your
mother, I do not expect that; but love and trust me as much
as you can."

"That will be a great deal," said Margaret, warmly, kissing the soft cheek.

"I suppose Robert is counting every moment that I keep
you from him, my dear. I am going to lie down for a little,"
and she drew her to the door, saying, "Robert, you may
have your Margaret to yourself for one hour."

"Where can Chloe be?" said Margaret, when Mr. Russell had led her to the lounge, and seated himself beside her.
"I have not once thought of the poor child."

"You must not think of her yet, Margaret; I cannot
spare one of your thoughts," and for a little while she could
not choose but give him every one.

In the meantime, Chloe, not in the least forgetful of
Margaret, but perhaps with an idea of saving the best till the
last, was visiting all her old haunts. She looked into the pig-
pen, the scene of her well-remembered overturn; went to the
barn, climbed to the hay-loft, examined all the nests, carefully counting the eggs, without touching one; ran down to
the sheep-lot to take a hasty survey of the sheep; set the
geese hissing and flying in every direction by suddenly dash-

ing in among them; and returned to the house, making sundry stops and observations by the way.

Why she did not go straight into the sitting-room, where she knew she should be likely to find Margaret, she could not have told, herself. Certain it is that she stood on tiptoe before each window, vainly trying to get a glimpse through the vines; she tiptoed back and forth before the door, peering this way and that; she mounted the gate-post; she climbed upon the outside of the porch, and finally, with many contortions and grimaces, and much hesitation, she went up the steps. Little by little her head appeared around the edge of the half-open door.

"Chloe!" cried Margaret, starting from her seat, "come here, child."

The sight of Miss Marg'et's face and the sound of her voice were too much for Chloe. Dropping on the floor, she drew her dress over her head, and broke into a sort of sobbing wail. Margaret bent over her, half inclined to cry herself, and tried to take the dress down, saying, "Chloe, I am so glad to have you here again. Let me look at you, Chloe."

But Chloe held her dress tight, and Margaret concluded that the best way was to let her take her own time. In a minute or two the wail suddenly ceased, the dress was withdrawn, and her eyes were shyly lifted to Margaret's.

"Are you glad to see me, Chloe?" asked Margaret.

"I reckon I is! Oh, Miss Marg'et!" Chloe got upon her knees, and throwing her arms around Margaret, laid her little black face against her, and broke anew into that wild wail.

Margaret could not speak for a moment. She wiped away her tears, and lifted Chloe to her feet.

"There, Chloe, don't cry any more. I want to see you look happy. I don't think you have grown or changed a bit, and I am glad of it—glad to have just our little Chloe again. Don't you want to see your old friends, George and Jack? They will be home soon."

Chloe nodded her head with her old vehemence. " I'se been all over."

" Have you? Have you been to the barn, and seen the pigs and the cows and the sheep ? "

" Yes, Miss Marg'et, an' I seen heaps o' eggs in dem ole nesses, but I nebber tetched one on 'em, an' dat's de trufe."

" I have no fear of your doing any mischief, Chloe. You have been a very good child, I know, since you left me."

" No I hain't allus," said Chloe, glancing at Mr. Russell, who stood watching the scene with the greatest interest, and she hung her head and dug her toes into the matting.

" I suppose Chloe is thinking of the time when she invaded my sanctum, and made an examination of my desk," he said, smiling. " She little knows what reason I have to bless her for that piece of audacity."

" And I too," said Margaret, returning his look.

" It was Miss Marg'et," said Chloe, dolefully, not comprehending what she heard, but feeling that she was under a cloud. " I nebber tetched nuffin else, on'y jes looked into dem' little draw's."

" Never mind that now, Chloe," said Margaret, " no one blames you."

" Well, Chloe," said Mrs. More, coming from the bedroom, " so you are with your dear Miss Marg'et once more. I have been thinking," she continued, turning to Mr. Russell and Margaret, " of the chain of little events that has brought you together. How strange it seems that a little child whom Margaret befriended, in the kindness of her heart, should have had so much to do with those events."

Here Chloe darted out of the house. She had seen Biddy before, but had been too busy to make her acquaintance. Now she followed her to the door of the kitchen, and sitting down on the steps, leaned her elbows on the floor just inside, her chin on her hands, and looked around.

" Whativer did yez come back here for ? " asked Bridget, who looked upon Chloe as Biddy's rival.

" I come back to live 'long o' Miss Marg'et. Dat ars

mine," she added, giving Biddy's dress, as she came near, a
little pull.   It had been Chloe's, but Margaret had given it
to Biddy, with other things that Chloe had left behind—the
two being about the same size.

"Yours indade!" cried Bridget, indignantly.   "Be aff
wid yez, an' don't come insultin' yere betthers."

"Gimme dat ar an' I'll gim you dis yer," said Chloe, in-
dicating the dress she had on.   "It's 'nuff sight han'somer."

Biddy thought to herself that it would be a fine bargain
—that nice brown dress and cape, trimmed with braid, for
her half-worn calico, but her mother quickly cut short her
speculations.

"Biddy, ye jist lave aff talkin' wid Chloe, she's benathe
yere notice; an' go sthraight an' git thim potaties an' be
afther palin' thim.   It's a'most dinner-time."

Bridget's looks and tones were wrathful, but Chloe remained on the steps, calmly watching operations, until she
heard shouts in the distance that made her start up.   Climbing the gate-post, she saw George and Jack coming across
the field from Miss Patty's.

"Hello, Chloe!" they cried every now and then as they
came towards her, which salutation she answered by kicking
her heels harder than ever, showing her white teeth and
nodding her head.

"Get down, Chloe, and let's see how you look," cried
George, as they reached the fence on the other side of the
road.   She did get down, and shot off behind the house,
with the boys after her; but before very long the three appeared at the sitting-room door, on very amicable terms.

George and Jack were introduced to Mrs. More, and had
a chat with Mr. Russell.   They took him out to show him
the lamb, whose wounded leg had nearly recovered, and who,
by dint of careful nursing and petting, had become quite interesting—besides some rare hens and turkeys which were
their own especial property.   When they came in, dinner
was ready.

The afternoon passed only too quickly.   Mrs. More felt

14

obliged to start for home before sunset, as the horses were not fresh, and they would have to drive slowly.

"I am sorry to take Robert away from you so early, Margaret," she said; "but you will see him again very soon."

"How shall I make my peace with Mrs. Davis, Aunt Clara?" asked Mr. Russell. "I promised that you should call there when you came to see Miss Crosby."

"But you see, my dear, I came to see *Margaret*. I might have cut short my visit to Miss Crosby, but I could not to Margaret."

"Of course you could not," exclaimed Mr. Russell.

Margaret smiled; she could not trust herself to speak.

"Well, my dear," said Mrs. More, "what about Chloe? I have no doubt that she will wish to stay with you, but will she not be in your way just now, until you have found a place for Biddy, and become a little used to Nancy?"

"I think Margaret has more than her share of dependents," said Mr. Russell; "I am afraid she will find difficulty in providing for them all."

"Oh, no," answered Margaret; "it can all be easily arranged; but I am inclined to think that, as I have had no time to prepare Chloe to meet Nancy, and Biddy would feel badly to go home to-night, Chloe had better go back with you; she can come some other time, if it seems best."

This was decided upon; but when the carriage came to the door, Chloe was nowhere to be found. The boys looked in every possible and impossible place—in the cellar, woodshed, barn, and where not—and shouted till they were tired. But no Chloe came to light. At length, Mr. Russell suggested that in all probability nothing would be seen of her until he and his aunt were gone, and the search was relinquished. Chloe, having taken her fate into her own hands, was left to it.

"I shall come again in a few days, my dear," Mrs. More said as she bade Margaret good-by; "then we will go together and call on your friend Mrs. Davis. And remember, that I must have a little visit from you before Robert goes home."

"I shall come to-morrow to see my darling," Mr. Russell said, as he took her hands and looked into her clear, gray eyes. "I must see her every day, for a time will come—a little time—when I shall be far away from her. But then another time will come—*not* a little time—"

With what a sweet contentment Margaret watched the carriage as it rolled away, seeing the uncovered head and the waving handkerchief until the turn in the road hid them from view. Then she looked down at the single, clear pearl upon her finger, in its old-fashioned setting. It had been his mother's. He would never have parted with it, save to her.

"There comes Nancy Stubbs," said Jack, while she still stood musing over her ring.

"Where can Chloe be!" exclaimed Margaret.

She turned to enter the sitting-room, and the first thing she saw was Chloe's head, emerging from under the chintz frill of the lounge.

"Why Chloe, have you been there all this time?" asked Margaret, laughing.

"No, I hain't; I jes' got in dat ar bedroom-winder while you was out to the gate. Oh, Miss Marg'et, lemme stay 'long o' you," she entreated, trying to look very miserable, as if she thought she might be sent away.

"You managed to stay, whether I would let you or no, Chloe," replied Margaret. "But I must tell you something, so come out from under the lounge and listen." Margaret proceeded to tell her about having seen Nance in St. Louis, and taken care of her when she was sick; about her having come there the night before, and how different she had become; and when George burst into the room, calling, "Is Chloe going to be afraid of Nancy?" she replied, bravely, "No, I ain't. I ain't a bit afeard." The only signs of her having any disagreeable remembrances of Nance, were the inquiring looks she gave her whenever she came near, and a little disposition to edge away.

Poor Nance! the sight of Chloe recalled so vividly that
terrible, suffering journey to St. Louis, and Simon's desertion,
that her case was far more pitiful than that of the child she
had persecuted.   Margaret felt that she had a strange household that night, but she disposed of them readily.   Biddy
was such a useful, sedate little body, that she knew she could
easily find a new home for her; and while Bridget would
miss her frequent day's-work at the farm, she would not suffer from the loss.   Of course, Nance and Chloe would stay
with her as long as she remained on the farm.

# CHAPTER XXVI.

All October's wealth of beauty
Seems a wedding gift for thee,
And our hearts bring loves and blessings
To endow thee royally.            ANON.

MARGARET remembered her promise to Miss Patty, and soon after breakfast Tuesday morning she set out in the farm-wagon, taking Chloe with her, and leaving the boys to keep house. She drove first to Mrs. Davis's, to ask her if she would like to take Biddy, or if she could think of any body who would. She little knew that her friend had been weaving a romance for her during the past five days, only equalled by the reality.

Mrs. Davis looked eagerly into Margaret's face, trying to discover if any thing had come to pass yet. But Margaret, unconscious of the scrutiny, pointed to Chloe, who sat in the wagon, holding the reins, not so steadily but that, if the horse had been less fond of standing still, he might have felt privileged to run away with her.

"Why, has Chloe come already?" exclaimed Mrs. Davis. "Chloe, how do you do?"

Chloe gave the reins an extra jerk and her head an extra dip, that nearly sent her over the dashboard.

"Be careful, Chloe, or you will fall out," cried Margaret.

"When did she come?" asked Mrs. Davis. "Did Mrs. More bring her?"

"Yes, she brought her over yesterday."

"Did Mr. Russell come too?"

"Yes," replied Margaret.

"And they never came here! Mr. Russell told me he would surely bring his aunt to see me when they came to your house! I shall give him a good scolding, and let him know that I am not to be trifled with in this style," said Mrs. Davis, with a great assumption of indignation, while in

her heart she was only weighing the probabilities that something *had* happened. "They just came for a call, I suppose?"

"No," answered Margaret, taken by surprise, and feeling
herself in rather a maze.

"No! did they spend the day?"

"Yes; but Mrs. More spoke of calling here some other
time."

"I shall be happy to see her. I wonder when Mr. Russell is going back to New York! I should like to see him
again very much."

"I dare say you will," said Margaret.

"Oh, then you think he will come with his aunt?"

"Yes, he intends to," replied Margaret, avoiding her
friend's bright eyes. "But I came of an errand. I must tell
you what it is, and hurry away, for I am going to take Miss
Patty to spend the day with me." She made known Nancy's arrival, with her plan for her, and her desire to find a
good home for Biddy.

"Well, well, it is something new for any one in these
regions to have such a superfluity of 'help,'" said Mrs.
Davis, laughing. "I'm glad its Biddy that you want to get
rid of, for I am sure she is just what Mrs. Thomas needs. She
would hardly undertake Nancy Stubbs, but I know she
would be delighted to have Biddy to mind the children."

"I am very glad," said Margaret; "Biddy is a nice
child, and I am very anxious that she should be under good
influences."

"Oh, mamma," said Charlie, coming into the room just
then, "I've cut my finger. Won't you put a rag on it?"

"Let me see the cut, Charlie," said Margaret; "is it a
very bad one?"

"Not very. I didn't know you were here, Miss Margaret. Did Jack and George come too?"

"No, I left them at home to keep house."

"You tie it up, Miss Margaret," said Charlie, as his
mother came with a bit of linen and a piece of thread.

"Of course I will, Charlie," replied Margaret, taking off her gloves, and hoping, as she bound up the wounded finger, that Mrs. Davis, who stood by, would not notice her ring.

"There, will that do?" she said, as she cut off the ends of the thread.

"Yes, thank you, that's very nice; ain't it, mother?" said Charlie.

"Very; now run away, my dear. Chloe is in the wagon. Go and ask her what she has been doing since she left Miss Marg'et. Margaret!" she cried, when Charlie was gone, "you must confess to me. Sit down again and tell me all about it."

"About Chloe's adventures?" questioned Margaret, smiling. She would rather have chosen her own time to make her confession.

"No, no! nothing about Chloe! Ah, Margaret! am I such a new friend, and do you trust me so little that you would go away without telling me? Where did you get that pearl ring?"

Margaret hesitated only a moment. Why should she shrink from letting her kind friend know what would give her so much pleasure?

"Mr. Russell gave me the ring. I am engaged to him," she said, meeting her friend's eyes with a proud happy light in her own.

"Oh, Margaret! my dear, my dear! I knew it, I was sure of it!" and Mrs. Davis threw her arms around her, and kissed her again and again.

"How did you know it?" Margaret asked, when Mrs. Davis gave her a chance.

"Oh, it's a long story. But sit down, and I'll tell you just how I found it out."

"If it is a long story I am afraid I cannot stay to hear it, much as I should like to. Miss Patty will think I have forgotten her."

"Well, it was only by putting this little thing and that little thing together. But I shall always comfort myself with the thought that I had a hand in making you happy. I'll tell you how, some day. I needn't ask if you have loved each other for years, for I know it; but how—oh, dear! well, this is a strange world. When is he coming over again?"

"To-day," replied Margaret.

"What! and Miss Patty going to be there!"

Margaret smiled at her friend's look of dismay. "I promised Sunday that I would go for her this morning, and I cannot disappoint her."

"But, dear me! how dreadfully poky and unromantic it will be to have the little old lady there. You'll feel as if you must make it pleasant for her, and she will just spoil every thing. Let me bring her here, instead."

"Oh, no, it isn't at all worth while. She longs to see the 'dear place,' as she calls the farm-house, and she will not spoil any thing."

"Well, I'm sorry that you should be so wilful; I know Mr. Russell will look cross when he sees her there. You think he can't look cross, I can tell by your eyes; but you'll find out!"

Margaret found Miss Patty watching for her, in her best dress, with her best cap pinned up in a paper, and her spectacles and knitting in her black-silk bag.

"Oh, there you are, my dear," she cried, as the wagon stopped at the gate. "Don't get out; I'm all ready but my bonnet and shawl, and I'll be there in a trice."

In a moment she came to the side of the wagon, and Margaret reached her hand down to help her in. At the moment a chaise drove up behind them, and Dr. Somers' voice called, "Hello, there! Wait a bit, and I'll lift you in," which he did, and shook hands with Margaret, giving a nod at Chloe.

"You see Chloe has come back to me," said Margaret.

"Yes, I see; and I've seen more than that, Miss. I suppose if I had dropped in unexpectedly yesterday I should have seen more yet. I can't stop here now to talk, for Mrs. Brown's baby is cutting a tooth! But I give you fair warn-

ing I shall be there this afternoon to hear what it all means
—a letter from one young man, and a visit from another, in
less than a week! Miss Hopkins, I wonder that you allow
her to carry on such flirtations."

"Flirtations!" cried Miss Patty, indignantly. "Fie on
you, doctor! I'm ashamed of you! as if Margaret didn't
know her own affairs, and wasn't to be trusted. Flirtations,
indeed!"

"I suppose she does know her own affairs, and I want to
know 'em too. It's all well and good if she can give a satisfactory explanation as to the person I saw in the carriage
with Mrs. More and Chloe yesterday, on the way from Jonesville. I'll see this afternoon;" and without giving Margaret
time to speak, he was in his chaise, driving away.

"I hope Nancy was not a trouble to you yesterday?"
said Margaret, when Miss Patty had inspected Chloe, never
having seen her before. "I could think of no other way to
dispose of her, so that she should not be at hand when Chloe
came."

"She wasn't a bit of trouble, my dear. She did the
washing very well, and I'm sure she'll make a very good
worker, and be very useful to you—that is, my dear, supposing that you were going to stay here."

"I have been thinking, Miss Patty," said Margaret, after
a little pause, "that perhaps you might like to let Jotham
have your house, and come to live in mine—when I am gone,
and keep Nancy to do your work and make you comfortable.
Your house is hardly large enough to admit of your taking
any body else into it, and I could never feel happy to leave
you alone, with your sister to take care of. If you had my
house, just as it is, with Nancy to do your work—don't you
think it would be very nice?"

"Indeed it would, my dear," replied Miss Patty, in a
plaintive little voice. "It's very kind of you to plan for me.
Are you going right away?"

"Oh, no, not for some time yet, dear Miss Patty; we
shall have many a pleasant day together before I go."

14*

As they sat together, Miss Patty with her knitting and Margaret with her sewing, they talked of Chloe and Nance and other things; and after a little silence, Margaret told Miss Patty her story. Notwithstanding its glad ending, Miss Patty's gentle heart was wrung with sympathy, and it was some time before the spectacles and the knitting were resumed.

"I hope I shall see Mr. Russell," she said then, with a sigh.

"You will see him this very day, Miss Patty," said Margaret. The knitting was dropped again, and the hands were lifted in amazement. "He is coming here to-day," added Margaret, "so you will have your wish sooner than you thought."

"I'll just stay to take one look at him, and hear him speak, and then run home. I wouldn't be in the way, for the world and all."

"You shall not run home, and you cannot be in the way," replied Margaret.

"Look!" cried George, as they left the dinner-table; "if there isn't Mrs. Davis' carriage, and Mrs. Davis and Charlie and Nellie!" He and Jack ran out to the gate, where Chloe was already stationed, and Margaret followed.

"I'm not going to stop a minute, Margaret," said Mrs. Davis; "has your friend arrived?"

Margaret shook her head.

"Well, I'm glad of it. I was afraid he might have the start of me. I'm going to Jonesville to get some things, and to make one or two calls, and I'm going to take Miss Patty and the boys with me. Wouldn't you like to go, boys?"

"Hurrah! I guess we would."

"Well, run and get your caps, and ask Miss Patty to come to the door. Miss Patty," she called, "don't you want to take a drive with me and the children? It will do you good."

Miss Patty said she should like it, very much, and assured Margaret of it again, when she begged her not to go, unless she would rather than not.

"I will take Biddy, too, if she'll go at such short notice without a fuss? I know Mrs. Thomas needs some one now, and I can stop and see Bridget about it."

Biddy was consulted, and found tractable. In a few minutes the noisy carriage-load departed, leaving Margaret to the quiet anticipation of Mr. Russell's visit; and she had not long to wait. Chloe, who divided her time about equally between outdoor and indoor duties—thus far generally self-appointed—espied him as soon as he came in sight at the turn of the road, and called, "Miss Marg'et, Massa Russell's a comin'! dar's Massa Russell down dar!"

Margaret saw that it was true. "Get down now, Chloe," she said; "can't you wipe the dishes for Nancy, and clean the knives?"

Chloe jumped down, and with her hands clasped over her head went slowly towards the kitchen, but stopped to ask if "dat ar little white gal was comin' back ag'in?"

"No, she isn't, Chloe. Why? do you want her to?"

"No, Miss Marg'et, I doesn't. I'se gwine to have my bed an' my clo'es back agi'n, now, ain't I?"

"Your bed, Chloe, but not your clothes. Poor Biddy has no dresses except what used to be yours, and I am sure you would not like to take them from her, when you have so many nice ones."

"Dey's mine," said Chloe, unwilling to give up her rights. She darted into the kitchen as Mr. Russell arrived at the gate.

She and Nancy were on very friendly terms now, apparently oblivious of the fact that they had ever been on any other, though Chloe was inclined to patronize Nancy, on the ground that she had lived there before, and was thoroughly posted as to Margaret's ways and wishes. Nancy took the patronage very meekly, recognizing Chloe's superiority in this respect.

"Oh, laus, Nance," exclaimed Chloe as she came to the

table, "you dunno how to wipe de dishes. Gimme dat tow'l
I'se gwine to show you how to do't." She seized a plate,
and expended strength and pains enough upon it to have
answered for a dozen. "You jes see now, Nance, how dat
ar shines. Dat's de way Miss Marg'et wants um to look."

"I reckon she don't want yer ter be all day at one on
'em," answered Nance, resuming her dishcloth.

"'Course she don't, an' who's a gwine to be all day?"
returned Chloe sharply, but the rest of the dishes were made
to shine in much less time.

The quiet, undisturbed hours of that summer afternoon
were full of sweetness to Margaret and Mr. Russell, the
more that, in the fuller interchange of thought and feeling,
they came upon no discords, born of time and separation.
Their experiences of life had been different, but they had
not to learn each other anew, as might have been the case,
after so many years. They only realized more and more the
strength and completeness of the bond that united them,
which no length of time or distance could break or lessen.

"Margaret," said Mr. Russell, as, late in the afternoon,
the conversation came back to their meeting in the woods,
"that day seems longer ago than the one in which I first
told you of my love. I can hardly believe that we have not
been walking side-by-side all our lives. I should like to see
if we can find the sweet little nook in the woods yonder that
I have a picture of in my mind. I am almost sure it was a
dream—the parting, and that meeting."

He looked into her face, and a shadow came over his
own. "Oh, Margaret, how dark and desolate my heart was
without the light of these dear eyes. I can only wonder how
I endured the loss."

"Dear Robert, did we not resolve that no vain regrets
should have place in our thoughts? I cannot bear to remember that you were ever desolate."

"Forgive me," Mr. Russell exclaimed, "for being un-
mindful of our resolve and bringing tears to these 'sweetest
eyes were ever seen.'"

They were just ready for their walk, when Dr. Somers appeared. Margaret withdrew her hand involuntarily from Mr. Russell's arm, and her cheeks glowed, for she felt the doctor's keen eyes peering into their relations to each other.

"You see I kept my promise," he remarked, getting out of his chaise, and tying his horse. "I hurried up other cases for the sake of attending to yours without delay. Where's Miss Patty?" he demanded in a tone that said as plainly as words, "Why isn't *she* looking after you?"

"She has gone to ride with Mrs. Davis," replied Margaret; and Dr. Somers having by that time come to her side, as she stood near Mr. Russell, she introduced them.

"How do you do, sir? I'm glad to make your acquaintance, Mr. Russell. You will excuse me if I attend to my patient at once. I am sorry to see that her symptoms are even worse than I anticipated," he said, anxiously.

"I was not aware that Miss Crosby was under medical treatment," said Mr. Russell, looking from the doctor to Margaret's laughing, blushing face.

"I am not. Dr. Somers is an incorrigible tease," she exclaimed.

"Look out, Miss Crosby!" cried the doctor; "remember how you excited my fears last week, and again yesterday, and—but I am in something of a hurry, and if Mr. Russell will excuse you for a few minutes, I will inquire further into your symptoms, and leave you a prescription."

Mr. Russell, a little mystified, bowed his assent, and the doctor led Margaret into the house.

"Now then—did you see that man for the first time when he came with Mrs. More yesterday?" he asked, when they were in the sitting-room.

"No, I did not," answered Margaret.

"When did you know him? in St. Louis, or long ago in New York?"

"Long ago in New York."

"You were very good friends then, and there came a misunderstanding, eh? And now he is going to take you away!

You needn't tell me—I know it; I saw it in his eyes when
he looked at you; and you don't object to going, I know, by
your looking so happy and contented. But what's going to
become of the young man from St. Louis? He made over's-
eyes at you too. You'll break his heart, you may depend."

"Do not say that, Dr. Somers," exclaimed Margaret,
earnestly. "He is a kind, true friend, and nothing more."_

"Well, never mind him now. Is Mr. Russell any relation
to Mrs. More?"

"He is her nephew."

"Is he the Mr. Russell that the Davises and Thomases
talk so much about?"

"Yes," answered Margaret, taking a step towards the
door.

"Wait a minute, child. Isn't he the man who started the
singing that Sunday at the school-house? That's it! I
thought I had seen him before. I had to leave before the
service was ended, but I remember his singing, and recall his
face. Did you see him that day?"

"I saw him, yes."

"But not to speak to him? Well, well. I understand
something now that I didn't before. Poor child, and happy
child. I congratulate you with all my heart," and he gave
her a fatherly kiss. "Stay here a moment; I want to speak
to Mr. Russell."

Margaret saw the smile which lighted Mr. Russell's face
as he received Dr. Somers's greeting, and that they shook
hands in the most cordial manner; but she did not hear what
was said. The doctor soon hurried away, and almost immediately after he was gone, Mrs. Davis stopped to say that she
had left Miss Patty at home, as it was late, and she was
going to take the boys home with her to tea; they and her
children had been concocting some wonderful amusement
for the evening; she would send them home before bedtime..

George and Jack were inclined to relinquish their plans
when they saw Mr. Russell, but Mrs. Davis prevented it

She shook hands warmly with Mr. Russell, her eager eyes
and flushed cheeks showing how much she had it in her heart
to say, if she but had an opportunity.

When they were gone, Margaret turned to Mr. Russell,
saying, " I feel so sorry for poor little Miss Patty; I am
afraid she was grieved at being taken home so unceremoniously."

She had already told him of Mrs. Davis's kind plot for
their benefit.

" We can make it all right, can we not, by going to see
her ?  It will not make our walk much longer to go on to
her house."

Margaret looked her thanks, and they made Miss Patty's
heart proud and glad by paying her a visit in her wee bit of
a parlor.  She did not say to herself in so many words, that
Margaret's " true prince " had come, but that was her idea,
which was ample proof of the lofty opinion she had formed
of Mr. Russell.

The two weeks of Mr. Russell's stay drew to an end
speedily, as weeks do that are filled with happiness, and he
was to leave Moresville on Tuesday.  The Saturday before,
Mrs. More came to the farm-house, and took Margaret and
the boys home with her, to spend the intervening days ;
and days they were that could not be surpassed for sweetness to Margaret and Robert.  They were pleasant days to
Mrs. More too, and each one made Margaret nearer and
dearer to her.

One morning, while Mr. Russell was giving the boys
another riding-lesson, and intense delight thereby, Mrs.
More, in her own gentle way, led Margaret to talk of her
plans, to which she added suggestions that at once com-
mended themselves to Margaret's good sense; and thankful
she was to feel that at length she had some one's judgment
to trust in besides her own.

" I am glad, my dear," Mrs. More said, in the course of
conversation, " that you feel kindly disposed towards the old
house, and do not mind the unfashionable location.  Robert

told me how you felt about it, and I must confess I was relieved. You know how old people regard old things, and I
did not like to think of having my dear brother's house go
into the hands of strangers. You know Robert intends to
refurnish it, and I think you will find it really pleasant
there."

"Robert did not speak to me of refurnishing it," said
Margaret; "if he had, I should have told him that I would
rather not have it done. I like old things too, and I should
be very sorry to have him put aside what must be so tenderly
associated with his earlier years. Will you not tell him how
I feel about it ? "

"You may tell him yourself, my dear. I know he will
be delighted to hear you say it. You will not be sorry, I am
sure, when you see the house, for the furniture suits it. It is
old-fashioned, of course, but it is rich and handsome, and very
well preserved, too. Janet is a careful body."

On Sunday, Margaret and Mr. Russell sat side by side
in the village-church; together their hearts arose in thanksgiving, and their hearts and voices united in the songs of
praise. How vividly the first tones of that clear, sweet ten-
or, recalled to Margaret the scene in the little red school-
house.

"Two months will seem very long, Margaret," Mr. Russell said, when the moment for parting came. "I am afraid
I shall hardly be a patient waiter; I shall count the hours
till they bring me to you again. But your letters will be my
solace. Good-by. The dear Father forever bless and keep
you."

Margaret wondered at herself that no sense of loneliness
came, as she lost sight of him she loved in the gray morning-
light, and said, "I shall not see him again for two whole
months." Mrs. More wondered, too, to see the cloudless
face at the breakfast-table an hour later. It was another
mark, Mrs. More thought, of Margaret's cheerful temper.
Margaret thought, "How foolish and ungrateful I should be,
if I could feel lonely and downcast now."

Honora's admiration for Margaret was beyond the power of even her extensive vocabulary to express. She embraced every opportunity to take a " good look " at her, and " made bold," when Mr. Russell was gone, to ask her into her wing-room, where she told the story of Chloe's invasion, and gave some intimations of the system " of hedication under which that foolish Miss Lucinda kept the child."

Margaret and the boys took their leave Wednesday morning, a little before Mrs. Rice and Lucinda were to ar-rive, and Mrs. More could not help sighing over the ex-change. Honora expressed her mind freely on the subject in her own department, and even to Mrs. More.

Margaret's first duty, when she was once more at home, was not a welcome one—that of informing her sister of her engagement. But she tried not to let the painful thoughts which pressed upon her as she wrote, cast more than a pass-ing shadow over her happiness.

Her letter to Dr. Doane, who had returned to St. Louis, leaving Fanny with her gay friends at the East, was such as a confiding sister might write to a kind brother. It speedily brought, as she knew it would, an answer full of warm and hearty congratulations. He insisted upon her coming to his house at once, and not leaving it until she went to her own in New York.

In due time Fanny's reply came, and its tone was much more sisterly than Margaret had expected.

The truth was, Fanny had been at first perfectly over-whelmed, fairly terrified, by the tidings from Margaret. She could almost have welcomed death, as an escape from the exposure and shame which, for the time, seemed inevitable. But she was soon able to reason away the incubus of fear and dread, and prepare to meet the event in a manner that should redound to her social honor and distinction.

She wrote, after expressing her pleasure at hearing of the renewal of the old engagement, that she had suffered tortures from the remembrances of her own homely wed-ding, and that it was not worth while for Margaret, as well as herself, to emerge into society and married life from a little farm-house on the prairies. She must come to St. Louis, and have a wedding that should be in keeping with the position she was to take as the wife of Robert Russell, the rich and influential New York merchant. It was settled in her own mind that she would astonish St. Louis by the style and elegance of the affair, but she did not think it necessary to tell Margaret the extent of her plans. "I shall be in New York in a few days," she wrote, "and will purchase your laces, dresses, etc. Ordinary things you can procure in St. Louis, where, of course, you will go as soon as you can dispose of the farm. Write me at once, as I shall hasten my return home, to prepare for the wedding."

Nothing could have been farther from Margaret's thoughts than to sell the farm, beyond the few acres that was needful to provide her outfit, or than having her wedding in St. Louis. She smiled at the idea of her ever being annoyed by memories of her humble home. It never seemed dearer to her than now; even the prospect of forsaking it for two or three weeks, and going to St. Louis, as Mrs. More had advised and she felt to be necessary, gave her many a pang. She longed to remain there quietly until the two months had passed.

In her reply to Fanny's letter she explained her wishes, expressing the hope that her sister would bear with her primitive notions—her only ambition with regard to her wedding being, that it might be in her own home, and that those she loved should be with her. She assured Fanny that she would profit by her experience, and not trust to country dressmakers and her own unsophisticated ideas, and would gladly avail herself of Madame L——'s skill, as well as of her sister's taste, in the matter of dresses and laces.

However disappointed and indignant Fanny might have been, she was obliged to submit to Margaret's decision, and consoled herself by looking forward to winter visits at Mrs. Robert Russell's. She referred to the fact that Mr. Doane had just joined her party at Newport, and that he did not seem in the least astonished when she told him of Margaret's engagement. But she did not speak of any plans of his own, so that Margaret was surprised, and very sorrowful to learn, when she next heard from Dr. Doane, that his cousin had returned home, and was intending to sail for Europe in a short time, much to the grief of his father and mother.

A few days later came a note of congratulation from Mr. Doane, assuring Margaret of his sincere and unchanging regard for her, and his high esteem for Mr. Russell, and wishing her all possible happiness. It had been the cause of real pain to Margaret, that such powers as Mr. Doane possessed should fail of their highest use. She longed to see him living a more earnest life, and it was with a deeper feeling than that of personal regret, that she heard of his intention to travel again.

August passed quickly by, and with the first of September, Margaret's arrangements for leaving home for a time being completed, she started alone to join Fanny on her way from New York. Miss Patty was left in charge of the boys and Nancy—Chloe being taken to Mrs. More's to await Margaret's return. The boys shed many tears at parting with their aunt. George, especially, was sadly incredulous as to the certainty that she would come back to be married. He had yielded his claims to his aunt as the head of his grand prospective home, very cheerfully; but he seemed possessed with the idea that Mr. Russell would not wait; that he would go to St. Louis, and take her in state to his grand house in New York; and it required all Margaret's skill to allay his fears of such a catastrophe.

When the sisters met, there were no tokens of unwelcome memories in Fanny's manner. As they talked of the approaching marriage, it was Margaret's eye that refused to seek her sister's—Fanny's never quailed.

Dr. Doane met them when they reached St. Louis, and the few weeks of separation seemed to have healed the little wounds in his love for Fanny, for he welcomed her with the tenderness of a satisfied lover.

"Why, Fred—cousin Fred!" cried Fanny, as, in passing through the depot, they came face to face with Mr. Doane. "Where are you going? You surely are not starting for Europe now, just as we arrive to enjoy your society?"

"I am indeed about to start for New York," answered Mr. Doane, shaking hands with her and with Margaret.

"You will not be at Margaret's wedding?" said Fanny. "What a pity! But I must say, you look as if you needed to go to Europe for your health. What have you been doing with yourself since you left Newport so suddenly?"

"Nothing unusual, I believe," replied Mr. Doane. And, as an acquaintance of Fanny's claimed her attention, he said to Margaret, who was perplexed and troubled by his altered manner, "I shall not be missed from the marriage-feast."

"Indeed, indeed, you will be missed," exclaimed Margaret. "I have not so many friends that I could fail to miss one of the very kindest I ever had. I am so glad to have met you now; I want to thank you for your kind note, and to tell you how heartily I wish you a pleasant journey and a safe return—but beyond all, I wish you could know what happiness is—the best and truest."

She said this rapidly, with her truthful eyes fixed on his, and as he listened, his pale face flushed and his lips trembled.

"Your kind wishes will be the best guarantee I could have of my safety, and of my attaining to that real happiness. I believe they will follow me like a holy spell, and I thank you for them. Good-by."

He held her hand in a close, firm clasp for a moment, with an expression in his eyes that haunted her for many a day, and, with a hasty good-by to Dr. Doane and Fanny, disappeared in the crowd.

Margaret's two weeks in St. Louis were very busy, and, on the whole, very pleasant ones. Fanny, still feeling the exhilaration of a gay, successful season, was bright and amiable, and never more attractive, as Margaret often said to

herself. If there was a tinge of envy in the contemplation
of her sister, as living in New York with her choice of its
society, she was too politic to let it appear. She might have
found it more difficult to conceal it, if Dr. Doane's position
had been less respectable, or her house less elegant, and if
she had been less beautiful, or less able to gratify her love
of dress and show.

In due time Margaret returned home, with only two short
weeks left before her marriage-day. That day pressed eagerly on, and when it came, it was as perfect as any that ever
queenly October granted to a bride; a day that June might
well have claimed, only that the fields and woods had laid
aside their summer robes of green, and were arrayed in those
of autumn's bright hues.

The little farm-house wore a holiday look, for a profusion
of choice and beautiful flowers that came to Moresville the
night before, had greeted Margaret when she first entered
the sitting-room, and they transformed it into a fair and fragrant place as she arranged them, her face the while telling
of happy, loving, and lovely thoughts.

Then there was Miss Patty, in her new cap and black
silk—Margaret's gifts; and Jotham and Nance in fine array,
busy and important as if the whole responsibility rested
with them. Chloe was everywhere, investigating and admiring; now watching operations in the kitchen, now peering in at the flowers; but chiefly she favored the gate-post,
as it gave her a bird's-eye view of the whole, and nothing
of importance could happen without her knowledge. The
boys were as excited and alert as Chloe herself, with no end
of questions to ask and comments to make, to all of which
Dr. Doane patiently listened and replied, while Fanny, animated and graceful in her rich lavender silk and point-laces,
was ready to receive the guests.

When Margaret had given the last touch to the flowers,
she went to her own little room, where Mrs. Davis awaited
her coming; and some minutes before Mrs. More's carriage
arrived, she sat in her bridal dress—a soft India muslin, with

white azalias in her hair, and on her bosom, where reigned a
serenity as sweet as Nature's own. No wonder that her
friend was silent from very lack of words that could express
her sense of that rare loveliness.

Margaret was dreamily conscious of Dr. Doane's coming
to her, and saying, with grave tenderness, that the bridegroom waited—and of descending with him to the parlor,
where she received a vague impression of friends and flowers, and the glad sunshine and bright landscape through the
open door. Nothing was real and distinct but the face and
voice of him who came to meet her; and it was sweetly,
solemnly real, when she stood by his side and heard Mr.
Thomas speak the words that united them forever, and listened to the earnest prayer for a blessing upon that union.

Dr. Doane and Fanny were the first after the bridegroom
to greet the bride; then came the boys, and Mrs. More.
What warm congratulations and fervent benedictions were
lavished by the friends—few, but tried and true—who were
gathered in that little room: Dr. and Mrs. Somers, Mr. and
Mrs. Davis, the Thomases, Miss Patty, and all. How they
rejoiced in Margaret's happiness—but how they grieved to
lose her.

As soon as the ceremony was over, Nancy had left her
corner, and gone sobbing into the kitchen, and Jotham and
Bridget followed, wiping their eyes; but Chloe remained,
and, mounted on a chair, looked on with absorbed attention,
until Margaret moved from her place, when she suddenly
darted to her side, and, with her usual contortions, held up a
little bouquet of the gayest autumn-flowers she had been able
to find. Margaret took it, but before she had time to speak,
the giver had disappeared.

A tasteful lunch was served under the direction of the
competent Honora, and by-and-by the time for the partings
came. Amid tearful smiles and loving words, followed by
many blessings, the carriage rolled away with Robert and
Margaret Russell.

# CHAPTER XXVII.

I have seen thy heart to-day,
Never open to the crowd,
While to love me aye and aye
Was the vow as it was vowed
By thine eyes of steadfast gray.

MRS. BROWNING.

IT is nearly a week since Margaret came to her new home, and she sits in the library where she can look out of the window, and at the same time feel the pleasant warmth of the fire. It is the first of November. The sun shone in the early part of the day, but the sky is overcast now, and large, feathery snow-flakes fill the air and cover the roofs, and cling to the garments of the passers-by, whom Margaret sees vaguely, while her eyes and heart keep watch for one. Now she turns from the window to a little stand near by, which holds a basket of flowers; she feasts on their beauty and fragrance, and listens to the sweet story they tell, and have been telling all the day. Then, as her eyes return to their watch, her thoughts go wandering down the track of the past year, and if she finds shadows and sadness and crosses, they only make the present more bright by contrast, when her thoughts are brought back from their wanderings by the sight of him for whom she waits. She receives his smile and bow, and hastens to open the door.

Her warm hands were taken in his cold ones as he bent to kiss her welcoming lips.

"What would be the consequence if my snowy coat should come in contact with your fine silk dress?"

"Injury to the dress," was the reply; and as Janet appeared with her switch-broom, Margaret stood at a safe distance while the snow was brushed off, and they went into the library.

"Those beautiful flowers, Robert! You cannot think
how much I have enjoyed them."

Mr. Russell took a cluster of white azalias, and fastened
them in her hair, saying, "I never knew, till a month ago,
how lovely azalias were; and white muslin, too. I wonder
that all brides do not wear those, instead of satin and silk
and lace and orange-blossoms."

"It was their fitness that made them pretty on me, Robert. If we had been married in some grand city-church or
drawing-room, instead of in a little farm-house sitting-room,
can you imagine me in white muslin, or any thing but satin
and point-lace?"

"I am glad we were married in a little farm-house parlor,
and in white muslin and azalias," said Mr. Russell.

"So am I," replied Margaret.

"Now that we are married, will you not always wear
gray silk dresses, like the one you have on," asked Mr. Russell demurely, "with such laces and pearls?"

"Why, only yesterday," replied Margaret, laughingly,
"you requested me always to wear black silk and corals.
And another day it was my carefully-preserved violet which
became me so well! Either your taste is fickle, or you have
the happy faculty of thinking that whatever is, is the most
desirable."

"Or else the face of my wife has the power to make
whatever she wears seem the very thing of all others to set
off its charms."

Mr. Russell left her for a few minutes to happy meditations by the fire. When he came back, Margaret said, "I
did not tell you, Robert, that Chloe had arrived. She came
with some friend of Dr. Somers; he assured me that she
behaved very well all the way."

"I am glad she has reached us safely," returned Mr. Russell. "What news did she bring of Miss Patty, and the rest
of the good people?"

"She has not been in a very talkative mood. She seemed
rather overpowered by her journey and her arrival. But she

brought me a letter from Miss Patty, written in the oddest
little hand, but very nicely expressed, which tells me that
they are all well, and that she and her sister are settled at
the farm-house with Nancy. Moreover, Jotham went to
Miss Patty the Sunday after we came away, dressed up in his
best, and informed her that he was going to be married to a
girl in Jonesville, requesting her to tell me when she wrote.
So, sure enough, there is a Mrs. Jotham Wright, as Jotham
intimated there might be, and they are living in Miss Patty's
house. But, from some hints he threw out, she thinks he
intends to own the farm some day, and live in the farm-
house. It will not be while Miss Patty cares to stay there."

"No, it would never do to let Mrs. Jotham usurp Miss
Patty's place as mistress-domo."

"I had a letter from Fanny, too, to-day, and, to my great
relief, they have decided to let George and Jack go to school,
instead of having a governess. Mademoiselle disappointed
them, and they could find no one to take her place. I only
hope they will have judicious teachers, who will appreciate the
good, while they correct what is faulty in their characters."

"They are splendid little fellows," said Mr. Russell;
"but they would pity themselves more than they do, for
being separated from their Aunt Margaret, if they knew how
much they have lost."

"Don't say 'lost,' Robert, for that implies that the good
I could have done is not to be made up to them."

"The good you have done them will prove an accumula-
tive possession, and there is no reason for your feeling anxious
on their account. They will make good men, and men of
mark, I do not doubt. By the way, Clara's letter has arrived
at length;" and he produced an envelope covered with
European postmarks, from which he took one directed to
Margaret.

"When you have read that, you may have mine," he said.
He watched Margaret's face while she read Mrs. Blake's
long-delayed letter, so affectionate and sisterly, regretting
so much that she could not be at the wedding; but antici-

15

pating the time, not far distant, when she should be able to
realize, what seemed too good to be true, that her dear
brother was happy at last, as he deserved to be.

"What does your sister say, Margaret?" asked Mr. Russell, as she folded the letter, and met his look.

"Very pleasant things," answered Margaret, handing it
to him, and taking the other, that brought tears to her
eyes and the warm color to her cheeks, so full was it of enthusiastic love for him, and of lavish praises of herself.
When she had read it, Mr. Russell gave her a little packet,
which she opened, and found to contain an exquisite sapphire
ring.

"It is the 'little token of a sister's love' that Clara
refers to," said Mr. Russell, taking the ring and placing it
upon her finger.

She looked into its clear blue depths a moment, and, with
her smiling eyes fixed on Mr. Russell's, she pressed her lips
to the pearl ring and the plain gold wedding-ring upon her
third finger.

"Several people have been here to-day," Margaret said,
as they sat at dinner a little later; and she mentioned several
names, among them those of Mrs. Thorne and Miss Thorne.

"I did not know that the Thornes had returned to town,"
said Mr. Russell. "Did you find them pleasant?"

"Very, indeed. I was particularly attracted to Claudia,
I think her mother called her. She has one of the sweetest
faces I ever saw, and her manners are such a pretty mixture
of womanly dignity and childlike simplicity. But I thought
she seemed sad, and did not look well. Isn't her health good?"

"It was not at all good in June, when I saw her last;
but I hoped she would have become strong again by this
time. I am sorry, too, to hear that she seemed sad—though
she has had reason for being down-hearted, poor child!—but
I believe brighter days will come yet."

"I was sure you were a special friend of hers," said Margaret, "for she listened eagerly whenever your name was
spoken, and expressed an earnest wish to see you."

"I was thinking, to-day," said Mr. Russell, "that I would tell you something about Claudia before she called, for I knew you would take her to your heart if you knew she was in trouble; she needs just such help as you could give her, if you would be a sort of elder sister to her. You can imagine that Mrs. Thorne would not be very leniently disposed towards an only child, who should dare to love a man whom she considered ineligible."

"Oh, Robert, is it a trouble like that?" exclaimed Margaret. "Poor Claudia, indeed! Mrs. Thorne is very gracious and affable, and evidently very fond and proud of her daughter; but I can imagine that her worldly wisdom would be severe and unbending;" and the sweet face, with its sorrowful shadow, came before her again and again, as she talked with her husband of other things.

After dinner, as they sat by the library-fire, Mr. Russell told her the story of Claudia's and Philip's love, as well as of the peril Philip had escaped, knowing that he could not more surely enlist her womanly interest for his young friend.

"But how can I help Claudia, Robert?" Margaret asked. "Do you think her mother will allow me to be her friend? Knowing that you are so much interested in Philip, will she not be suspicious of my influence with Claudia?"

"I think not, Margaret. If it were not that I received a rebuke for my conceit from Aunt Clara, last summer, upon a kindred topic, I would just hint at a reason for Mrs. Thorne's being especially on her guard—to save her pride; as it is, I forbear."

"I thought as much," cried Margaret, laughing. "But oh, Robert, I don't see that you profited by your aunt's rebuke."

"Do you not? Well—at least it is worth the effort, to give Claudia more cheerful views of life; to teach her how trials may be made the means of continual growth in strength and grace. I might point your instructions, by giving her a little chapter from your life, my darling."

"If she does not know the one source of grace and

strength, I don't see how she can bear her burden. I should like to teach her where to lay it. But I feel hopeless of getting near enough to any one, in this great, busy city, to be of use."

"Never fear, dearest, but that you will find means of giving help and comfort. I know plenty of humble, sorrowful homes, where you may, and will be, the ministering angel; plenty of wayward hearts, that need just your guiding, helping hand. Tell me, now, what you have been doing to-day besides receiving visitors."

"I've been such an idler of late, Robert, that I find it very hard to be any thing else. But I think I have succeeded in convincing Janet that I am not going to be a fine lady, restricting my attentions to the drawing-room; that is something."

"She has been supreme so long, that I am afraid she does not yield very gracefully," said Mr. Russell.

"She does very well, only she finds it difficult to appreciate that one fact. I think we shall get on very amicably. Well—I kept house and read the papers, and practised, and Chloe came, and visitors, and I enjoyed my flowers and watched for you! You see, it has not been a very profitable day. I hope to have a better record before long."

"I think you have no reason to find fault with this day's record: but when are you going to take possession of my little room? I want you to make whatever changes you like, and consider it your sitting-room—and mine, too, you know. I am tired of seeing it look like a bachelor's den."

"It never did," said Margaret; "it could not have a more charming air than it has now."

"Yes, it could; and it will, when your work-basket and books and writing-desk are there, and I am sure of finding you there when I come home, as I shall be, if you take the afternoon, as the least liable to interruptions, for your books and music, making that your study."

"Do you suppose you will never sigh for the quiet possession of your sanctum, Robert?"

"Always, when my wife is in it; never, when she is not. What did you practise to-day? Let me hear you sing—some of the old songs."

"Oh, Robert, let us sing our old duets," said Margaret; "I looked over some of the accompaniments to-day." They went to the piano—a new and excellent one, which Margaret found in the library on her arrival—and sang several duets. Then they fell to talking of old times, and as something suggested it, Margaret asked Mr. Russell to show her the picture of herself that Chloe had found. He led her into the sanctum and opened the desk, displaying the withered leaves and rosebuds, and reminding her of the time when she had taken them from her dress and given them to him, in memory of the happy hour.

"I had not looked at them or the picture for nine years, Margaret, when Chloe brought them to light."

"Ah, Robert!" sighed Margaret, pityingly. "Tell me, did I ever look like this?" she added, examining the miniature.

"The fact that Chloe knew it for her 'Miss Marg'et' shows very conclusively that you look like it now, don't you think so? And then only think of *my* recognizing you the moment I saw you, the night of my first visit to the farm!"

"And only think of my knowing you across the meadow, Robert! What conclusive proof that you are the same—as young and handsome as you were ten years ago!"

"Miss Marg'et."

It was Chloe's voice in the library.

"Wait, Margaret," said Mr. Russell; "see if she will venture into this memorable place. Chloe, come in."

"I want to say suthin' to Miss Marg'et," answered Chloe, in a muffled voice.

"Well, come in and say it, Chloe," said Mr. Russell, pleasantly. "Miss Marg'et is here."

Chloe's head presently appeared at the door; but it bobbed back again instantly, and when Margaret went to see what had become of her, she was sitting on the floor near the door

"Chloe, what are you afraid of?" she asked. "Why didn't you come in, when Mr. Russell said you might?"

"Dunno," whispered Chloe.

"Were you afraid your feet would walk to the desk, and your hands open the drawers in spite of yourself?" asked Mr. Russell, laughing at the quick, inquiring look she gave him out of the corners of her eyes.

"Dunno," answered Chloe again.

"Stand up, Chloe, and tell me what you wanted to say," said Margaret.

"You said I mout fetch in dem teapots an' cups an' things," said Chloe, hanging her head and digging her toes.

"So I did, Chloe. What is the trouble?"

"Dat ar Jan't says I can't, an' I'se afeard she ain't gwine to lemme."

"Go back, Chloe, and when the things are ready she will let you bring them, for I told her that it should be your task. She thinks you are too little, perhaps; but you must show her that you are quite big enough."

Chloe went hopping briskly from the room.

"What a queer little thing she is," said Mr. Russell. "She continually surprises one by the droll things she does, and the good feeling and genuine amiability she displays;" and he told Margaret of her act of kindness to the little Irish child. They were still talking of that and other of her doings, when she came in with the tray, and arranged the tea-things upon the table with an air of mingled shyness and importance.

"That is very well done, Chloe," said Margaret. "I think Janet will be willing to trust you after this."

Chloe gave a little chuckle of delight, and darted out of the room.

"I think I must begin to mend Chloe's manners," said Margaret. "Her odd little ways have been such a source of amusement to the boys and me that I couldn't bear to check them. But now that we are not countryfolk any more, but have the dignity of a city-house to maintain, I must teach her to walk out of my presence, instead of darting and hopping, and not to dig her toes and make grimaces and contortions."

"It seems hard to make her walk by rule, like ordinary Chloes and Marthas," said Mr. Russell. "Will it not do to let her take her own time to lay aside such specialties?"

"I am afraid not, Robert. Imagine Mrs. Thorne witnessing such an exit as she made just now! She would set me down as an utter heathen. Chloe will learn quickly. She is wonderfully susceptible of improvement, and I can hardly comprehend it, when I think what her life must have been before she came to me."

"An affectionate heart like Chloe's is a ready medium for reaching a benighted soul," said Mr. Russell. "Instruction and discipline are generally fruitless, without kindness and human sympathy. If all Chloes could be so fortunate as to find 'Miss Marg'ets'—but how can they, poor things, when there is but one in all the world!"

"What a misanthropical sentiment, Robert!" exclaimed Margaret.

The next day was Sunday, and clear and bright, with only a patch of snow here and there in shady places, to show that there had been a foretaste of winter the day before.

In the morning Mr. Russell and Margaret went to church. In the afternoon, leaving Janet to take Chloe with her, they went down to the tenement houses, where Mr. Russell had established a Sunday-school, composed of all the grown people and children in the building, who could attend, and as many from without as could be accommodated in the large room set apart for the purpose.

Margaret was introduced to many, and was received with a homely friendliness that went to her heart. Her heart was full, as she saw, by the respectful, earnest attention they gave to every word he spoke, and by the confidence with which troubles and anxieties were poured into his ear, what her husband was to these people.

Would she ever know how closely and by how many "bands of love and service" he was bound to the "world's sad heart?" Never, she thought, until Christ says to him, Inasmuch as ye did it unto these, ye did it unto me.

When the service—which was made so varied that the smallest child was kept interested to the last—was over, Mr. Russell took Margaret to visit one or two families where there was sickness or trouble, and saw how readily her gentle, sympathizing words won trust and love.

"Well, Margaret," he asked, as they walked homeward, "what do you think now, about the probability of your having work to do, and getting near to any one in this great city?"

"I am only afraid of not being able to fulfil the great trust," answered Margaret; "but you will help me, Robert?"

"No, you will help me, my beloved," Mr. Russell replied.

In the evening Janet and Reuben, and Martha and Chloe, came to the library. Mr. Russell read in the Bible, giving simple practical explanations of what he read, and he and Margaret sang, those who could joining with them, and after Mr. Russell had prayed, all repeated the Lord's Prayer, and the servants said good-night, and departed.

In the course of a week, Margaret and Mr. Russell returned Mrs. Thorne's and Claudia's call.

"Do you think," Margaret asked, as they walked, "that the Thornes know of Mr. Ventnor's being a professor?"

"I think it doubtful," replied Mr. Russell, "as they have been absent all the summer and autumn; and they would not be likely to seek any knowledge of him."

"Can't you contrive to make it known to them, Robert? Is it not possible that they might overlook his not being rich, if they knew he was respected and had a fine position?"

"Mr. Thorne would give Claudia and Philip his blessing, gladly, if he had the occasion. It is only the worldly mamma who has such lofty aspirations for her daughter. But I shall certainly be on the watch for an opportunity to mention Philip's improved fortunes."

The opportunity was not wanting, for it happened that Mr. Wells, the gentleman to whom Mr. Russell had recommended Philip, was there, being an old friend of Mr. Thorne's. In the course of the conversation, he referred to the appointment of Mr. Ventnor as having proved eminently satisfactory. "We are greatly indebted to you for naming him," he said.

"What are you speaking of?" asked Mr. Thorne, who had caught the name.

"Of the election of Mr. Ventnor to the Professorship of Belles-Lettres in —— University," replied Mr. Russell.

"What! the Philip Ventnor whom we know—who used to visit here—Professor of Belles-Lettres?"

"You seem surprised," Mr. Wells remarked. "Have you not heard of it before, and Mr. Ventnor an acquaintance, too? He entered upon his duties in September."

Mr. Thorne looked at his wife, but she was at the moment speaking to Margaret; and he turned to Claudia, nodding his head in a very expressive manner, as he met her happy eyes.

"We've been out of town for several months," he said to Mr. Wells, "travelling about most of the time, and have not been in the way of hearing any news of our friends. But I rejoice in this; I always liked Mr. Ventnor. Helen, did you hear what Mr. Wells said of Mr. Ventnor?"

"Yes, I heard, my dear, and with great pleasure. I was just remarking to Mrs. Russell how entirely Mr. Ventnor had dropped from our circle of late. I am not at all surprised to learn that his talents have gained him such a position."

"When is the next vacation?" asked Mr. Thorne.

"Not until the Christmas holidays," answered Mr. Wells; and the subject was dropped.

When Margaret and Mr. Russell rose to go, Mrs. Thorne said that she hoped Mrs. Russell would not look upon them in the light of mere acquaintances. She felt that they had a claim upon her, as her husband had been a friend so long.

15*

As Margaret responded, her eyes sought Claudia's, which were fixed wistfully upon her; and when she held out her hand, Claudia clasped it in both of hers, saying, with the impulsiveness of a child, "Will you be my friend? I love you already." Her eyes fell, and her cheeks flushed, as she realized that not only Mrs. Russell, but her mother and Mr. Russell, had heard her overture.

"Indeed, I will," returned Margaret earnestly, holding the trembling little hands in hers; "and you shall show me that you really desire it by coming to see me very soon, and very often."

"Thank you," said Claudia, in a low tone.

"You do not know what a pertinacious child my Claudia is," said Mrs. Thorne, laying her hand on Claudia's shoulder. "You must not let her encroach upon your time too much, Mrs. Russell, as I see she will be in danger of doing from her enthusiasm at this early day of your acquaintance. But who can marvel at it?" she added, with an air of the most well-bred flattery.

One day, not long after this, Margaret had a visit from Mrs. Sarelli and Paul and Angelica.

Mr. Russell had interested her in their sad story, but he had not prepared her for the account they gave of his generous kindness, and for their fervent gratitude. As Mrs. Sarelli said, it was a relief to express what they felt, and to talk about their kind friend to one who could appreciate it, as his own wife could.

Margaret insisted upon their taking lunch with her, and the charm of her manner won even Angelica from her timid reserve. They all, in turn, won Margaret's heart.

"I have heard so much of the beauty of your little ones, Edith and Mary, Mrs. Sarelli, that I am impatient to see them. I wish you would all come and spend a whole day with me," Margaret said, as they were preparing to leave her.

"Oh, thank you," exclaimed Mrs. Sarelli; and Paul and Angelica looked their delight. "You don't know what pleasure it would give us. But will Saturday be a convenient day for you? It is the only one in which I am at liberty."

"It will be quite as convenient as any other day," replied Margaret. "Will your little school continue through the winter?"

"Oh, yes; I shall lose one or two of my smaller scholars, but most of them live near enough to come during the winter."

"What will you do without Paul?" asked Margaret; "he must be such a help to you in every way."

"He is, indeed; but I shall do very well, knowing that he is happy, and improving in his art."

"I think Mr. Russell said he was to begin his studies in about a month," said Margaret.

"Yes, the first of December," replied Mrs. Sarelli.

"We will try to find him a boarding-place near us," said Margaret, "and not let him feel quite alone, without his mother and sisters."

"You are very kind," replied Mrs. Sarelli. "I shall feel perfectly at ease about him, if he has such oversight."

The Christmas holidays came, and with them came Philip. His mother and sisters were envious of every hour that he was out of their sight, but he managed to spend a good many with Mr. Russell and Margaret. He and Margaret speedily became excellent friends. Claudia had grown to be a constant visitor. She came nearly every day, to read or sing or talk with Margaret. But it was tacitly understood that, while Philip was in town, and liable to drop in at any time, her visits should be discontinued; and as the days of the short vacation passed, Margaret began to fear that their happiness was to be still deferred.

However, one day Philip appeared with a joyful face, exclaiming, almost before he had shaken hands with Margaret, "Mrs. Russell, are you going to Mrs. Thorne's to-night?"

"Yes, we are," answered Margaret, catching at the pleasant truth, and Philip confirmed her conjecture.

"So am I!" he cried. "I found the most polite invita-

tion at my grandfather's last night—you can imagine my
emotions. I scarcely credit it—that I am to be received into
that house once more, and allowed to see Claudia. Do I
look as if I were dreaming?"

"Not in the least. It is, without doubt, a happy reality.
But you will make up your mind to be patient, even if the
meeting is not altogether satisfactory?"

"Yes," answered Philip, a little doubtfully.

Claudia was standing by Margaret when Philip entered
her mother's drawing-room that evening, and Margaret saw
the flash of joy that lighted up the sweet face, as they noted
Mrs. Thorne's cordial reception of Philip. One would surely
have thought that he had always been one of her most
favored and honored guests. Mr. Thorne, of course, welcomed him in the heartiest manner.

Philip's eyes met Claudia's in an eloquent glance, before
he was at liberty to go to her; and when he took her hand,
though only for an instant, and though not a word was spoken, it seemed as if life had no greater joy than that which
he felt then.

Before he returned to ———, their happiness was complete and cloudless, for they were engaged with the full
consent and blessing of Mr. and Mrs. Thorne. Mr. Thorne
would have had the day of their marriage fixed at once,
declaring that he had an ample marriage portion laid by for
his daughter, but Philip and Claudia felt that the time had
not come. So Philip went back to his work with an increased earnestness, looking bravely and hopefully in the face
of all difficulties, determined to master them.

Claudia, only regretting that she had been so slow in
learning her life-lessons, tried to be, in her home, so far as
differing circumstances would admit, what Margaret was in
hers, and to dispense sunshine to some who had little or
none.

Early in the spring a sorrow came to Margaret in the
death of her friend, Mr. Doane. A letter from Mrs. Blake
brought the sad tidings.

She, and her husband's father and mother, with whom she was travelling, on their way to Rome had stopped at a little town, and heard accidentally that there was an American gentleman at the inn, very ill with a fever. On making inquiries, and learning that it was Mr. Doane, they gave up all thought of going on, and devoted themselves to caring for him. The doctors had already given up hope of his recovery; but he was conscious to the last, and again and again assured them of its being the greatest comfort to have friends about him, and to feel that he should not be buried by strange hands in a strange land. "I want to lie in the old burying-ground at home," he said, "where my poor mother can have the satisfaction of looking at my grave, and planting flowers beside it."

"I shall never cease to be thankful," Mrs. Blake wrote, "to the kind Providence which directed us to him, when he was alone and suffering. The afternoon that he died, I was sitting beside him, and, hearing him speak my name, though in the faintest whisper, I bent over him to hear what he wished to say, feeling that death must be near. He spoke with difficulty, but I did not lose a word. 'Tell her—Mrs. Russell'—he had already sent messages to his parents and a few friends—'tell her that I found the happiness she wished for me, 'the best and truest,' and that I shall meet her in the better country. I can sing in my heart, Rock of ages, cleft for *me*.' I never shall forget his heavenly expression as he said this, and it should be a life-long joy to you, dear Margaret, if you were instrumental in making his dying hour so peaceful and happy, and giving him so sure a title to the blessedness of heaven."

That it was a deep joy in the midst of her grief, who can doubt?

# CHAPTER XXVIII.

Roll on, O blessed years,
For though ye bring us sorrows, and the mournful tears
May sometimes at your bidding start,
Ye also bring such rich and precious treasure,
Such large reward for every weak endeavor,
Such gentle chastening for the wayward heart.    ANON.

"Now, Chloe, bring the basket and the scissors, and we will gather the flowers while the dew is on them," said Margaret Russell, one June morning of the second summer after her marriage. "O gift of God, O perfect day," she repeated to herself, as she stood upon the broad piazza of her country-home on the Hudson, and looked over the lawn, woods, river, and hills, all bright with morning sunlight and canopied by the sapphire sky.

Roses were in their glory, as well as pansies and heliotrope and verbenas and daisies, and all the other June flowers, and Chloe's basket was soon filled.

"Is you gwine to put 'em in every single room, Miss Marg'et?"

"Yes, Chloe; I think they will all like to have them, don't you?"

"I reckon dey will. Be dey comin' dis mornin'?"

"Not till towards night. You will be glad to see them, Chloe."

"Yes, Miss Marg'et. I jes' wish I could take car' o' dat ar little baby 'at's a comin'."

"I dare say Mrs. Doane will let you help, if she sees that you are very careful. But the baby's nurse, Rosa, is coming too."

"Is Rosa a nigger, Miss Marg'et?"

"She is a very nice colored girl."

"Won't she t'ink dis yer's a mighty fine, mos' beaut'ful house!" said Chloe, with a solemn shake of her head.

"Oh, here you are," said Mr. Russell, coming into the little room where Margaret had taken her flowers to arrange them. "I have been looking for you everywhere. You are sure to be missing, if I have something very important to say to you."

"You mean that if I am missing for three minutes, Robert, you are sure to have something very important to say to me."

"I think of tying a string to your wrist, and keeping hold of the other end, so that I need only to follow it in order to find you."

"I will tie you to my apron-strings, if you like," responded Margaret, laughing; "but what is the important thing you wish to say to me now?"

"That I am going to take a walk to the village, and desire your company."

"You shall have it, if you will wait until I have finished my bouquets. The flowers would fade if I left them."

"Of course I will wait. It is early yet, and will be cool enough for a walk, even in the middle of the day."

"Did you ever know such a superb day as this, Robert? I feel as if I could set Longfellow's 'Day of Sunshine' to the most triumphant music, and sing it like an angel, only that it doesn't need to be set; it is music in itself."

"I have been repeating that, too, Margaret, and wondering that such days as this never inspired me to write just such a poem. My presumption surpasses yours."

"I think it at least equals it. Now, Chloe, I will let you put these in the rooms; there is one for each," she said, having finished the bouquets. "Then you can gather up all these stems and leaves, and put the basket away. Robert, you may help to carry these into the parlor;" and she gave Mr. Russell a glass dish of rosebuds, heliotrope, and geranium leaves, and took one herself filled with scarlet verbenas, the white sweet wood and some dark rich green.

"Ise gwine to put the han'somest in your room, Miss Marg'et," said Chloe, with one of her old contortions.

"You may please yourself, Chloe," Margaret replied, knowing that in her eyes the prettiest would be the gayest.

"Shall I dust while you's gone?"

"Yes, and then ask Janet what she has for you to do."

Margaret and Mr. Russell had their walk, and the rest of the day was spent in the busy, not unprofitable idleness, befitting days wherein it is enough "not to be doing, but to be."

Towards night the expected guests arrived, and the meeting was a joyful one, though it was not the first time Margaret and Mr. Russell had seen their western friends since their marriage; for when Mrs. Blake returned from Europe they went with her to St. Louis, and spent a few days with Mrs. More, of course paying Miss Patty a little visit.

The boys were wild with joy at seeing their aunt once more, and being at her home in the country; even Fanny was warm in her greetings.

"Give me the baby, Rosa," said Margaret, and she carried the little blue-eyed, golden-haired girl into the house, followed by the others.

"She has grown since you saw her, Margaret," said Dr. Doane.

"Yes; she is not quite the atom of humanity that she was then. How sweet she is! How you must love her, Walter."

"Indeed, you will think so," cried Fanny. "I verily believe he thinks there is nothing else in the world worth looking at, or thinking of, but Margie."

"And Margie's mother, and her aunt Margaret, and her brothers," added Dr. Doane.

"That dear little thing has been as good as never was, all the way," said George, pressing the soft, rosy cheeks, and kissing the tiny mouth, and he was rewarded for his compliment by a merry baby-laugh.

"I suppose these travellers are tired and dusty and hungry, Margaret," said Mr. Russell.

"Oh, yes; I quite forgot that, in my admiration for my namesake. Follow me, all of you," she said, leading the way, with the baby in her arms. At the door of Fanny's room she delivered her charge to Rosa, and went with Mrs. More to hers.

"Well, my dear, I never expected to come so far from home again," Mrs. More said, as Margaret helped her to take off her dusty garments.

"I was sure I should have the delight of welcoming you to my house, dear Aunt Clara," answered Margaret. "I do really think you look younger than you did when I saw you last, even after your long journey."

"I don't know, Margaret; I feel pretty old, I can assure you. But I am very glad to be with you, my dear, and to see your beautiful home. I suppose this is Robert's compensation to you for living in such an old-fashioned house in the winter?"

"No, indeed, Aunt Clara. You know I did not need any compensation for that. I love the old house dearly. But we both wished to be in the country six months of the year, so Robert bought this place. It is lovely; isn't it?"

"Oh, those hills!" cried Mrs. More, looking from the window. "I never should grow weary of gazing at them. The 'everlasting hills!'"

"Do you love them so?" asked Margaret, thinking of her own longing for hills when she lived on the prairie-farm.

"Oh, yes, I love such scenery as this, but I love the prairies too. My dear child, I do not know what earthly thing there is left to wish for in your lot."

"There is nothing, my dear aunt. I have every conceivable blessing. My cup runs over."

"I know you are grateful, my dear, and that earthly joys cannot make you lose sight of the heavenly."

"If I could not feel that my earthly joys were the gift of my Father in heaven, and sanctified by His love, they would be worthless," said Margaret, earnestly.

"I was sure of it," returned Mrs. More.

When they went down-stairs, they found Mr. Russell, Dr. Doane, and the boys, on the piazza.

"Oh, boys," cried Margaret, as they ran to her, "how you do grow! You, Georgie, are almost as tall as I am now. Jackie, you don't grow quite so fast, but you are getting to be a very big boy, too."

"I'm taller than any boy in school that isn't any older than I am," cried George.

"And just think, Aunty, he got the medal for being the best scholar," said Jack, eagerly.

"Why! did you, Georgie? I am delighted."

"I got it," answered Georgie, "but I only tried for it cause I didn't want Bill Morton to have it. He's so awful mean. He whips all the little boys, and never goes near a big boy when he wants to fight."

"You whipped him pretty well when he came at me once," cried Jack.

"I'll bet I did!"

Here the boys ran away to look after something that had attracted their attention, and Dr. Doane said to Margaret, "I am afraid, from all accounts, that your elder nephew has rather the reputation of a belligerent than a peaceful member of society."

"It is something for him to fight in the defence of the small and oppressed," said Mr. Russell.

"Yes, he is the champion of all the small boys in the school and the neighborhood; but I do not think he had afflicted himself with much studying, until there was danger that Bill Morton, as he calls him, would get the prize."

"Well, Fanny dear, how do you feel now?" asked Margaret, as her sister came out upon the piazza. "No one could imagine from your looks that you had been travelling all day; you are as fresh and fair as an apple-blossom."

"I seldom have the credit of feeling weary," returned Fanny, "because any little excitement gives me color. I am very much fatigued, notwithstanding my looks."

"I think you ought to be glad of it, mother," said

George, who had come back from his race with the dog in time to hear his mother's remark. "I do like to see any body always look nice and pretty, as you do when you are dressed up."

"Thank you, George," said his mother; "I believe you appreciate my good looks, if I have any."

Chloe helped to wait upon the tea-table, and did herself much credit, only once or twice losing herself in absorbed contemplation of the familiar faces with new surroundings.

"Chloe has not changed in the least; has she, Margaret?" said Mrs. More, when they left the table, "except that she is more quiet and sedate."

"She is the very same Chloe, Aunt Clara; only, as you say, somewhat improved in her manners. She occasionally does some droll thing that shocks Janet and Martha, and amuses Robert and me, but she will be a real treasure when she is older. She is now. I would not part with Chloe for a great deal."

"And she certainly would not part from 'Miss Marg'et,'" added Mr. Russell. "I suppose you have observed that she continues to dignify my wife by her old title."

"Yes; and how absurd it is," exclaimed Fanny. "Why do you allow it, Margaret?"

"I tried to impress her with the fact that I was Mrs. Russell," replied Margaret, "but I grew tired of correcting her every time she spoke to me, and concluded to let her take her own time. If she ever thinks of my being any body but 'Miss Marg'et' now, I have no proof of it."

"Margaret," said Mrs. More, "I have not told you yet that I drove over to the farm-house before I came away, so that I could bring you the latest tidings of all your friends."

"My dear Aunt, how good of you! Are they all well?"

"Yes, very well. I saw Mrs. Davis, and Mr. and Mrs. Thomas, and they all sent a great deal of love to you. Poor Miss Patty Hopkins is in affliction. Her sister is dead. She was buried the day before I was there."

"Poor Miss Patty!" exclaimed Margaret. "Her sister

was never much of a comfort to her, but I know she mourns for her as if she had been the best sister in the world. Did she say any thing about leaving the farm-house ? "

" No ; I presume she hopes to live and die there. She sent her love to you, my dear, and hoped you would write to her."

" I certainly will write at once. Poor little woman ! I wish I could have her near enough to see that she is comfortable and happy. Did she speak of Nancy ? "

" Yes ; she said that Nancy was very kind, and was devoted to her sister during her last illness. She takes the charge of every thing, and Miss Patty considers herself very fortunate in having such a woman to live with her. Jotham took occasion to tell me that he should like to move into the farm-house now, if Miss Patty could go to her own house with Nancy."

" Jotham must be patient, or he shall never have the farm-house at all," said Margaret.

" I even saw Bridget, and she and Nancy both sent their love to you."

In the course of the evening, Mrs. More asked Mr. Russell about Mrs. Sarelli and her family.

" I remember our visit there so well, Robert ! " she said. " Are they in the same pretty place ? "

" Mrs. Sarelli and the girls are there, but Paul is in Italy. He developed so much genius, that it seemed only right for him to have every advantage, and he went to Rome last winter. He will be a distinguished artist one of these days."

" His mother still keeps her school, I suppose ?."

" Yes ; and Angelica is attending school in town, and studying music ; so that she will be able to assist her mother before long, and they will open on a larger scale."

" Where is Mr. Ventnor, Robert—your young friend that I admired so much ? "

" He is still Professor in —— University, and is to be married in about two weeks to Miss Claudia Thorne, one of the loveliest girls that ever lived. They are coming to make us a visit in September; if you would only stay till then, Aunt Clara, you would see them."

"I should not need that inducement, Robert; if I could stay, I should be content to see only you and Margaret. But think of my dear children, whom I shall never visit again. And I must get home before the cold weather comes."

Mrs. More left Margaret's happy home in two weeks, and Dr. Doane went back to St. Louis about the same time, leaving the boys and little Margie and Fanny to spend the summer with Margaret, at her earnest entreaty.

It was an unmixed pleasure for her to have the boys and the baby there; and Fanny's presence might have been an added pleasure, if she had not seemed to find quiet country-life so tedious and irksome. Fortunately for all, some friends, whom she had been with at Newport the summer before Margaret's marriage, had taken a cottage at Long Branch, and she was invited to spend the month of August there. The invitation was eagerly accepted, and the congenial variety made the summer endurable.

The little Margie she petted and caressed at times as if she were her only comfort, and she was extremely fond of her—as who could help being of the winsome little creature? But it was not a love so absorbing and solicitous that she could not readily leave her to the care of Margaret and Rosa, while she enjoyed the gayeties of the sea-shore.

"What will Walter do without the baby?" Margaret said to Mr. Russell, the evening after Dr. Doane's departure. "It is almost painful to see what an intense, yearning love he has for the little thing."

"She is a real blessing to him now, and will be a still greater blessing when she is older," returned Mr. Russell. "I wonder if Walter is in any serious trouble, pecuniarily?'

"I am afraid he is; he seems to consider the cost of things so carefully, while he used to spend freely, almost thoughtlessly. And he has that harassed, absent look, so much of the time."

"They are evidently economizing closely."

"Yes, and I am thankful. Fanny says the house they live in now is as plain as plain can be, and that all their elegant furniture is sold. I know that what few new dresses she has, were not made by Madame Larisse. I am happily disappointed, for I was afraid that Walter would involve himself more and more deeply, in his dread of distressing Fanny. She says he is determined to pay his debts without touching the sum he settled upon her at their marriage, though she would have preferred that he should take that, rather than leave their handsome house."

"He is very wise," said Mr. Russell, "and I have no doubt he will come out all right in the end."

"Fanny bears the trial better than I expected. It is a severe mortification to her, I know; but I do think she loves Walter, and, with little Margie, they may be reasonably happy yet. I feel more concerned about the boys than any body else."

"An idea has just occurred to me, Margaret. I will at once submit it to your judgment. What do you think of proposing to Fanny and the Doctor—I wish I had thought of it before he went away—to let the boys remain at the East, and prepare for college in ——, under Philip's oversight? They could spend their vacations with us. It strikes me as a fine plan in every view."

"I think it the best one of all that could be devised, Robert," responded Margaret, warmly.

The arrangement was made with little objection, even from Dr. Doane, who saw its advantages too clearly to let any selfish feeling weigh against it. And they are now in ——, pursuing their studies under Mr. Ventnor's eye, and their progress and general improvement are a source of real satisfaction to Margaret and Mr. Russell. Philip's home, where Claudia presides with grace and dignity, is almost as much a home to George and Jack as their aunt's. It is a perfect gem in its way, and there is no one in ———— more admired and beloved than Mrs. Ventnor.

The boys have spent their vacation thus far with Mar

garet, but the coming summer they are to make Mrs. More a
visit. Dr. Doane and their mother and Margie are to meet
them there. They are looking forward to this with eager
pleasure, and have already planned excursions on horseback
or on foot—whichever seems most attractive when the time
comes—to the farm, and see Dr. Somers, and Charlie, and
Nellie Davis, and the rest of their old friends. They are even
saving as much of their pocket-money as they can spare—
their allowance is not large—to buy a present for Miss Patty.

Dr. Doane is free from debt, but they continue to live in
the plain house. He insists that it is large enough for comfort, and as tasteful as could be desired—which is very true.
He shrinks, beyond expression, from the possibility of a renewal of his late perplexities.

Fanny avoids society, because she cannot dress and receive as of old, and her visits to New York are the oases in
her life. At home she is low-spirited and sad, but the health-
ful, kindly atmosphere which she breathes when with her sister and Mr. Russell, has its effect for the time. The little
Margie makes music and sunshine in the otherwise quiet
house. She charms the gloom from her father's heart, and is
to him as the apple of his eye ; and she returns his devotion
with an ardor that would seem almost incredible in a child
of two or three years. Fanny sees this gladly ; for, deep
down beneath her self-love, lies the stinging consciousness
that she has not realized the hopes of her husband ; that she
has been a blight rather than a blessing to his life ; and she
welcomes the comfort which her child brings, while too inert
to make an effort herself.

Mrs. Blake lives with her husband's parents, in St. Louis,
but makes frequent visits to Margaret and Robert, to whom
her sweet presence is ever welcome.

Mrs. More has lost the valuable companionship of Mrs.
Rice and Lucinda, as Lucinda gave her hand and her wounded heart to a " dry-goods merchant " in a neighboring town
a few months since, and her mother lives with her ; she continues to make verses upon all subjects that touch her sensi-

bilities. But Mrs. More does not suffer by the loss; for, besides having the gentle, unobtrusive Miss Patty with her, she always has some one from among her loving, admiring children and grandchildren, nieces and nephews, to enliven her home.

Miss Patty gladly acceded to Mrs. More's kind proposal that she should come and take Mrs. Rice's place; for, notwithstanding Nancy's fidelity and devotion, she found her life at the farm very lonely, after her sister's death. And the idea of being with Mrs. More, whom she agrees with Chloe in regarding as only second to Ma●●●t in goodness, and who is, besides, related to that darling of her heart, is like a taste of heaven below. Nancy is with Mrs. Davis, and has already made herself indispensable in that lady's domestic economy.

Jotham and his wife are in happy possession of the farmhouse; and the farm, still owned by Margaret, is in a profitable condition. In a year or two more, without doubt, Jotham will be able to buy it.

John Heath has entered upon his theological studies, and is pursuing them with earnestness. His brother, having decided that his taste is not particularly for books, has just gone into business; and Mr. and Mrs. Heath are still living tranquilly at Rockdale.

Chloe has her especial duties, which she performs in the most satisfactory manner. But all her spare moments are devoted to Master Robbie Russell, the son and heir, the pet and darling of the house—who never fails to greet her with a crow of delight. She groans in spirit that she is not big enough to take the entire charge of him, and regards his nurse with envious eyes, while she waits as patiently as she can for the time when Robbie shall run alone. Then she has been promised the coveted responsibility. She can read and write, and is sure to become an intelligent and trustworthy woman.

The charms of their happy home do not absorb the interest and sympathies of Margaret and Robert Russell. Their daily record is in hearts and homes but for them dark and joyless; and their influence is felt in all that is true, noble, and Christ-like.

www.ingramcontent.com/pod-product-compliance
Lightning Source LLC
Chambersburg PA
CBHW021106270326
41929CB00009B/750